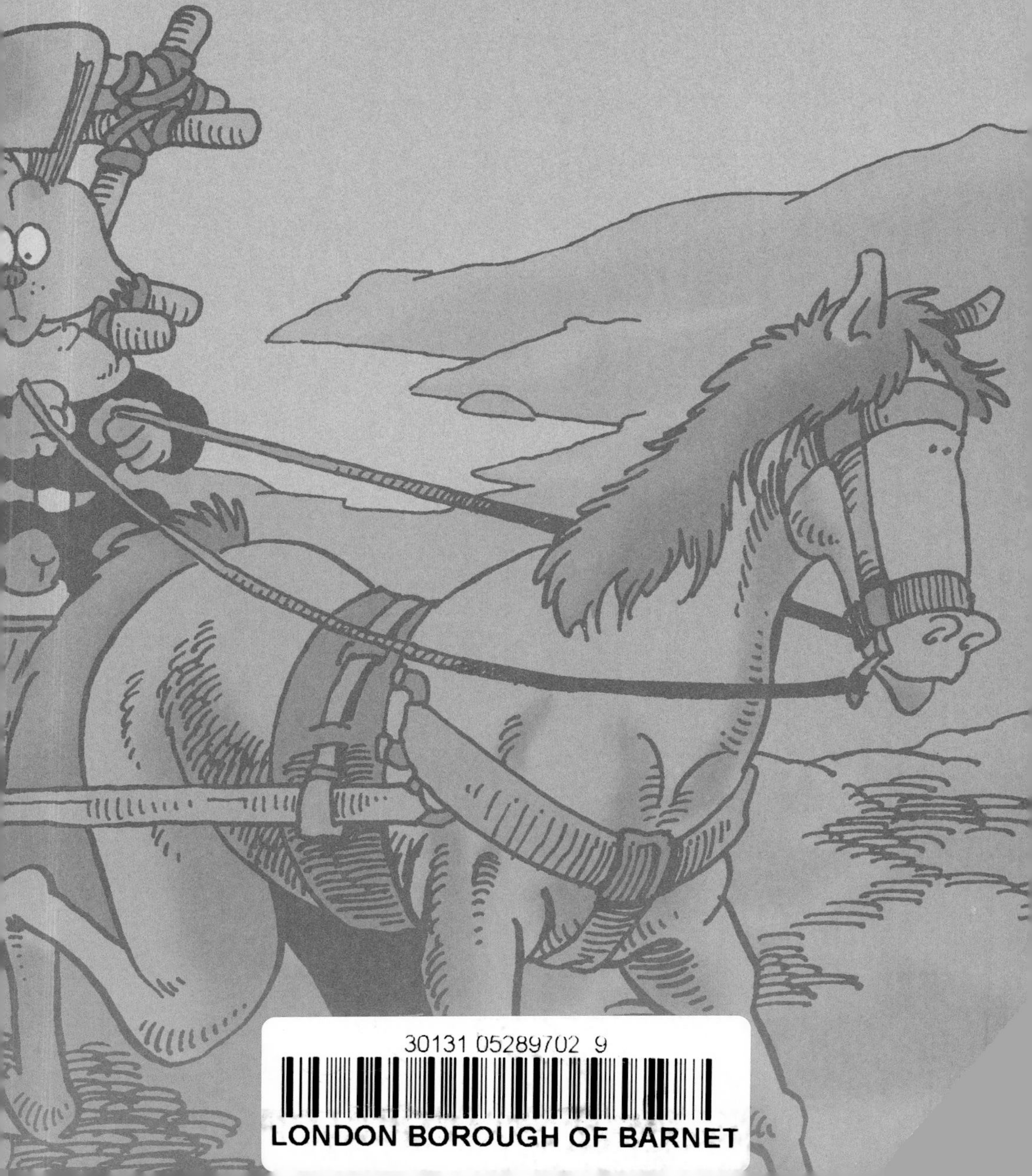

THE ADVENTURES OF
NiLSON ™
GROUNDTHUMPER

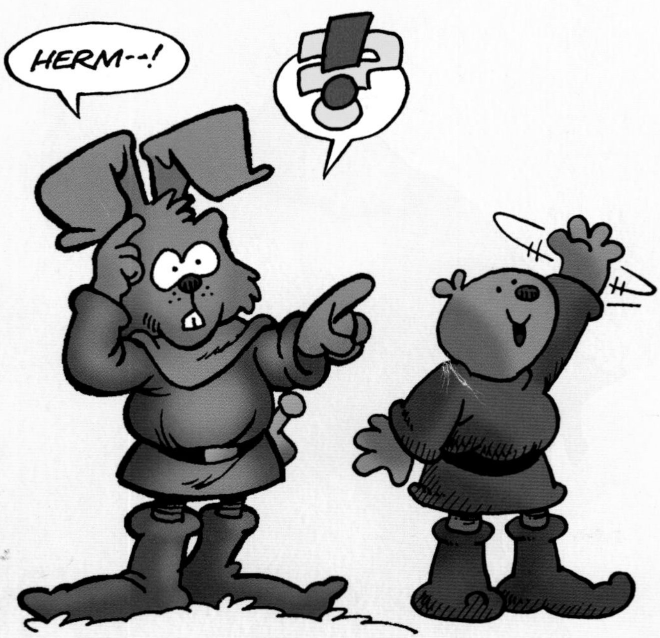
HERM--!

THE ADVENTURES OF NILSON GROUNDTHUMPER AND HERMY™

Created, Written,
and Illustrated by

Stan Sakai

Colored by

Tom Luth
and
Ryan Hill

DARK HORSE BOOKS

DIGITAL PRODUCTION AND DESIGN
Cary Grazzini

ASSISTANT EDITOR
Ian Tucker

EDITOR
Brendan Wright

PUBLISHER
Mike Richardson

This volume collects stories from issues *Albedo* #1 and #5, published by Thoughts & Images; *Critters Special* #1, *Critters* #5, #16, and #27, *Usagi Yojimbo vol. I* #19, *Usagi Yojimbo Color Special* #1–#3, published by Fantagraphics Books; *Usagi Yojimbo vol. II* #9, published by Mirage Studios; and *Dark Horse Presents vol. 2* #30, published by Dark Horse Comics.

Published by Dark Horse Books
A division of Dark Horse Comics, Inc.
10956 SE Main Street
Milwaukie, Oregon 97222

DarkHorse.com

Library of Congress Cataloging in Publication Control Number: 2013047596

First edition: March 2014
ISBN 978-1-61655-341-8

1 3 5 7 9 10 8 6 4 2
Printed in China

INTRODUCTION

I am best known as the writer and artist of the *Usagi Yojimbo* series, but before Usagi there was Nilson Groundthumper. I mean that two ways. Usagi made his first published appearance in *Albedo* #2 in 1984; however, Nilson and Hermy were in the first issue of that comic-book anthology. Also, the creation of Nilson predates Usagi by a good year or so. Usagi was to have been a secondary character in *The Nilson Chronicles*, a 2,500-page graphic novel, imagined even before the term "graphic novel" was coined. Usagi was to have made his appearance at about page 1,000. However, I fell in love with the samurai rabbit immediately after I finished his first short story and have stuck with him ever since.

The Nilson Chronicles was to have told the story of why there are anthromorphs, or intelligent human-like animals, and of the rise of the goblins, which would eventually become humans. It would start off with short humor stories of the meeting of friends, and show their relationship and abilities mature over time. The stories would become longer and more dramatic, as Nilson rose in stature to become a king. It would also tell of the humans, led by the Sauron-like Lord Hikiji. At one point in the storyline, Hermy would be kidnapped for certain knowledge in his possession, and taken to the Japans. Nilson would, of course, follow to rescue his friend, and there he would meet up with a very capable samurai rabbit. Together, they would rescue Hermy, and begin to gather other heroes.

The anthromorphs would make their last stand in a castle, which I had envisioned as similar to the abbey at Mont Saint-Michel, France, surrounded by the humans. I had a glorious death planned for Usagi, and an even more spectacular one for Nilson. The only ones to escape the castle would be Hermy and Nilson's young son. The entire series would have ended with the eventual death of Hermy.

It would have been a great story. However, this is one of those projects that will never be completed. As I said, I really enjoy working on *Usagi Yojimbo* and, aside from the occasional short story, have no plans to return to Nilson. The last remnant of the Nilson storyline actually appeared in an early Usagi story, where, for one panel, I drew Lord Hikiji as human.

People often ask which of my characters I identify with the most. My reply is always, "Hermy." I like his simple innocence, his naiveté, and his sincerity. We had a "What animal is Hermy?" contest in the early days, and the reader who put forward the most persuasive argument received an original drawing of Nilson and Hermy.

Hermy is a guinea pig.

Stan Sakai

Stan Sakai
October 2013

This one is for Kim Thompson,
the first editor I worked with,
and a good friend.

TABLE OF CONTENTS

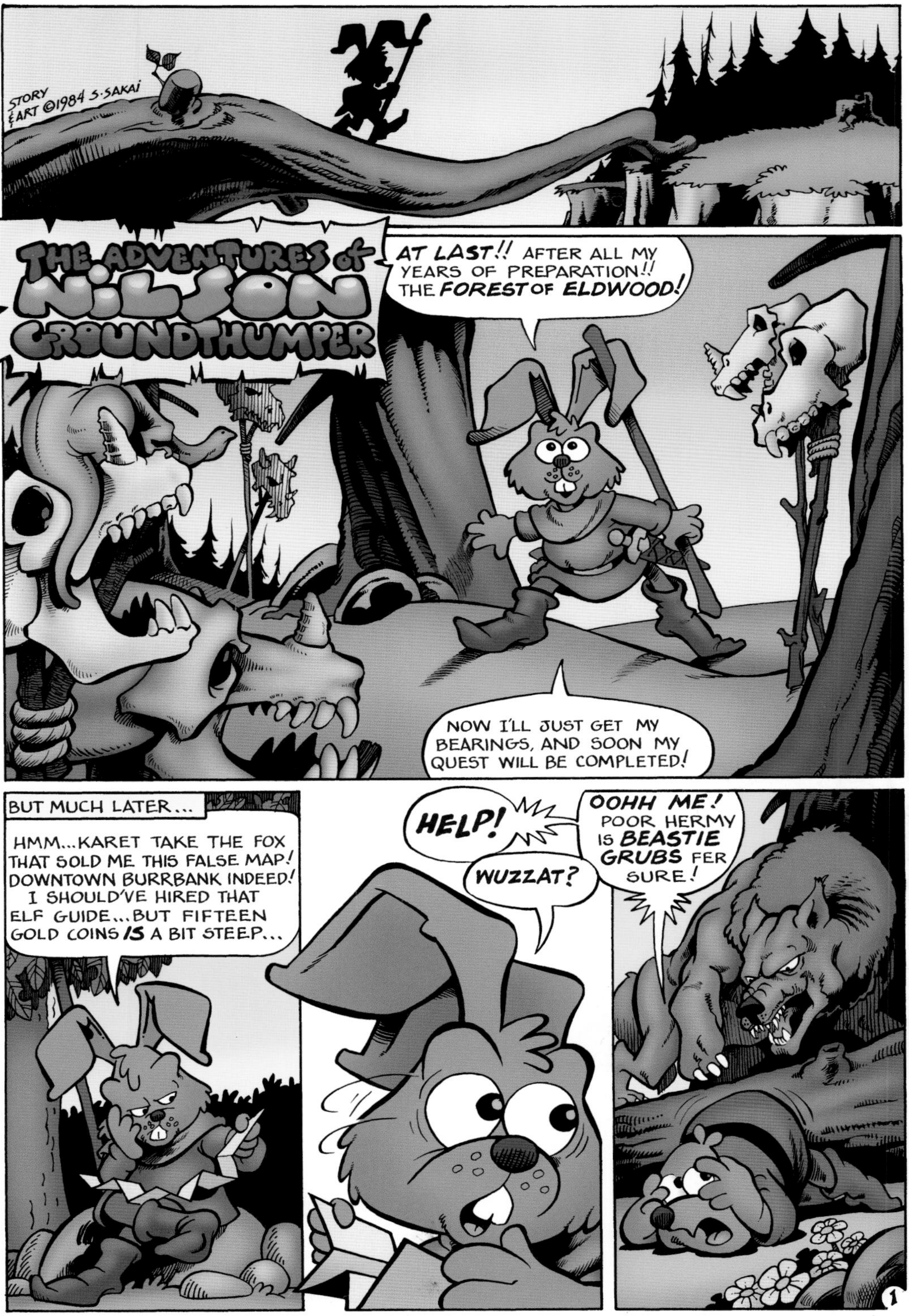
STORY & ART ©1984 S. SAKAI
THE ADVENTURES of NILSON GROUNDTHUMPER
AT LAST!! AFTER ALL MY YEARS OF PREPARATION!! THE FOREST OF ELDWOOD!
NOW I'LL JUST GET MY BEARINGS, AND SOON MY QUEST WILL BE COMPLETED!
BUT MUCH LATER...
HMM...KARET TAKE THE FOX THAT SOLD ME THIS FALSE MAP! DOWNTOWN BURRBANK INDEED! I SHOULD'VE HIRED THAT ELF GUIDE...BUT FIFTEEN GOLD COINS IS A BIT STEEP...
HELP!
WUZZAT?
OOHH ME! POOR HERMY IS BEASTIE GRUBS FER SURE!
1

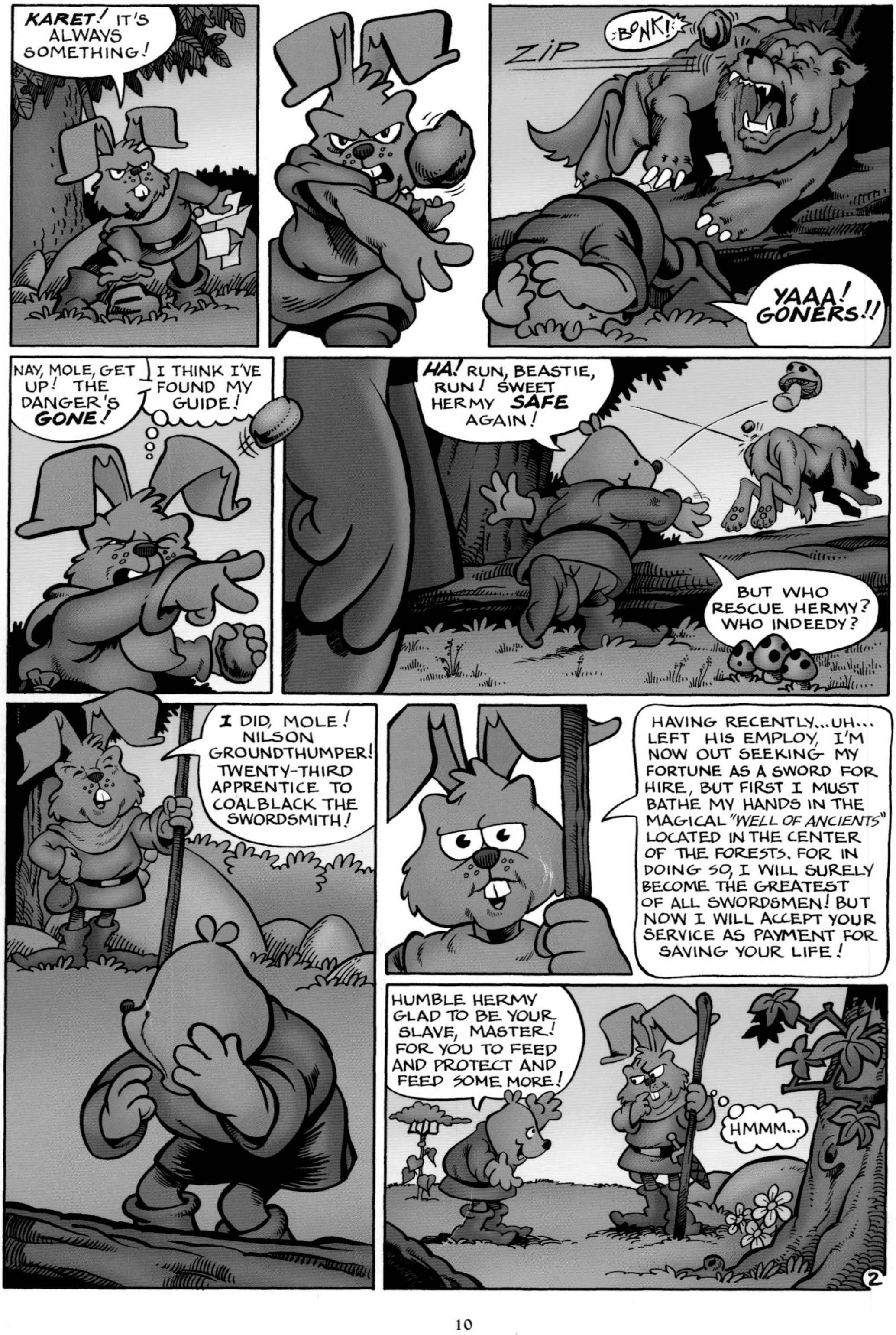
KARET! IT'S ALWAYS SOMETHING!
ZIP
BONK!
YAAA! GONERS!!
NAY, MOLE, GET UP! THE DANGER'S GONE!
I THINK I'VE FOUND MY GUIDE!
HA! RUN, BEASTIE, RUN! SWEET HERMY SAFE AGAIN!
BUT WHO RESCUE HERMY? WHO INDEEDY?
I DID, MOLE! NILSON GROUNDTHUMPER! TWENTY-THIRD APPRENTICE TO COALBLACK THE SWORDSMITH!
HAVING RECENTLY... UH... LEFT HIS EMPLOY, I'M NOW OUT SEEKING MY FORTUNE AS A SWORD FOR HIRE, BUT FIRST I MUST BATHE MY HANDS IN THE MAGICAL "WELL OF ANCIENTS" LOCATED IN THE CENTER OF THE FORESTS. FOR IN DOING SO, I WILL SURELY BECOME THE GREATEST OF ALL SWORDSMEN! BUT NOW I WILL ACCEPT YOUR SERVICE AS PAYMENT FOR SAVING YOUR LIFE!
HUMBLE HERMY GLAD TO BE YOUR SLAVE, MASTER! FOR YOU TO FEED AND PROTECT AND FEED SOME MORE!
HMMM...
2

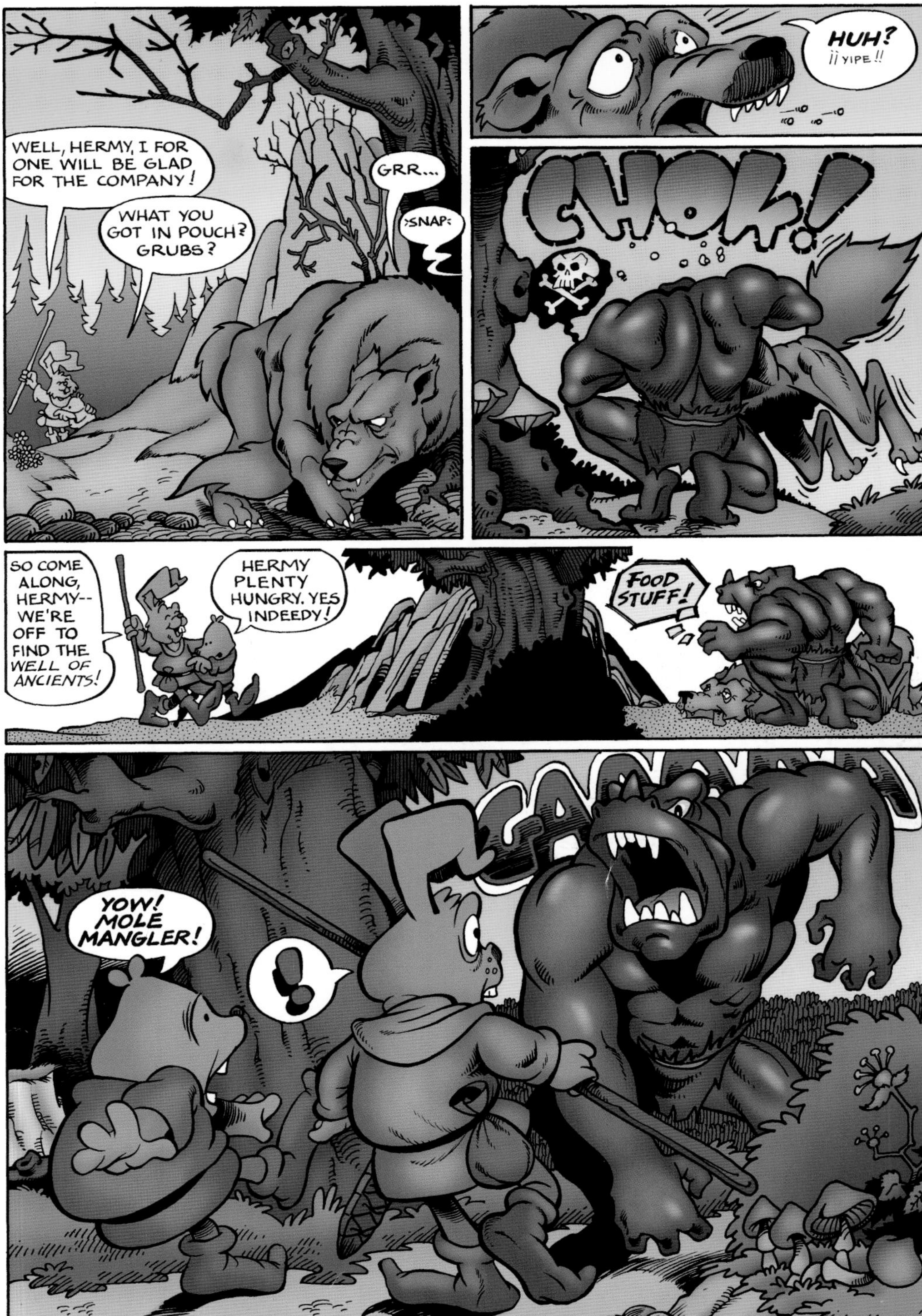
WELL, HERMY, I FOR ONE WILL BE GLAD FOR THE COMPANY!
WHAT YOU GOT IN POUCH? GRUBS?
GRR...
>SNAP<
HUH?
¡¡YIPE!!
CHOK!
SO COME ALONG, HERMY-- WE'RE OFF TO FIND THE WELL OF ANCIENTS!
HERMY PLENTY HUNGRY. YES INDEEDY!
FOOD STUFF!
YOW! MOLE MANGLER!
!
3

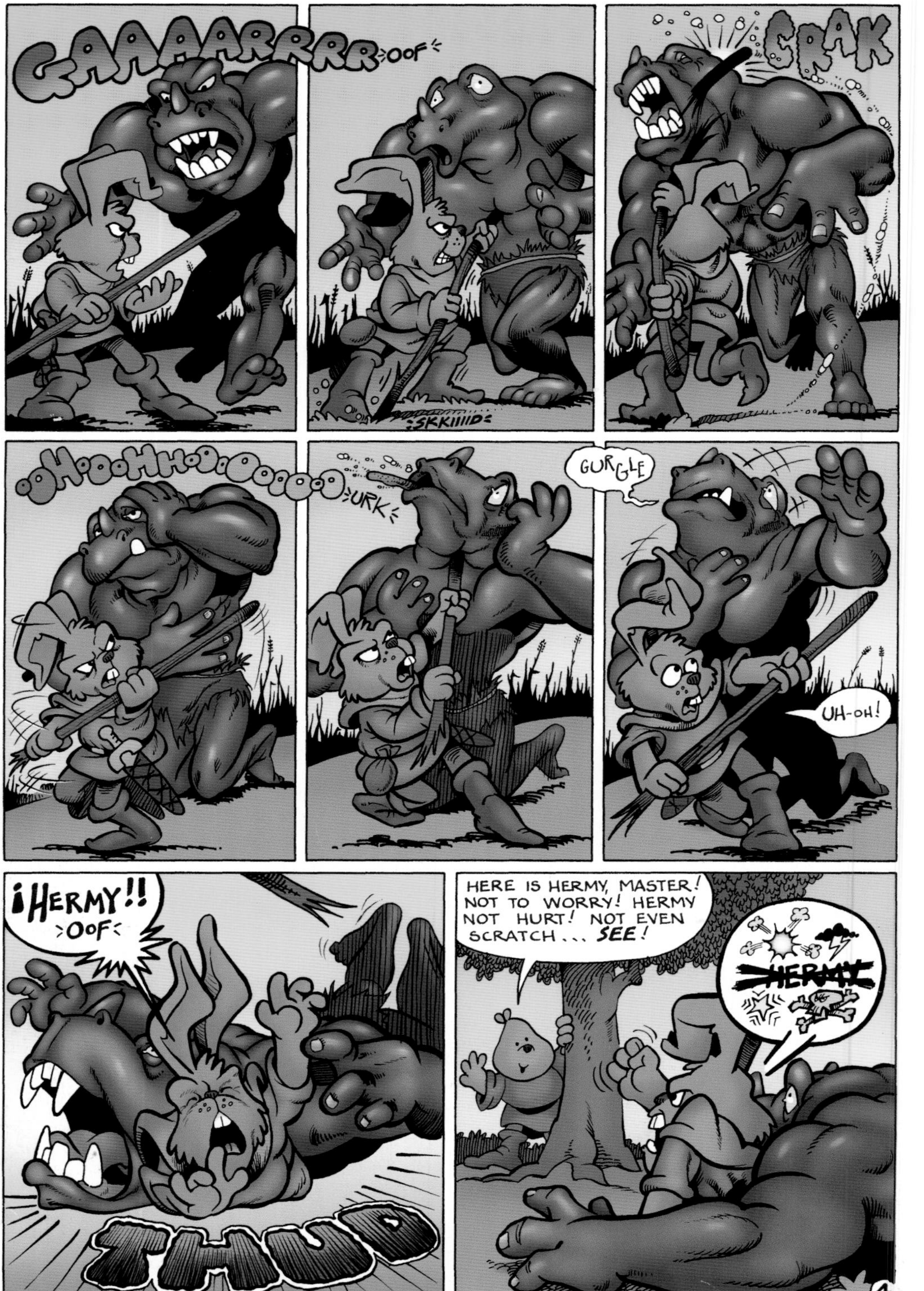
GAAAARRRR
OOF
SKKIIIID
CRAK
OOHOOOHHOOOOOOOOOO
URK
GURGLE
UH-OH!
¡HERMY!!
OOF
THUD
HERE IS HERMY, MASTER! NOT TO WORRY! HERMY NOT HURT! NOT EVEN SCRATCH ... SEE!
HERMY
4

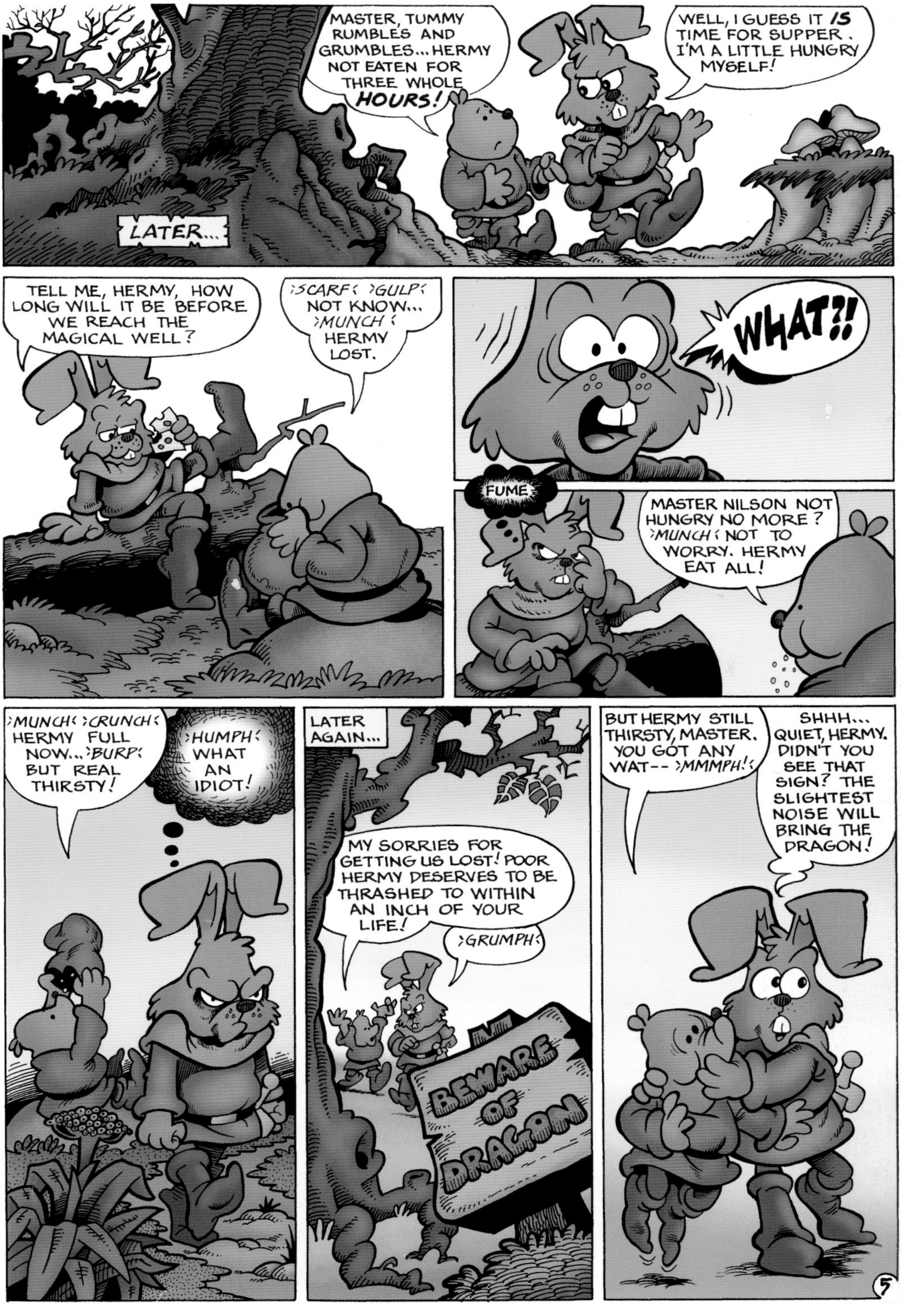

LATER...
MASTER, TUMMY RUMBLES AND GRUMBLES... HERMY NOT EATEN FOR THREE WHOLE HOURS!
WELL, I GUESS IT IS TIME FOR SUPPER. I'M A LITTLE HUNGRY MYSELF!
TELL ME, HERMY, HOW LONG WILL IT BE BEFORE WE REACH THE MAGICAL WELL?
›SCARF‹ ›GULP‹ NOT KNOW... ›MUNCH‹ HERMY LOST.
WHAT?!
FUME
MASTER NILSON NOT HUNGRY NO MORE? ›MUNCH‹ NOT TO WORRY. HERMY EAT ALL!
›MUNCH‹ ›CRUNCH‹ HERMY FULL NOW... ›BURP‹ BUT REAL THIRSTY!
›HUMPH‹ WHAT AN IDIOT!
LATER AGAIN...
MY SORRIES FOR GETTING US LOST! POOR HERMY DESERVES TO BE THRASHED TO WITHIN AN INCH OF YOUR LIFE!
›GRUMPH‹
BEWARE OF DRAGON
BUT HERMY STILL THIRSTY, MASTER. YOU GOT ANY WAT-- ›MMMPH!‹
SHHH... QUIET, HERMY. DIDN'T YOU SEE THAT SIGN? THE SLIGHTEST NOISE WILL BRING THE DRAGON!
5

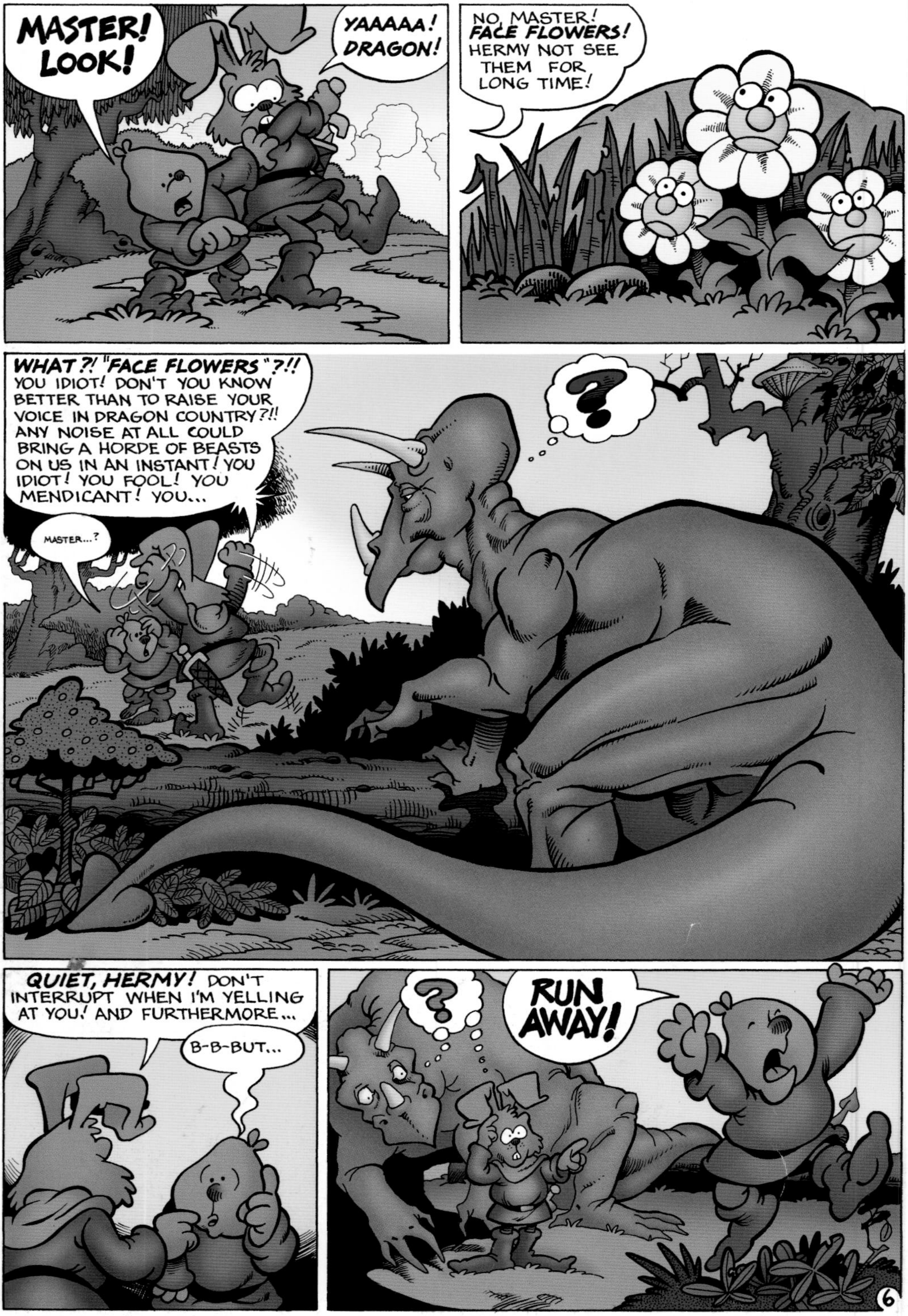
MASTER! LOOK!
YAAAAA! DRAGON!
NO, MASTER! FACE FLOWERS! HERMY NOT SEE THEM FOR LONG TIME!
WHAT?! "FACE FLOWERS"?!! YOU IDIOT! DON'T YOU KNOW BETTER THAN TO RAISE YOUR VOICE IN DRAGON COUNTRY?!! ANY NOISE AT ALL COULD BRING A HORDE OF BEASTS ON US IN AN INSTANT! YOU IDIOT! YOU FOOL! YOU MENDICANT! YOU...
MASTER...?
QUIET, HERMY! DON'T INTERRUPT WHEN I'M YELLING AT YOU! AND FURTHERMORE...
B-B-BUT...
RUN AWAY!
6

GURK?

UH... OH...

YAAAAAAAAAAAAAAAAAAAAAAAA

FIVE KILOMETERS LATER...

THERE YOU ARE, MASTER, HERMY HAVE NICE RUN, BUT RUNNING MAKE HERMY THIRSTIER STILL!

PANT PUFF PANT

PANT PUFF PANT

WELL OF ANCIENTS

LOOK, MASTER! TRIED-AND-TRUE RANGER-GUIDE HERMY BRING YOU RIGHT TO WHERE YOU WANT TO GO!

WELL OF ANCIENTS

PRAISED!

HA! HERMY DRINK LOTS NOW!

WELL OF ANCIENTS →

7

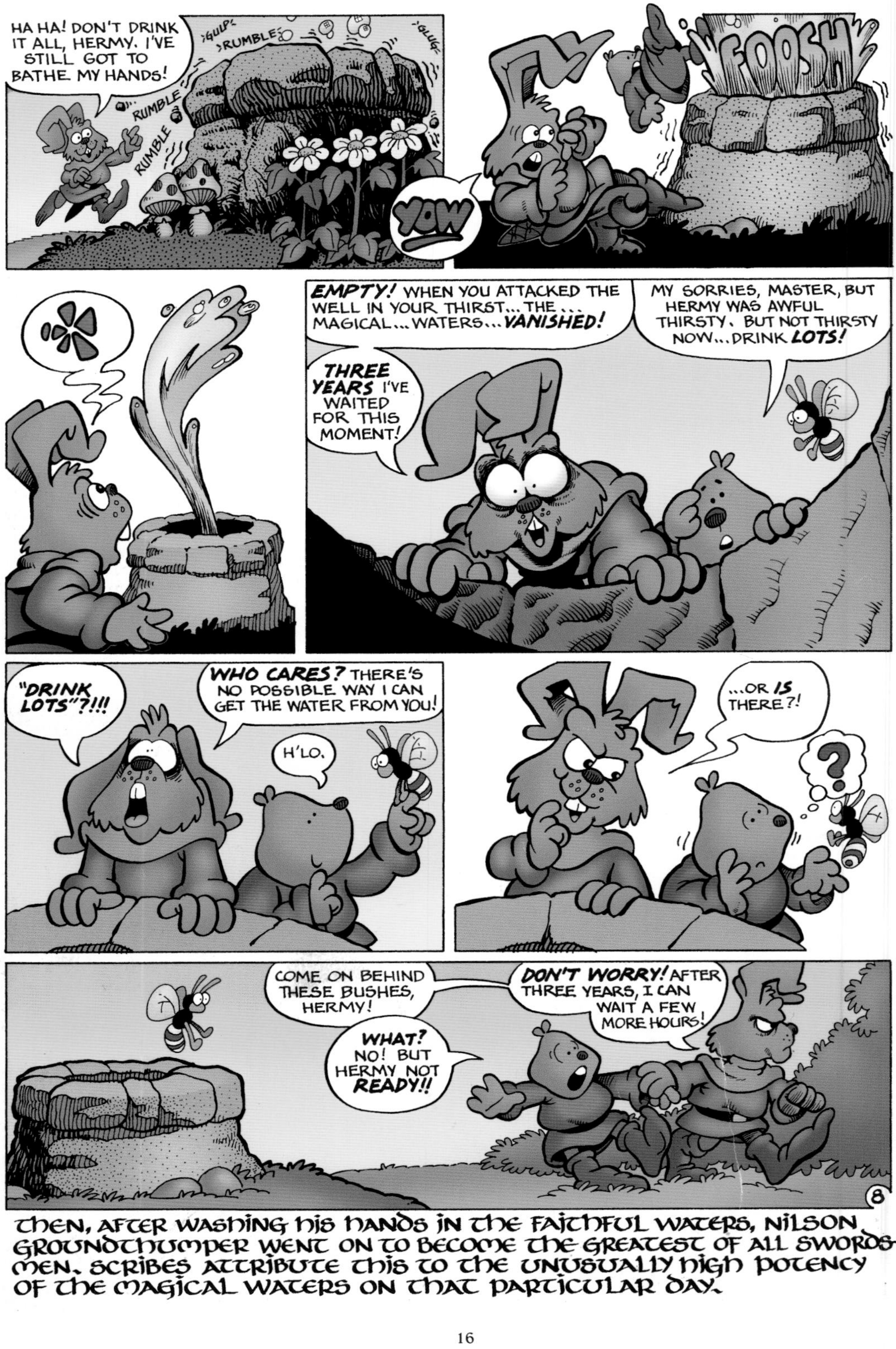
HA HA! DON'T DRINK IT ALL, HERMY. I'VE STILL GOT TO BATHE MY HANDS!
GULP
RUMBLE
GLUG
RUMBLE
RUMBLE
FOOSH
YOW
EMPTY! WHEN YOU ATTACKED THE WELL IN YOUR THIRST... THE... MAGICAL... WATERS... VANISHED!
THREE YEARS I'VE WAITED FOR THIS MOMENT!
MY SORRIES, MASTER, BUT HERMY WAS AWFUL THIRSTY. BUT NOT THIRSTY NOW... DRINK LOTS!
"DRINK LOTS"?!!!
WHO CARES? THERE'S NO POSSIBLE WAY I CAN GET THE WATER FROM YOU!
H'LO.
...OR IS THERE?!
COME ON BEHIND THESE BUSHES, HERMY!
DON'T WORRY! AFTER THREE YEARS, I CAN WAIT A FEW MORE HOURS!
WHAT? NO! BUT HERMY NOT READY!!
8

THEN, AFTER WASHING HIS HANDS IN THE FAITHFUL WATERS, NILSON GROUNDTHUMPER WENT ON TO BECOME THE GREATEST OF ALL SWORDSMEN. SCRIBES ATTRIBUTE THIS TO THE UNUSUALLY HIGH POTENCY OF THE MAGICAL WATERS ON THAT PARTICULAR DAY.

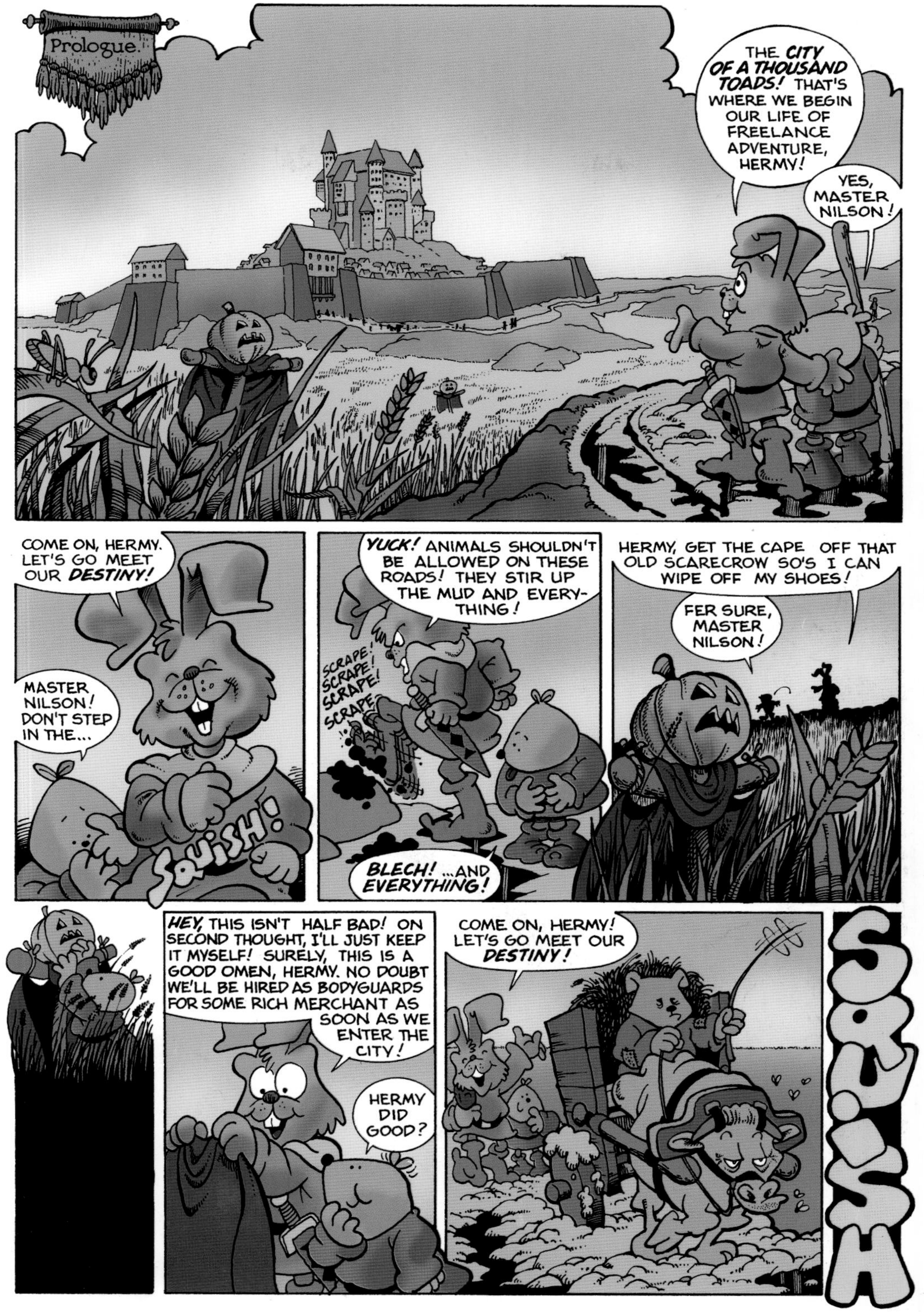
Prologue.
THE CITY OF A THOUSAND TOADS! THAT'S WHERE WE BEGIN OUR LIFE OF FREELANCE ADVENTURE, HERMY!
YES, MASTER NILSON!
COME ON, HERMY. LET'S GO MEET OUR DESTINY!
MASTER NILSON! DON'T STEP IN THE...
SQUISH!
YUCK! ANIMALS SHOULDN'T BE ALLOWED ON THESE ROADS! THEY STIR UP THE MUD AND EVERYTHING!
SCRAPE! SCRAPE! SCRAPE! SCRAPE
BLECH! ...AND EVERYTHING!
HERMY, GET THE CAPE OFF THAT OLD SCARECROW SO'S I CAN WIPE OFF MY SHOES!
FER SURE, MASTER NILSON!
HEY, THIS ISN'T HALF BAD! ON SECOND THOUGHT, I'LL JUST KEEP IT MYSELF! SURELY, THIS IS A GOOD OMEN, HERMY. NO DOUBT WE'LL BE HIRED AS BODYGUARDS FOR SOME RICH MERCHANT AS SOON AS WE ENTER THE CITY!
HERMY DID GOOD?
COME ON, HERMY! LET'S GO MEET OUR DESTINY!
SQUISH

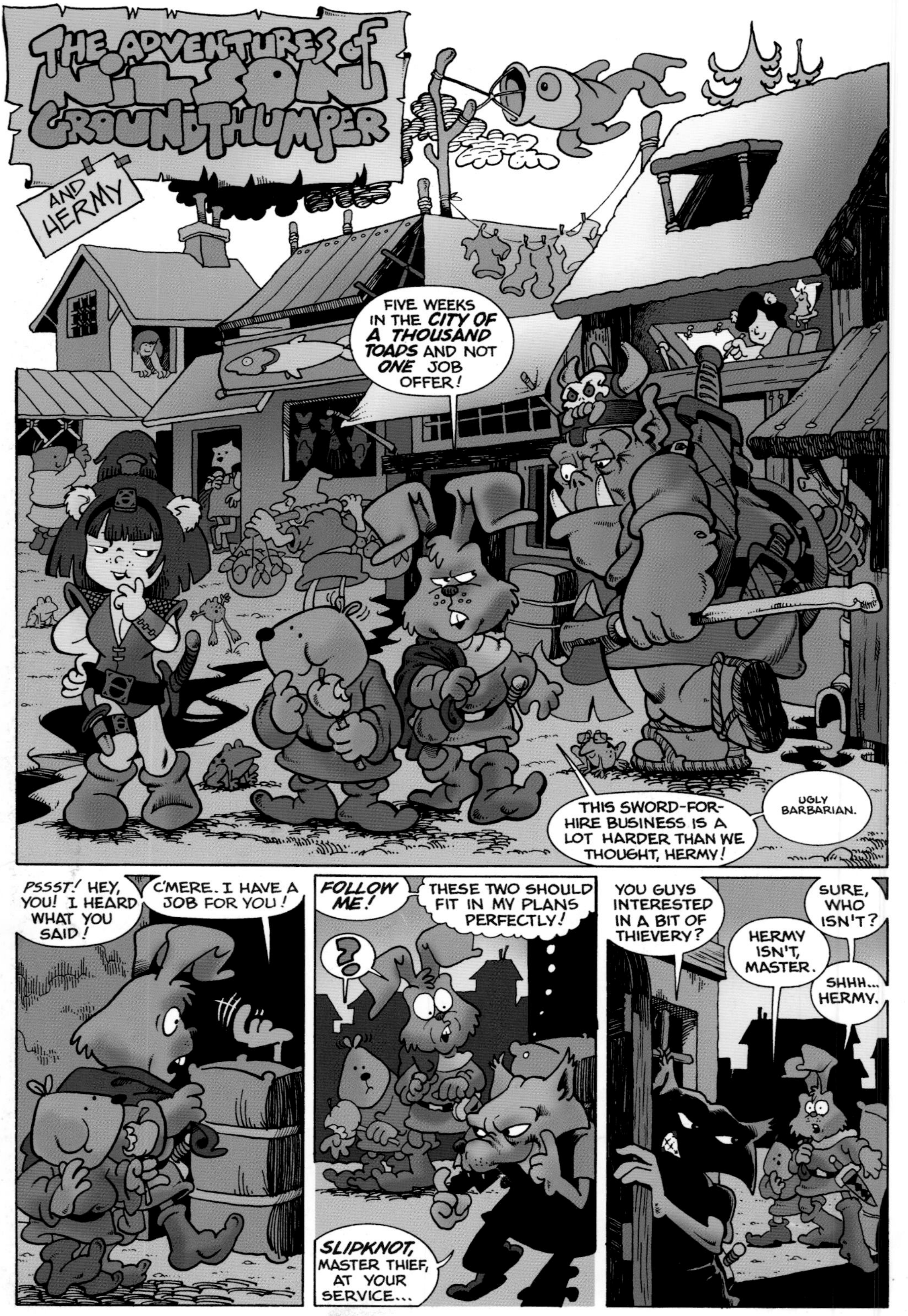
THE ADVENTURES OF NILSON GROUNDTHUMPER
AND HERMY
FIVE WEEKS IN THE *CITY OF A THOUSAND TOADS* AND NOT *ONE* JOB OFFER!
THIS SWORD-FOR-HIRE BUSINESS IS A LOT HARDER THAN WE THOUGHT, HERMY!
UGLY BARBARIAN.
PSSST! HEY, YOU! I HEARD WHAT YOU SAID!
C'MERE. I HAVE A JOB FOR YOU!
FOLLOW ME!
THESE TWO SHOULD FIT IN MY PLANS PERFECTLY!
?
SLIPKNOT, MASTER THIEF, AT YOUR SERVICE...
YOU GUYS INTERESTED IN A BIT OF THIEVERY?
SURE, WHO ISN'T?
HERMY ISN'T, MASTER.
SHHH... HERMY.

THEN FOLLOW ME!

I'VE BEEN WATCHING YOU TWO EVER SINCE YOU ENTERED THE CITY...

...AND YOU LOOK LIKE EXCELLENT CRIMINAL MATERIAL.

WHAT'RE YOUR NAMES?

I'M NILSON GROUNDTHUMPER AND THIS IS MY COMPANION, HERMY!

H'LO.

COME IN HERE, I'VE GOT JUST ONE MORE QUESTION TO ASK...

WHAT'S THAT?

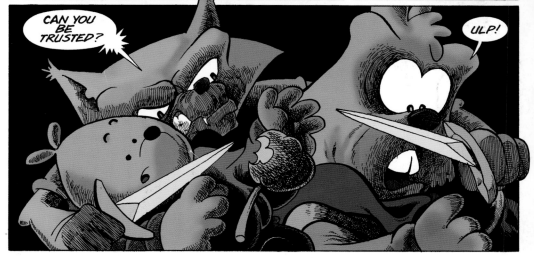

CAN YOU BE TRUSTED?

ULP!

OF COURSE! WE'RE *TRUSTWORTHY* THIEVES! WE CAN EVEN GIVE YOU REFERENCES!

OKAY, BUT ONE WRONG MOVE AND YOU'RE BOTH *DEAD MEAT!* NOW LIGHT THE LAMPS!

Y-YES, SIR!

HA! THE FOOLS SHOULD ASK IF *I* CAN BE TRUSTED...

... I'VE DOUBLE-CROSSED SO MANY PEOPLE IN THE CITY OF A THOUSAND TOADS THAT I'VE BEEN FORCED TO RECRUIT STRANGERS TO HELP ME PULL MY JOBS!

SO WHAT'S THE DEAL, SLIPKNOT?

OKAY, HERE'S THE CAPER...WE'RE GOING AFTER THE CROWN JEWELS OF KING KILBUN. INTERESTED?

HA! JUST THE KIND OF JOB WE'RE SUITED FOR!

ER...MIND IF I HANG MY CAPE?

>PSST< ONCE WE LEARN HIS *PLAN*, WE'LL TURN HIM IN TO THE KING AND COLLECT A *BIG REWARD!*

I'LL LET THESE TWO TAKE ALL THE RISKS, AND ONCE I GET MY HANDS ON THE ROYAL JEWELS, I'LL LET THEM TAKE THE RAP! HA! HA!

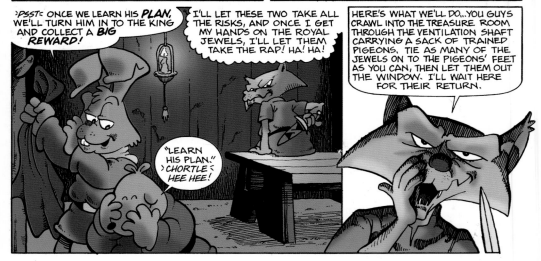

HERE'S WHAT WE'LL DO...YOU GUYS CRAWL INTO THE TREASURE ROOM THROUGH THE VENTILATION SHAFT CARRYING A SACK OF TRAINED PIGEONS. TIE AS MANY OF THE JEWELS ON TO THE PIGEONS' FEET AS YOU CAN, THEN LET THEM OUT THE WINDOW. I'LL WAIT HERE FOR THEIR RETURN.

"LEARN HIS PLAN." >CHORTLE< HEE HEE!

AND WE CRAWL BACK OUT THROUGH THE VENTILATION SHAFT AND MEET BACK HERE TO SPLIT THE LOOT! CLEVER *PLAN!*

"PLAN"!

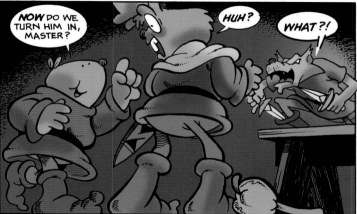

NOW DO WE TURN HIM IN, MASTER?

HUH?

WHAT?!

TRAITORS!!

STAND BACK, BLABBERMOUTH!

THUD!

CLAK!

SKULKING IN THE SHADOWS IS MORE YOUR STYLE OF FIGHTING, SLIPKNOT...

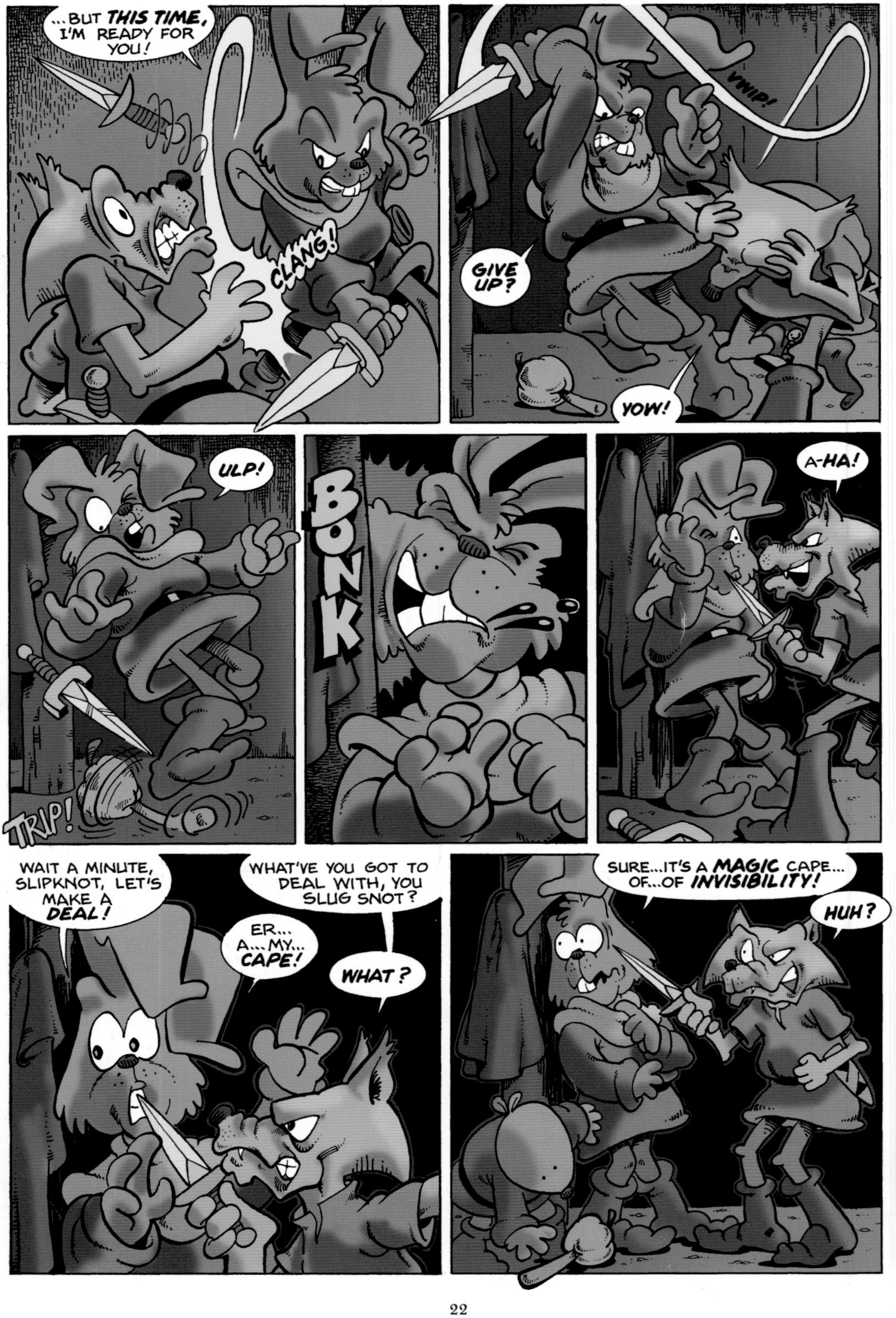

...BUT THIS TIME, I'M READY FOR YOU!
CLANG!
VWIP!
GIVE UP?
YOW!
ULP!
TRIP!
BONK
A-HA!
WAIT A MINUTE, SLIPKNOT, LET'S MAKE A DEAL!
WHAT'VE YOU GOT TO DEAL WITH, YOU SLUG SNOT?
ER... A...MY... CAPE!
WHAT?
SURE...IT'S A MAGIC CAPE... OF...OF INVISIBILITY!
HUH?

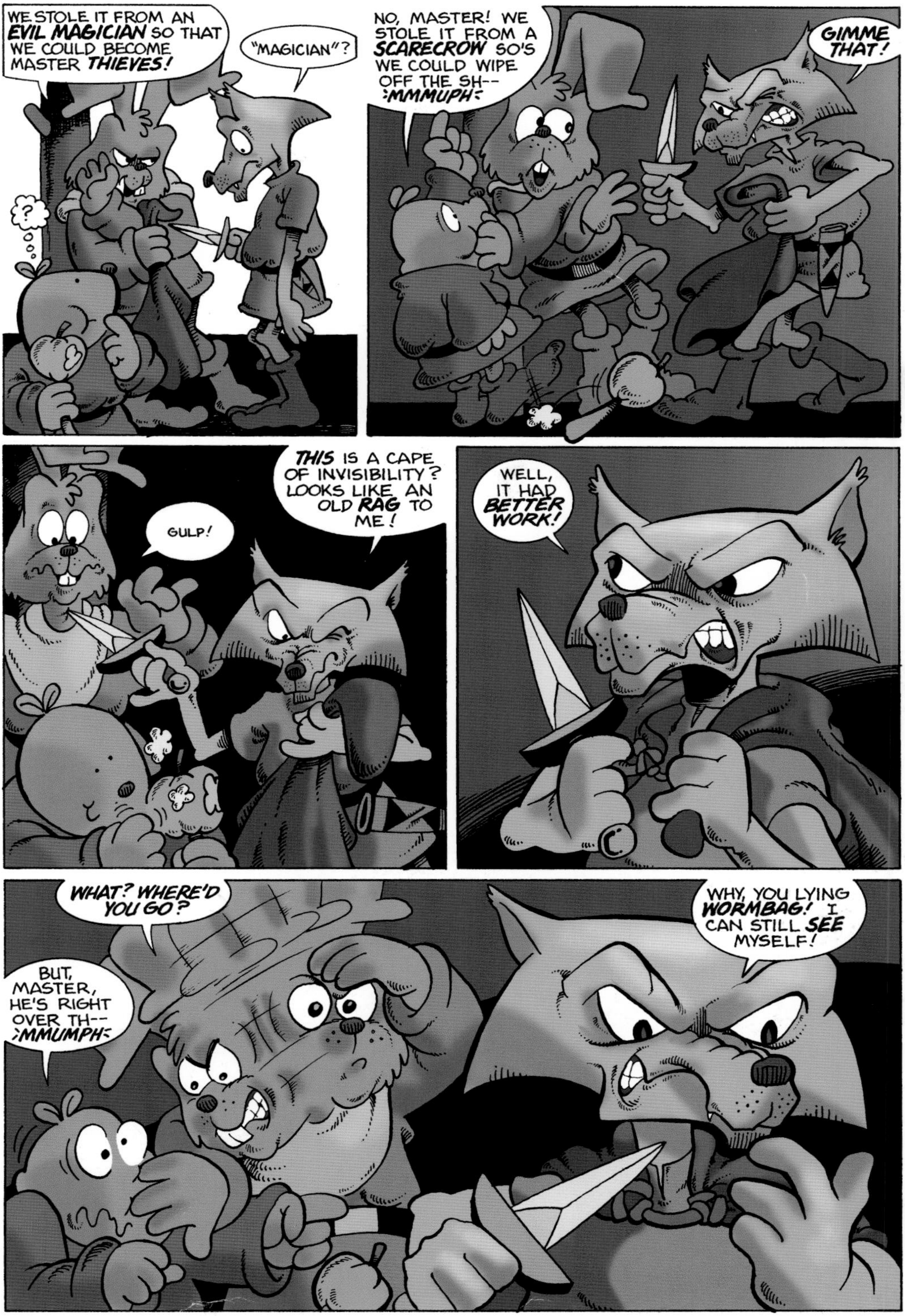
WE STOLE IT FROM AN EVIL MAGICIAN SO THAT WE COULD BECOME MASTER THIEVES!
"MAGICIAN"?
?
NO, MASTER! WE STOLE IT FROM A SCARECROW SO'S WE COULD WIPE OFF THE SH-- ›MMMUPH‹
GIMME THAT!
GULP!
THIS IS A CAPE OF INVISIBILITY? LOOKS LIKE AN OLD RAG TO ME!
WELL, IT HAD BETTER WORK!
WHAT? WHERE'D YOU GO?
BUT, MASTER, HE'S RIGHT OVER TH-- ›MMUMPH‹
WHY, YOU LYING WORMBAG! I CAN STILL SEE MYSELF!

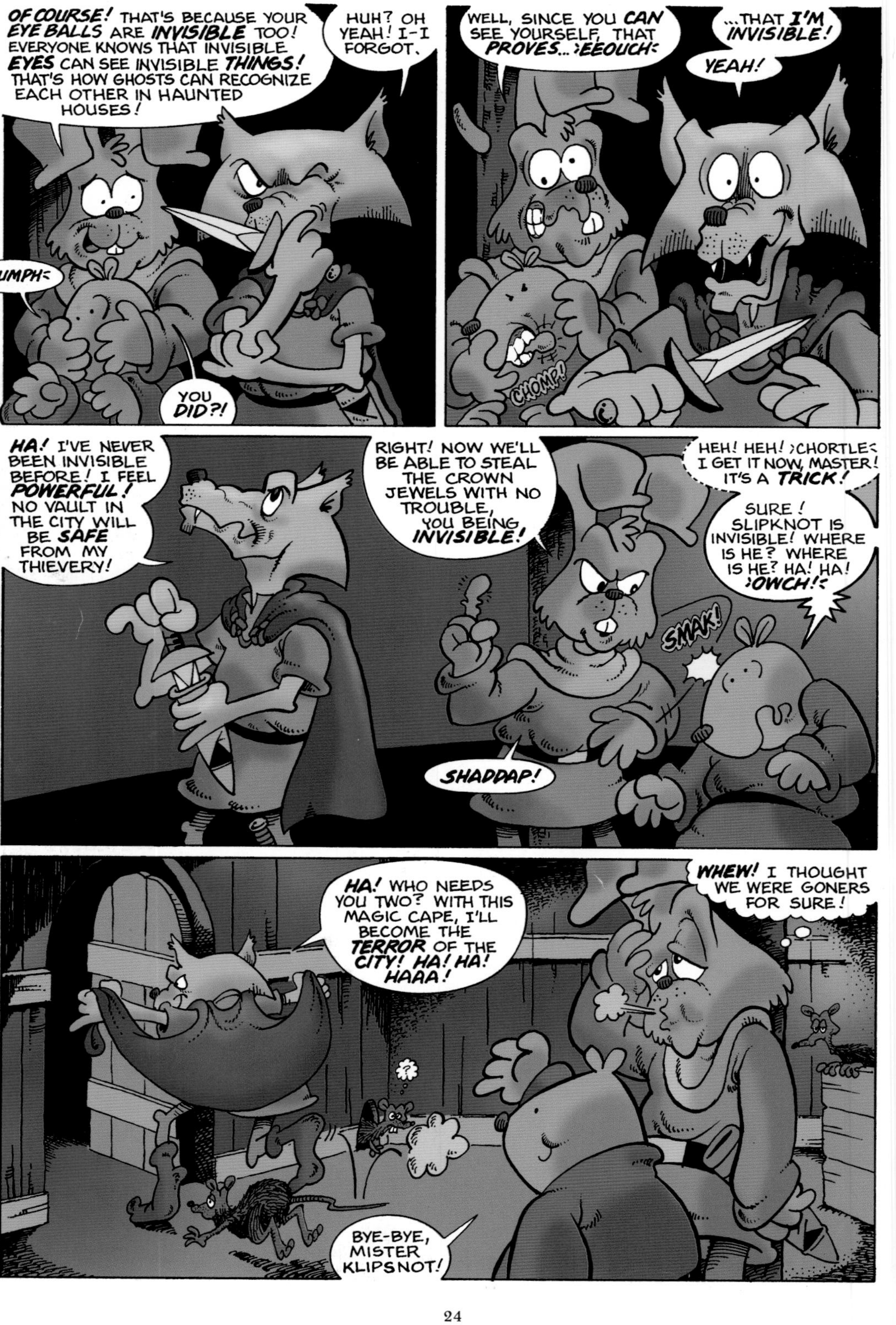

OF COURSE! THAT'S BECAUSE YOUR EYE BALLS ARE INVISIBLE TOO! EVERYONE KNOWS THAT INVISIBLE EYES CAN SEE INVISIBLE THINGS! THAT'S HOW GHOSTS CAN RECOGNIZE EACH OTHER IN HAUNTED HOUSES!
HUH? OH YEAH! I-I FORGOT.
>MUMPH<
YOU DID?!
WELL, SINCE YOU CAN SEE YOURSELF, THAT PROVES... >EEOUCH<
...THAT I'M INVISIBLE!
YEAH!
CHOMP!
HA! I'VE NEVER BEEN INVISIBLE BEFORE! I FEEL POWERFUL! NO VAULT IN THE CITY WILL BE SAFE FROM MY THIEVERY!
RIGHT! NOW WE'LL BE ABLE TO STEAL THE CROWN JEWELS WITH NO TROUBLE, YOU BEING INVISIBLE!
HEH! HEH! >CHORTLE< I GET IT NOW, MASTER! IT'S A TRICK!
SURE! SLIPKNOT IS INVISIBLE! WHERE IS HE? WHERE IS HE? HA! HA! >OWCH!<
SMAK!
SHADDAP!
HA! WHO NEEDS YOU TWO? WITH THIS MAGIC CAPE, I'LL BECOME THE TERROR OF THE CITY! HA! HA! HAAA!
WHEW! I THOUGHT WE WERE GONERS FOR SURE!
BYE-BYE, MISTER KLIPSNOT!

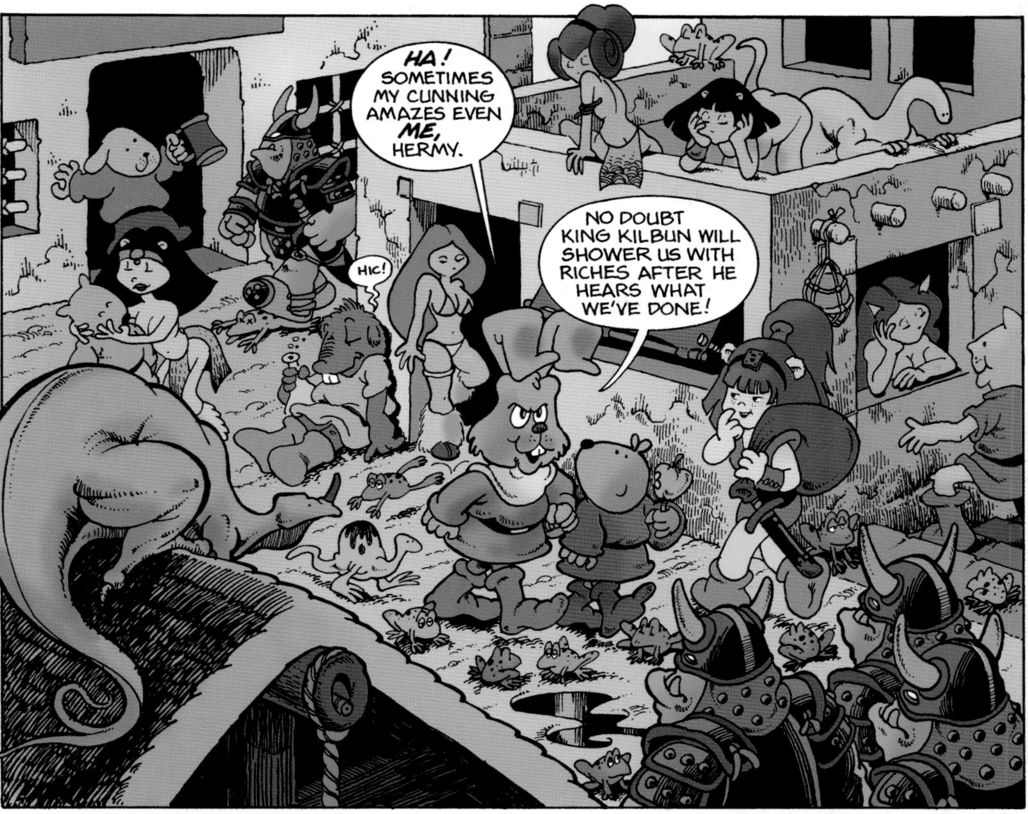
HA! SOMETIMES MY CUNNING AMAZES EVEN ME, HERMY.
HIC!
NO DOUBT KING KILBUN WILL SHOWER US WITH RICHES AFTER HE HEARS WHAT WE'VE DONE!

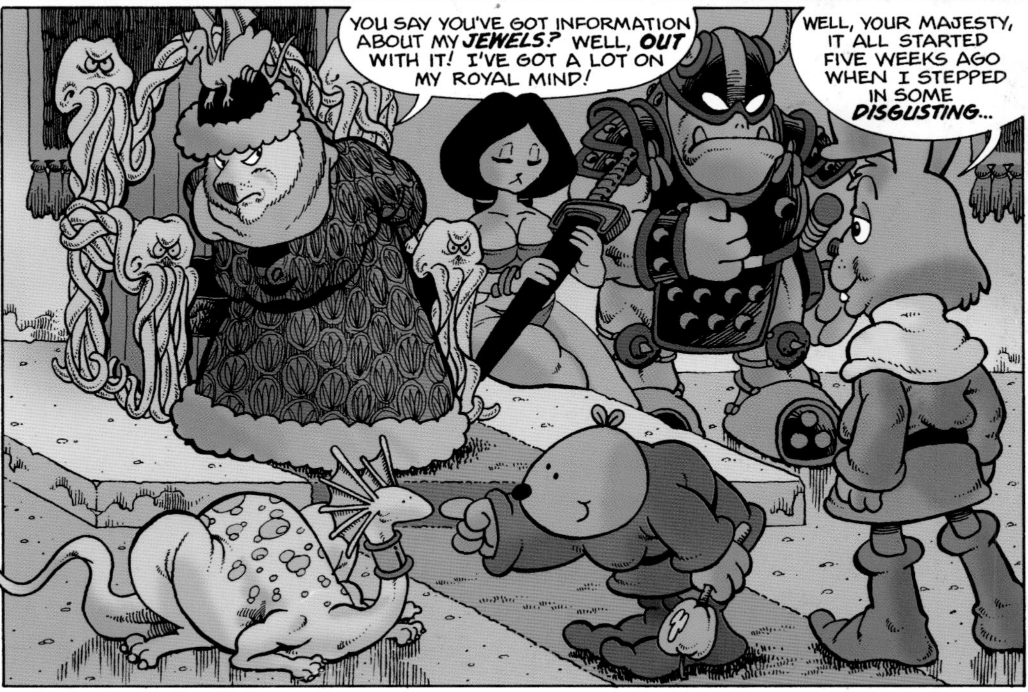
YOU SAY YOU'VE GOT INFORMATION ABOUT MY JEWELS? WELL, OUT WITH IT! I'VE GOT A LOT ON MY ROYAL MIND!
WELL, YOUR MAJESTY, IT ALL STARTED FIVE WEEKS AGO WHEN I STEPPED IN SOME DISGUSTING...

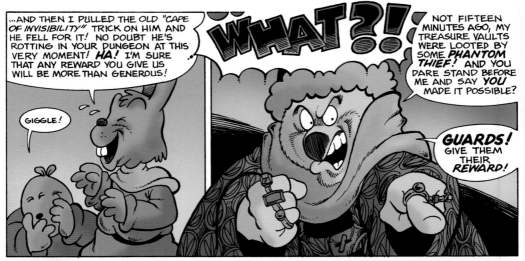

"...AND THEN I PULLED THE OLD "CAPE OF INVISIBILITY" TRICK ON HIM AND HE FELL FOR IT! NO DOUBT HE'S ROTTING IN YOUR DUNGEON AT THIS VERY MOMENT! *HA!* I'M SURE THAT ANY REWARD YOU GIVE US WILL BE MORE THAN GENEROUS!

GIGGLE!

WHAT?!

NOT FIFTEEN MINUTES AGO, MY TREASURE VAULTS WERE LOOTED BY SOME *PHANTOM THIEF!* AND YOU DARE STAND BEFORE ME AND SAY *YOU* MADE IT POSSIBLE?

GUARDS! GIVE THEM THEIR *REWARD!*

HERMY DOESN'T LIKE THIS REWARD, MASTER NILSON. MAYBE WE SHOULD HAVE KEPT THE MAGIC CAPE SO WE COULD SNEAK OUT OF HERE, INVISIBLE LIKE.

BUT IT WAS A TRICK, HERMY! A *TRICK!* THE MAGIC CAPE DOESN'T WORK!

..OR DOES IT?

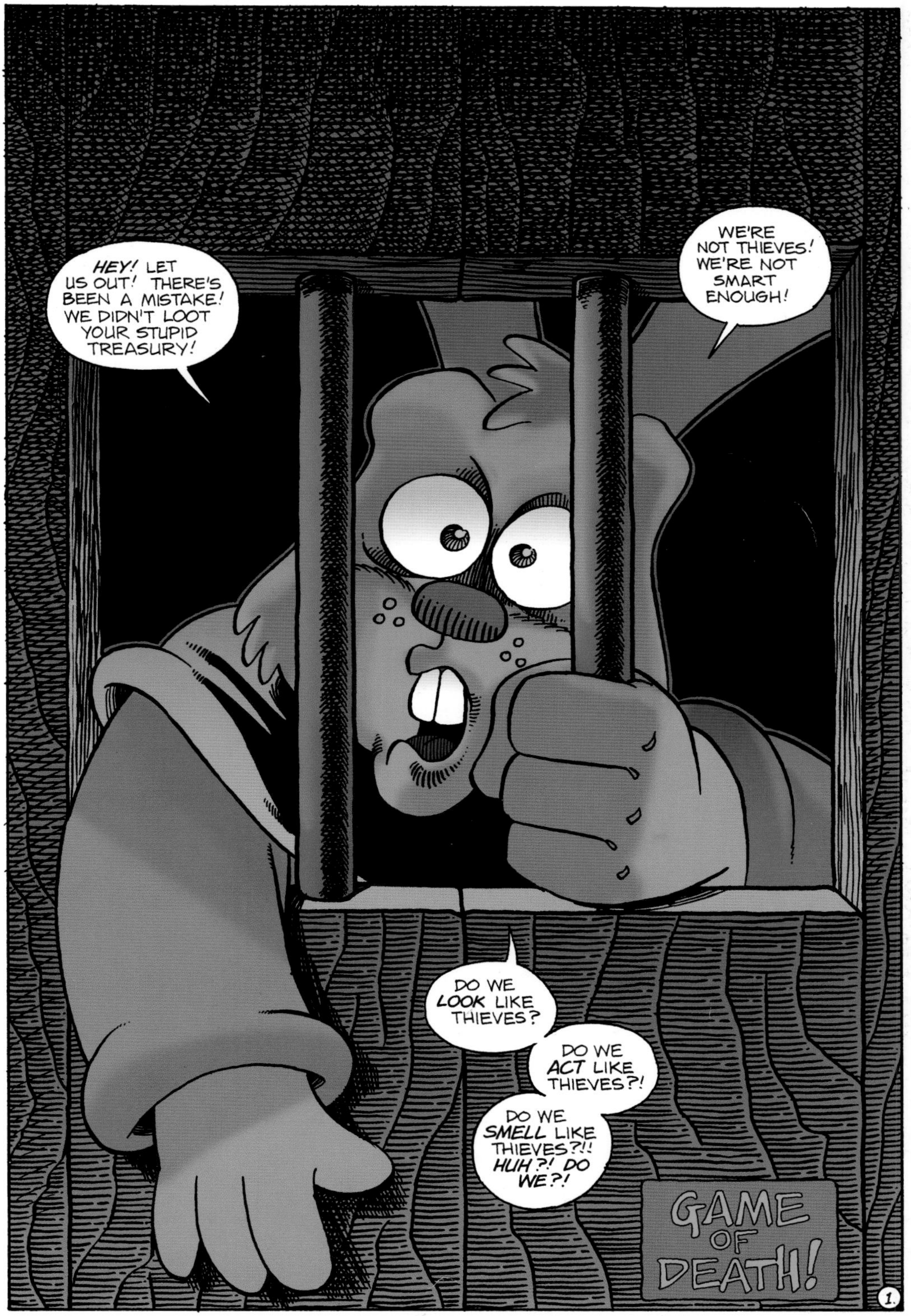
HEY! LET US OUT! THERE'S BEEN A MISTAKE! WE DIDN'T LOOT YOUR STUPID TREASURY!
WE'RE NOT THIEVES! WE'RE NOT SMART ENOUGH!
DO WE LOOK LIKE THIEVES?
DO WE ACT LIKE THIEVES?!
DO WE SMELL LIKE THIEVES?!! HUH?! DO WE?!
GAME OF DEATH!
1.

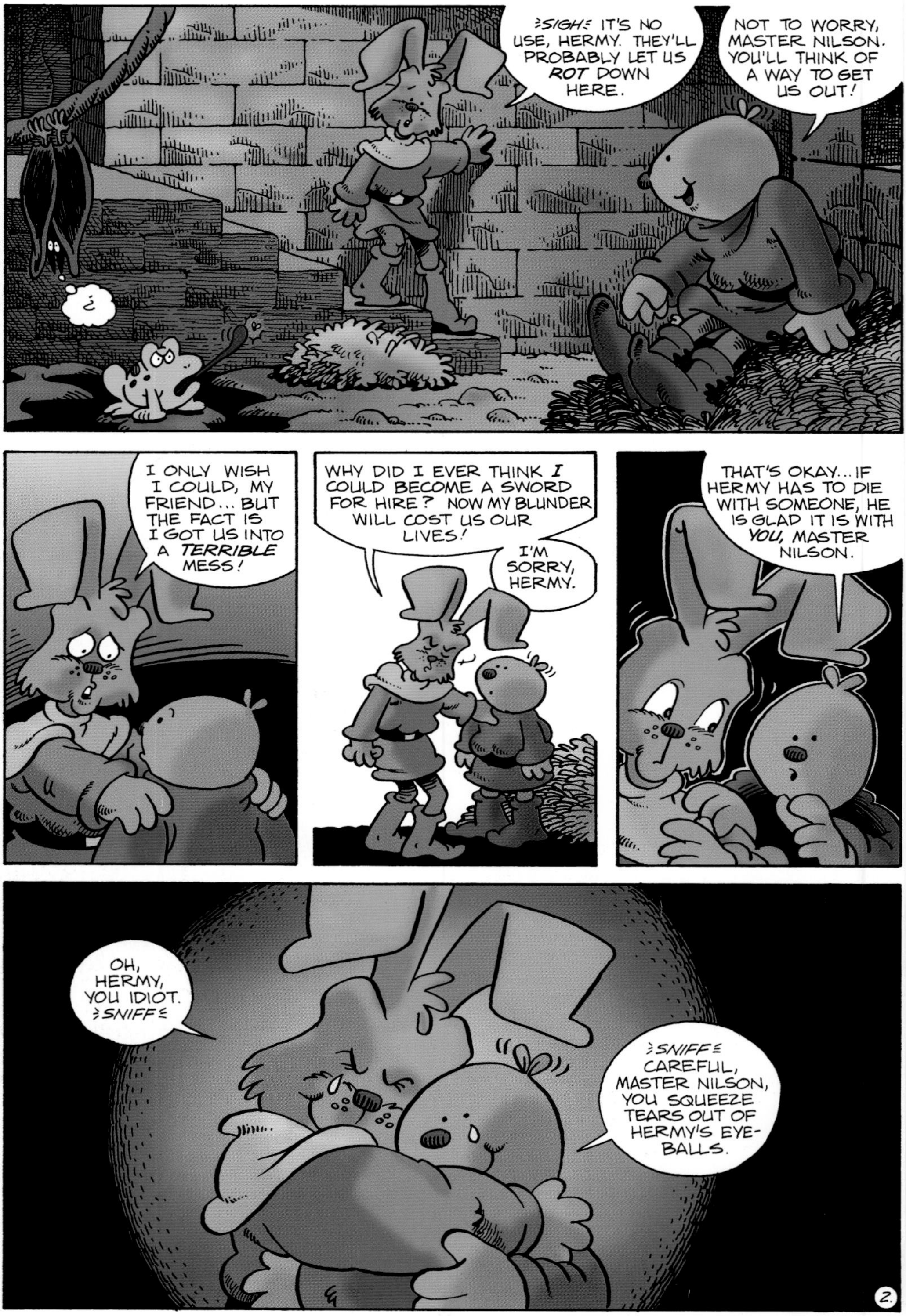

SIGH IT'S NO USE, HERMY. THEY'LL PROBABLY LET US ROT DOWN HERE.
NOT TO WORRY, MASTER NILSON. YOU'LL THINK OF A WAY TO GET US OUT!
I ONLY WISH I COULD, MY FRIEND... BUT THE FACT IS I GOT US INTO A TERRIBLE MESS!
WHY DID I EVER THINK I COULD BECOME A SWORD FOR HIRE? NOW MY BLUNDER WILL COST US OUR LIVES!
I'M SORRY, HERMY.
THAT'S OKAY... IF HERMY HAS TO DIE WITH SOMEONE, HE IS GLAD IT IS WITH YOU, MASTER NILSON.
OH, HERMY, YOU IDIOT. SNIFF
SNIFF CAREFUL, MASTER NILSON, YOU SQUEEZE TEARS OUT OF HERMY'S EYE-BALLS.
2.

HARRR! WHAT A TOUCHING SIGHT! NOW UP AGAINST THE WALL, SCUMS! IT'S ME, YOUR JAILER, LUMPBACK CLUBFOOT!

WHAT DO YOU WANT, JAILER?

STAY BACK, HERMY.

HARRR! I'M HERE TO FREE YOU!

KING KILBUN IS CONVINCED THAT YOU DID NOT RAID HIS TREASURY... BUT HE IS ALSO CONVINCED THAT YOU ARE NOT ENTIRELY BLAMELESS, SO HAS DECIDED TO FREE JUST *ONE* OF YOU!

JUST ONE?

JUST ONE.

HIS MAJESTY IS AN AVID SPORTS FAN AND HAS ARRANGED FOR YOU TO FIGHT EACH OTHER IN THE ARENA. THE WINNER WILL BE FREE TO LEAVE.

AND THE LOSER?

YUMMY!

IT'S A FIGHT TO THE DEATH! THE LOSER WILL BE LEFT WHERE HE FALLS... A TREAT FOR THE CARRION!

GULP!

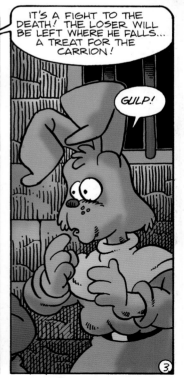

③

THE KING, IN HIS GENEROSITY, HAD ME BRING YOU A LAST MEAL TO PREPARE YOU FOR THE ARENA!

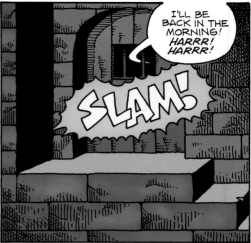

I'LL BE BACK IN THE MORNING! HARRR! HARRR!

SLAM!

ONLY ONE DAY BEFORE WE HAVE TO FIGHT EACH OTHER TO THE DEATH!

WHAT TO DO?

WHAT TO DO?

WHAT TREATS, MASTER NILSON!

STALE BREAD, MOLDY CHEESE, AND SOUR WINE!

YUMMY!

BUT HERMY DOESN'T LIKE WINE.

WHAT TO DO? ONLY ONE OF US WILL BE FREED--THE OTHER DIES! HERMY HAS NEVER HELD A SWORD IN HIS LIFE, SO I COULD WIN EASILY...

...BUT I'VE NEVER SLAIN ANYONE BEFORE EITHER. IT WOULD BE A SHAME TO START WITH MY BEST FRIEND...

BUT I CAN'T LET HIM KILL ME!

WHAT TO DO?

WHAT TO DO?

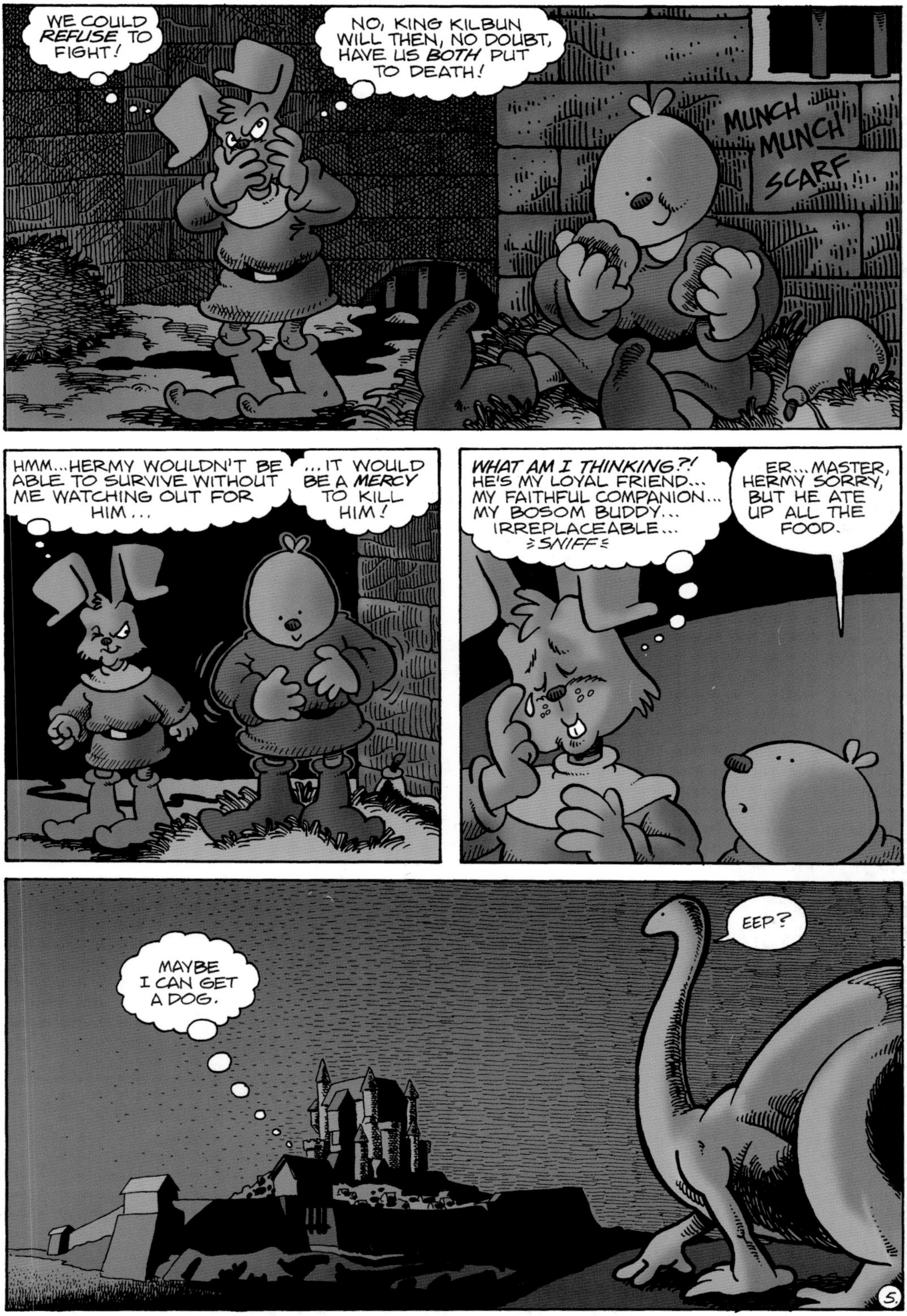
WE COULD *REFUSE* TO FIGHT!
NO, KING KILBUN WILL THEN, NO DOUBT, HAVE US *BOTH* PUT TO DEATH!
MUNCH MUNCH
SCARF
HMM...HERMY WOULDN'T BE ABLE TO SURVIVE WITHOUT ME WATCHING OUT FOR HIM...
...IT WOULD BE A *MERCY* TO KILL HIM!
WHAT AM I THINKING?! HE'S MY LOYAL FRIEND... MY FAITHFUL COMPANION... MY BOSOM BUDDY... IRREPLACEABLE... *SNIFF*
ER...MASTER, HERMY SORRY, BUT HE ATE UP ALL THE FOOD.
MAYBE I CAN GET A DOG.
EEP?
5.

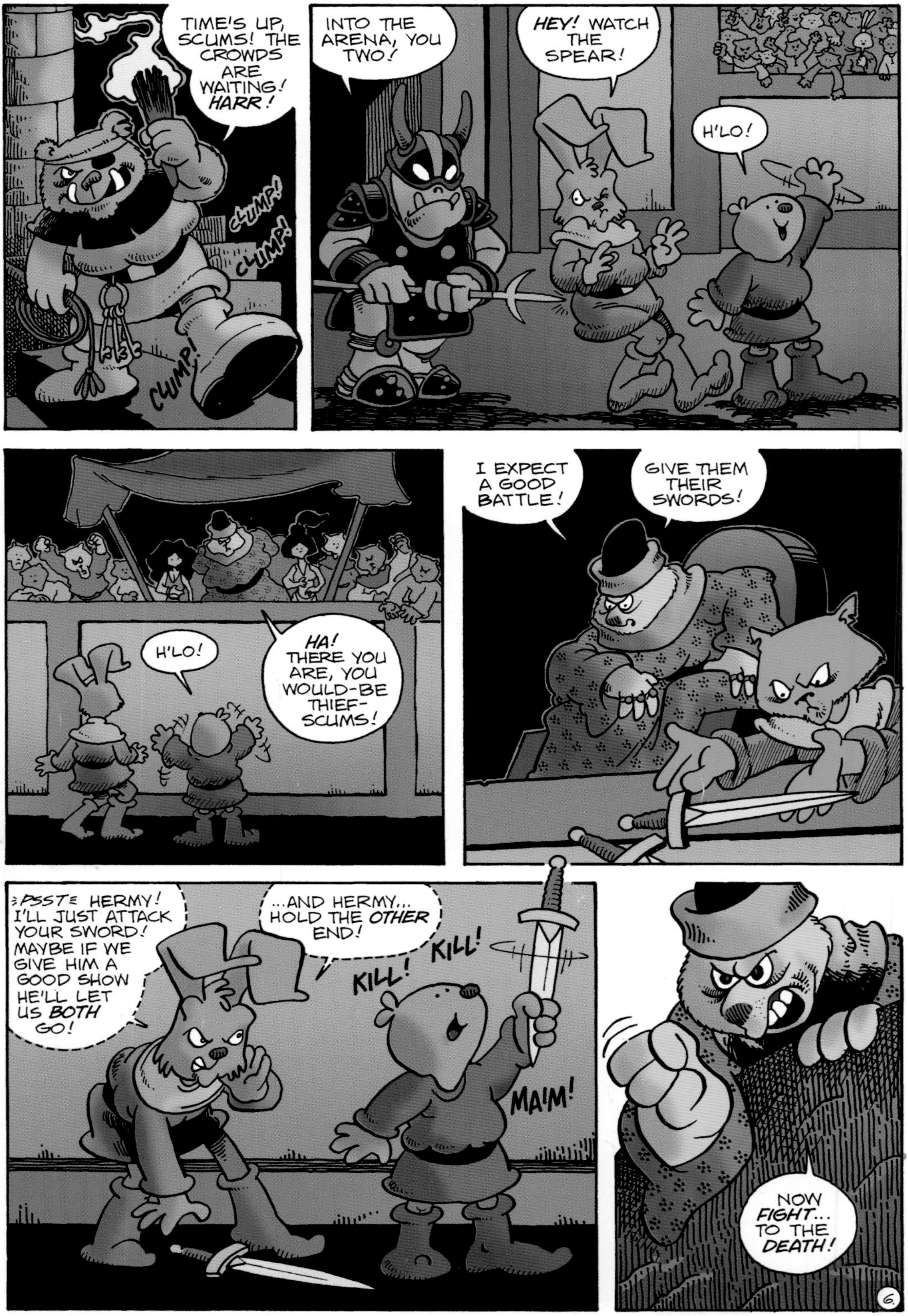
TIME'S UP, SCUMS! THE CROWDS ARE WAITING! HARR!
CLUMP!
CLUMP!
CLUMP!
CLUMP!
INTO THE ARENA, YOU TWO!
HEY! WATCH THE SPEAR!
H'LO!
H'LO!
HA! THERE YOU ARE, YOU WOULD-BE THIEF-SCUMS!
I EXPECT A GOOD BATTLE!
GIVE THEM THEIR SWORDS!
PSST HERMY! I'LL JUST ATTACK YOUR SWORD! MAYBE IF WE GIVE HIM A GOOD SHOW HE'LL LET US BOTH GO!
...AND HERMY... HOLD THE OTHER END!
KILL!
KILL!
MAIM!
NOW FIGHT... TO THE DEATH!
6.

YOW!

CLANG!

DIE! HAMSTER PIG!

PICK IT UP, STUPID!

UGH! HE DUCKED! I MISSED!

SWISH

HOLD ON TO IT THIS TIME!

HII—**YAA**

YES, MASTER NILSON.

NOW YOU ATTACK *ME* FOR A WHILE.

SURE THING, MASTER NILSON!

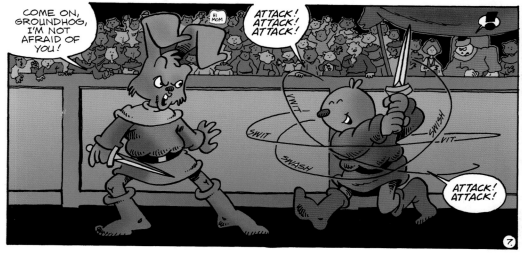

COME ON, GROUNDHOG, I'M NOT AFRAID OF YOU!

HI MOM

ATTACK! ATTACK! ATTACK!

VWIT

SWIT

SWASH

SWISH

—VIT—

ATTACK! ATTACK!

⑦

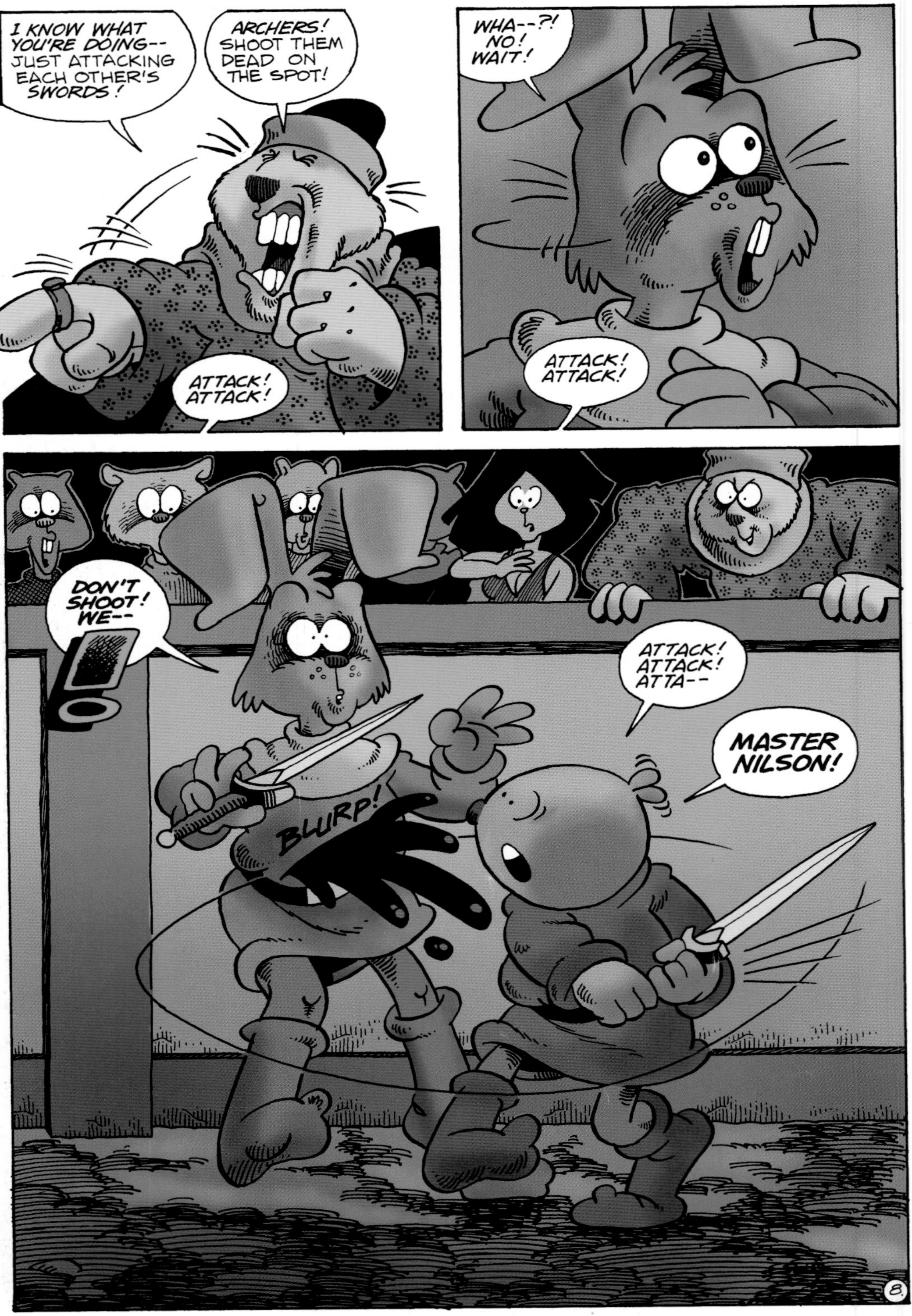
I KNOW WHAT YOU'RE DOING-- JUST ATTACKING EACH OTHER'S SWORDS!
ARCHERS! SHOOT THEM DEAD ON THE SPOT!
ATTACK! ATTACK!
WHA--?! NO! WAIT!
ATTACK! ATTACK!
DON'T SHOOT! WE--
ATTACK! ATTACK! ATTA--
MASTER NILSON!
BLURP!
8

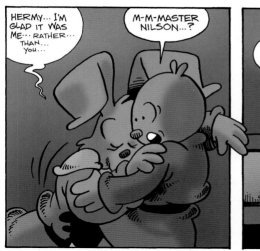

HERMY... I'M GLAD IT WAS ME... RATHER... THAN... YOU...

M-M-MASTER NILSON...?

MASTER NILSON?

HA! IT WAS A GOOD SHOW AFTER ALL.

THE MOLE GOES FREE.

COME, MY DEAR.

MASTER NILSON!

≥SOB≥

OH, MASTER NILSON! HERMY WISHES HE WAS DEADED... AND NOT YOU!

OooG! DON'T SQUEEZE TOO HARD! DO YOU WANT ME TO CHOKE?!

ARE THEY ALL GONE?

MASTER NILSON! YOU'RE ALIVE!

SQUEEZE!

GURK!

LET... ≥GASP≥ GO...!

9.

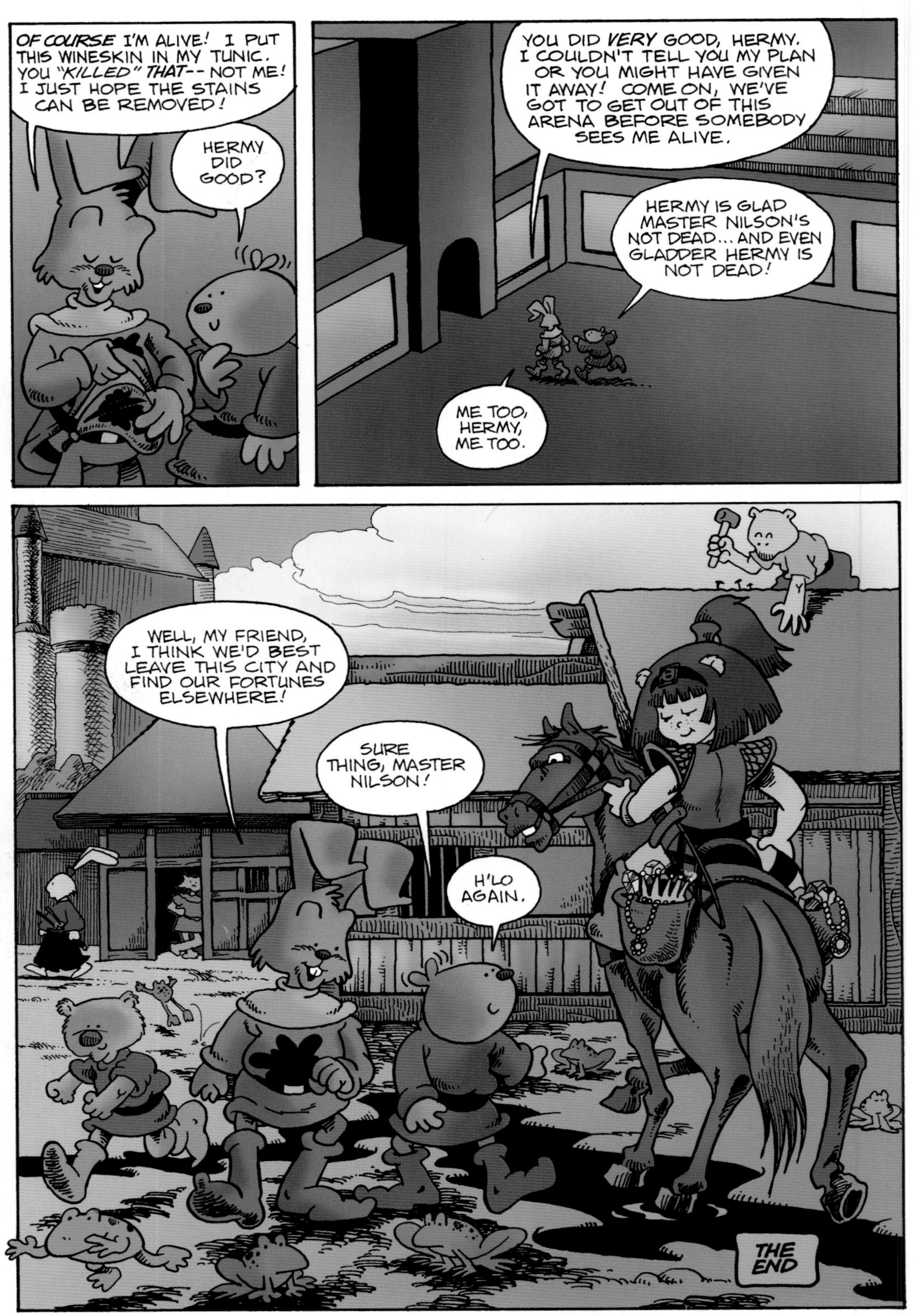
OF COURSE I'M ALIVE! I PUT THIS WINESKIN IN MY TUNIC. YOU "KILLED" THAT-- NOT ME! I JUST HOPE THE STAINS CAN BE REMOVED!
HERMY DID GOOD?
YOU DID VERY GOOD, HERMY. I COULDN'T TELL YOU MY PLAN OR YOU MIGHT HAVE GIVEN IT AWAY! COME ON, WE'VE GOT TO GET OUT OF THIS ARENA BEFORE SOMEBODY SEES ME ALIVE.
HERMY IS GLAD MASTER NILSON'S NOT DEAD... AND EVEN GLADDER HERMY IS NOT DEAD!
ME TOO, HERMY, ME TOO.
WELL, MY FRIEND, I THINK WE'D BEST LEAVE THIS CITY AND FIND OUR FORTUNES ELSEWHERE!
SURE THING, MASTER NILSON!
H'LO AGAIN.
THE END

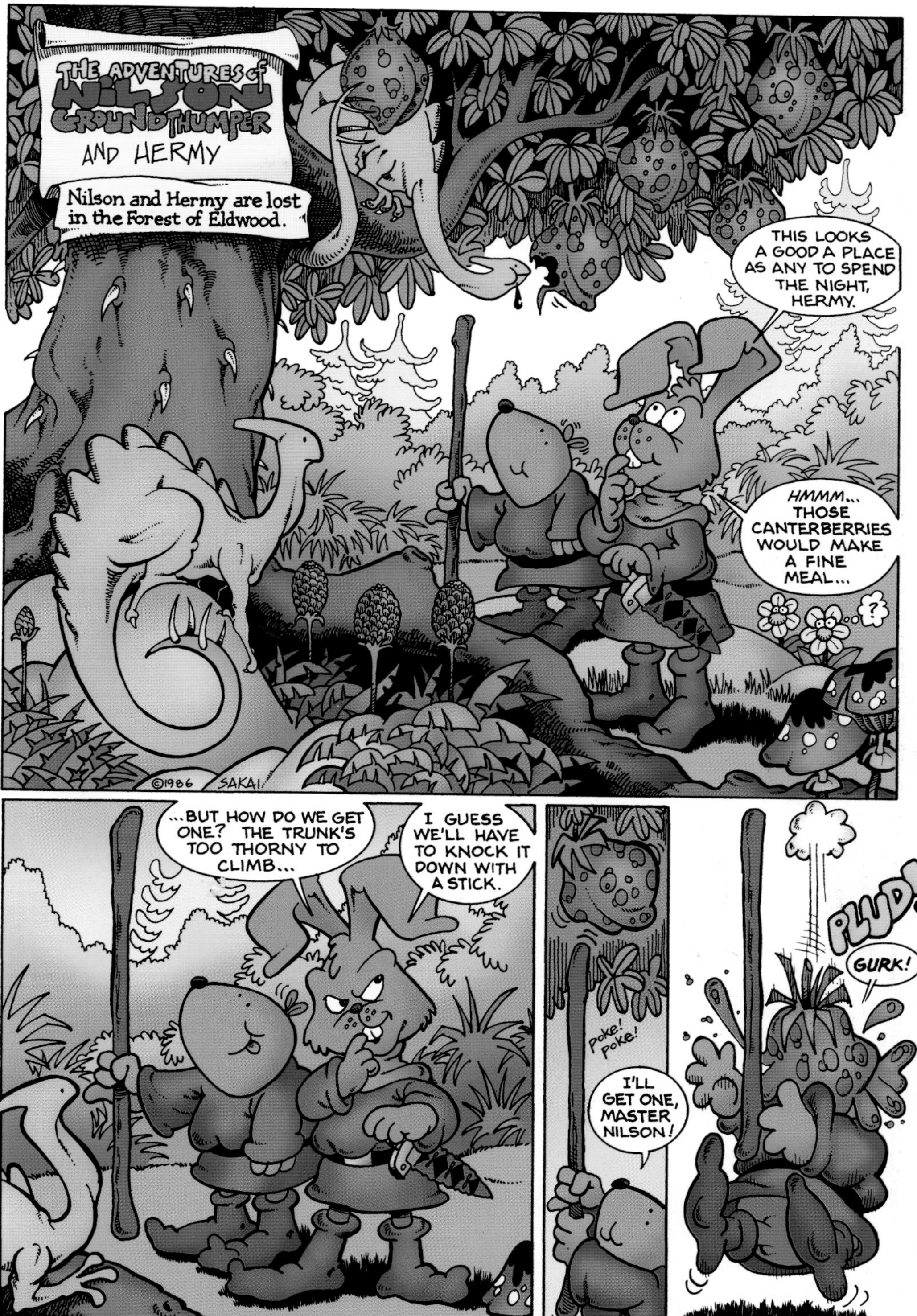

THE ADVENTURES of NILSON GROUNDTHUMPER
AND HERMY
Nilson and Hermy are lost in the Forest of Eldwood.
THIS LOOKS A GOOD A PLACE AS ANY TO SPEND THE NIGHT, HERMY.
HMMM... THOSE CANTERBERRIES WOULD MAKE A FINE MEAL...
?
©1986 SAKAI
...BUT HOW DO WE GET ONE? THE TRUNK'S TOO THORNY TO CLIMB...
I GUESS WE'LL HAVE TO KNOCK IT DOWN WITH A STICK.
poke! poke!
I'LL GET ONE, MASTER NILSON!
PLUD!
GURK!

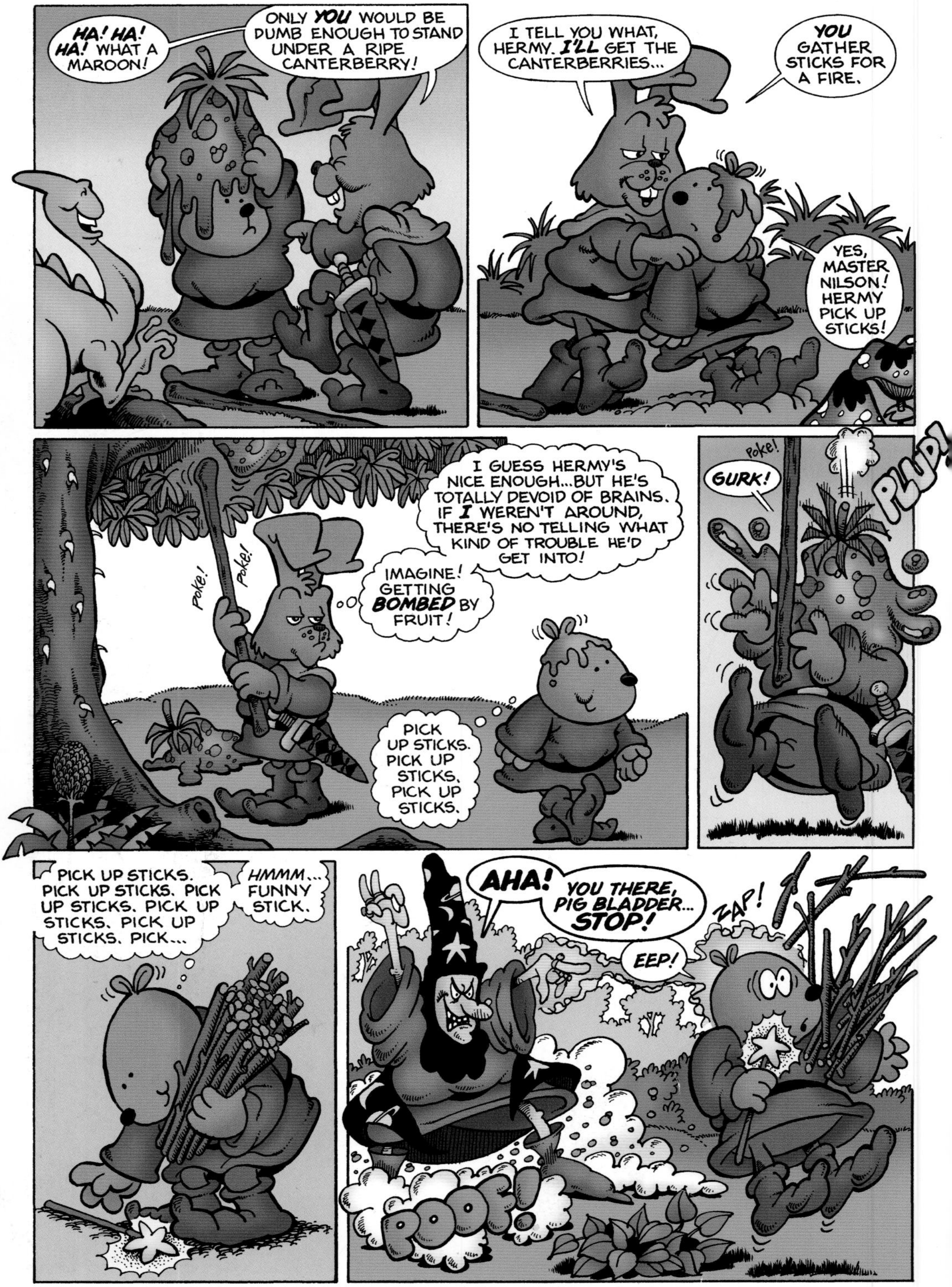
HA! HA! HA! WHAT A MAROON!
ONLY YOU WOULD BE DUMB ENOUGH TO STAND UNDER A RIPE CANTERBERRY!
I TELL YOU WHAT, HERMY. I'LL GET THE CANTERBERRIES...
YOU GATHER STICKS FOR A FIRE.
YES, MASTER NILSON! HERMY PICK UP STICKS!
POKE! POKE!
I GUESS HERMY'S NICE ENOUGH...BUT HE'S TOTALLY DEVOID OF BRAINS. IF I WEREN'T AROUND, THERE'S NO TELLING WHAT KIND OF TROUBLE HE'D GET INTO!
IMAGINE! GETTING BOMBED BY FRUIT!
PICK UP STICKS. PICK UP STICKS, PICK UP STICKS.
POKE!
GURK!
PLUD!
PICK UP STICKS. PICK UP STICKS. PICK UP STICKS. PICK UP STICKS. PICK UP STICKS. PICK...
HMMM... FUNNY STICK.
AHA!
YOU THERE, PIG BLADDER... STOP!
ZAP!
EEP!
POOF!

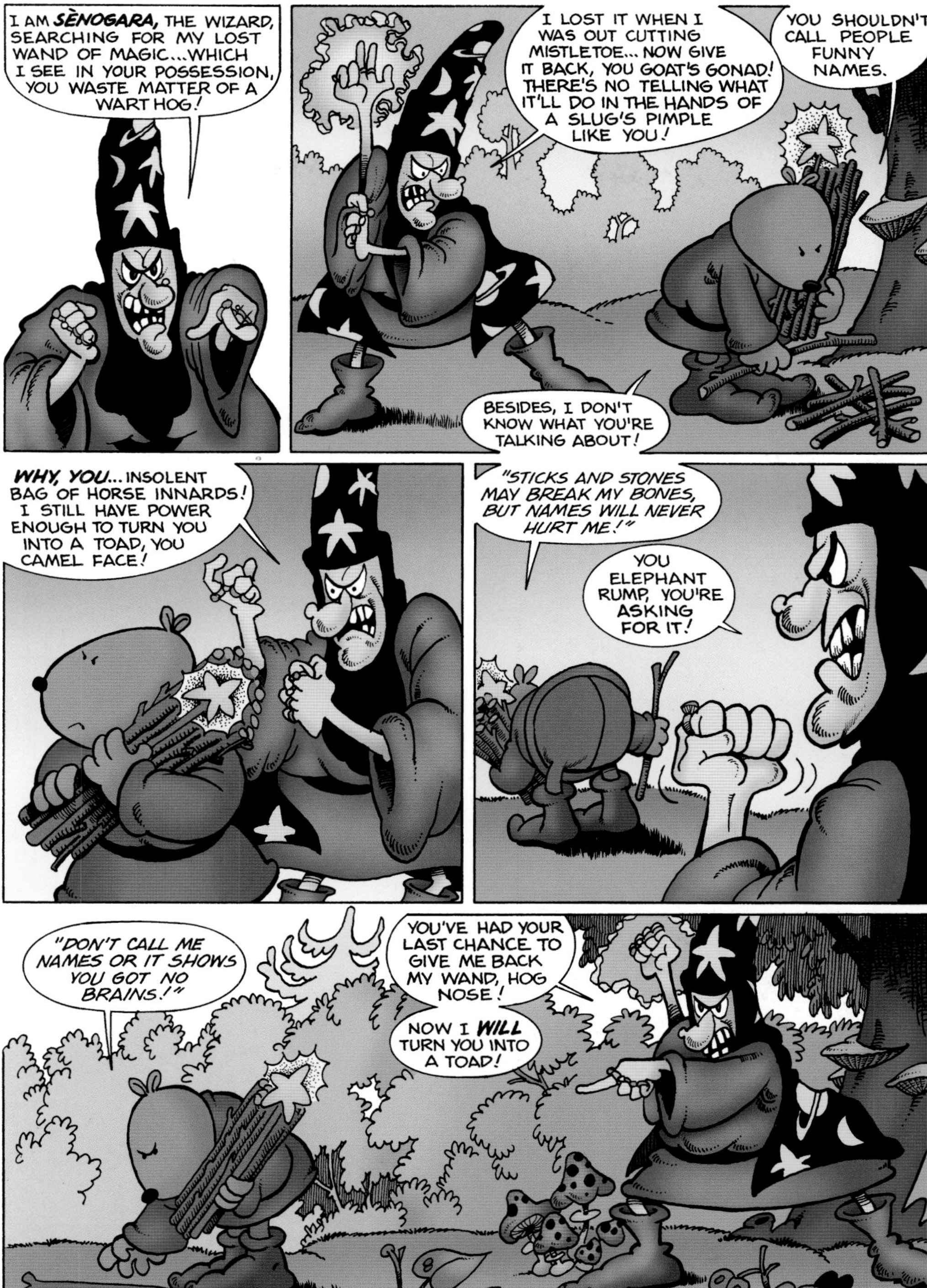
I AM **SÈNOGARA,** THE WIZARD, SEARCHING FOR MY LOST WAND OF MAGIC... WHICH I SEE IN YOUR POSSESSION, YOU WASTE MATTER OF A WART HOG!
I LOST IT WHEN I WAS OUT CUTTING MISTLETOE... NOW GIVE IT BACK, YOU GOAT'S GONAD! THERE'S NO TELLING WHAT IT'LL DO IN THE HANDS OF A SLUG'S PIMPLE LIKE YOU!
YOU SHOULDN'T CALL PEOPLE FUNNY NAMES.
BESIDES, I DON'T KNOW WHAT YOU'RE TALKING ABOUT!
WHY, YOU... INSOLENT BAG OF HORSE INNARDS! I STILL HAVE POWER ENOUGH TO TURN YOU INTO A TOAD, YOU CAMEL FACE!
"STICKS AND STONES MAY BREAK MY BONES, BUT NAMES WILL NEVER HURT ME!"
YOU ELEPHANT RUMP, YOU'RE ASKING FOR IT!
"DON'T CALL ME NAMES OR IT SHOWS YOU GOT NO BRAINS!"
YOU'VE HAD YOUR LAST CHANCE TO GIVE ME BACK MY WAND, HOG NOSE!
NOW I ***WILL*** TURN YOU INTO A TOAD!

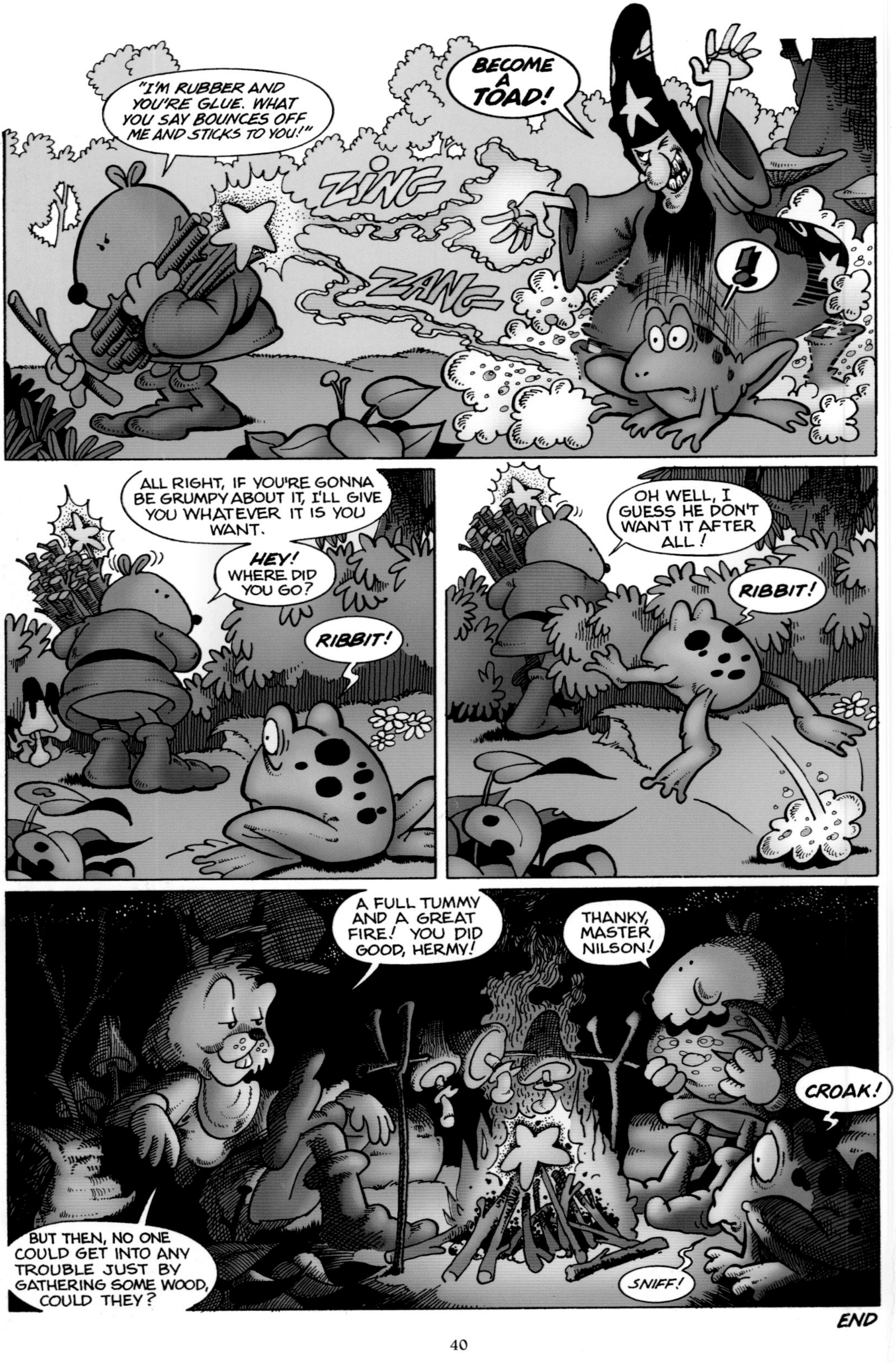
"I'M RUBBER AND YOU'RE GLUE. WHAT YOU SAY BOUNCES OFF ME AND STICKS TO YOU!"
BECOME A TOAD!
ZING
ZANG
!
ALL RIGHT, IF YOU'RE GONNA BE GRUMPY ABOUT IT, I'LL GIVE YOU WHATEVER IT IS YOU WANT.
HEY! WHERE DID YOU GO?
RIBBIT!
OH WELL, I GUESS HE DON'T WANT IT AFTER ALL!
RIBBIT!
A FULL TUMMY AND A GREAT FIRE! YOU DID GOOD, HERMY!
THANKY, MASTER NILSON!
CROAK!
BUT THEN, NO ONE COULD GET INTO ANY TROUBLE JUST BY GATHERING SOME WOOD, COULD THEY?
SNIFF!
END

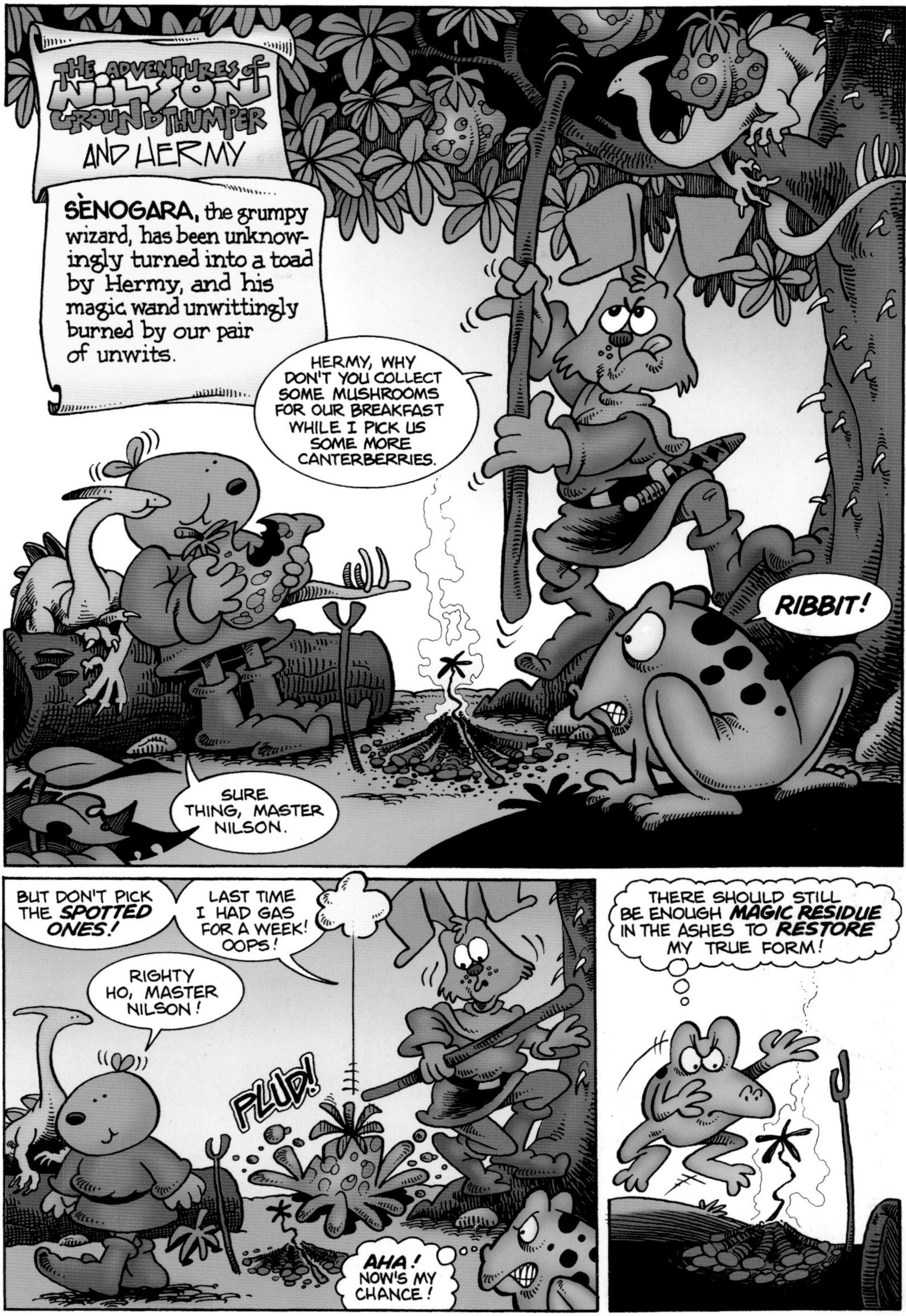
THE ADVENTURES OF NILSON GROUNDTHUMPER AND HERMY
SÈNOGARA, the grumpy wizard, has been unknowingly turned into a toad by Hermy, and his magic wand unwittingly burned by our pair of unwits.
HERMY, WHY DON'T YOU COLLECT SOME MUSHROOMS FOR OUR BREAKFAST WHILE I PICK US SOME MORE CANTERBERRIES.
RIBBIT!
SURE THING, MASTER NILSON.
BUT DON'T PICK THE SPOTTED ONES!
LAST TIME I HAD GAS FOR A WEEK! OOPS!
RIGHTY HO, MASTER NILSON!
PLUD!
AHA! NOW'S MY CHANCE!
THERE SHOULD STILL BE ENOUGH MAGIC RESIDUE IN THE ASHES TO RESTORE MY TRUE FORM!

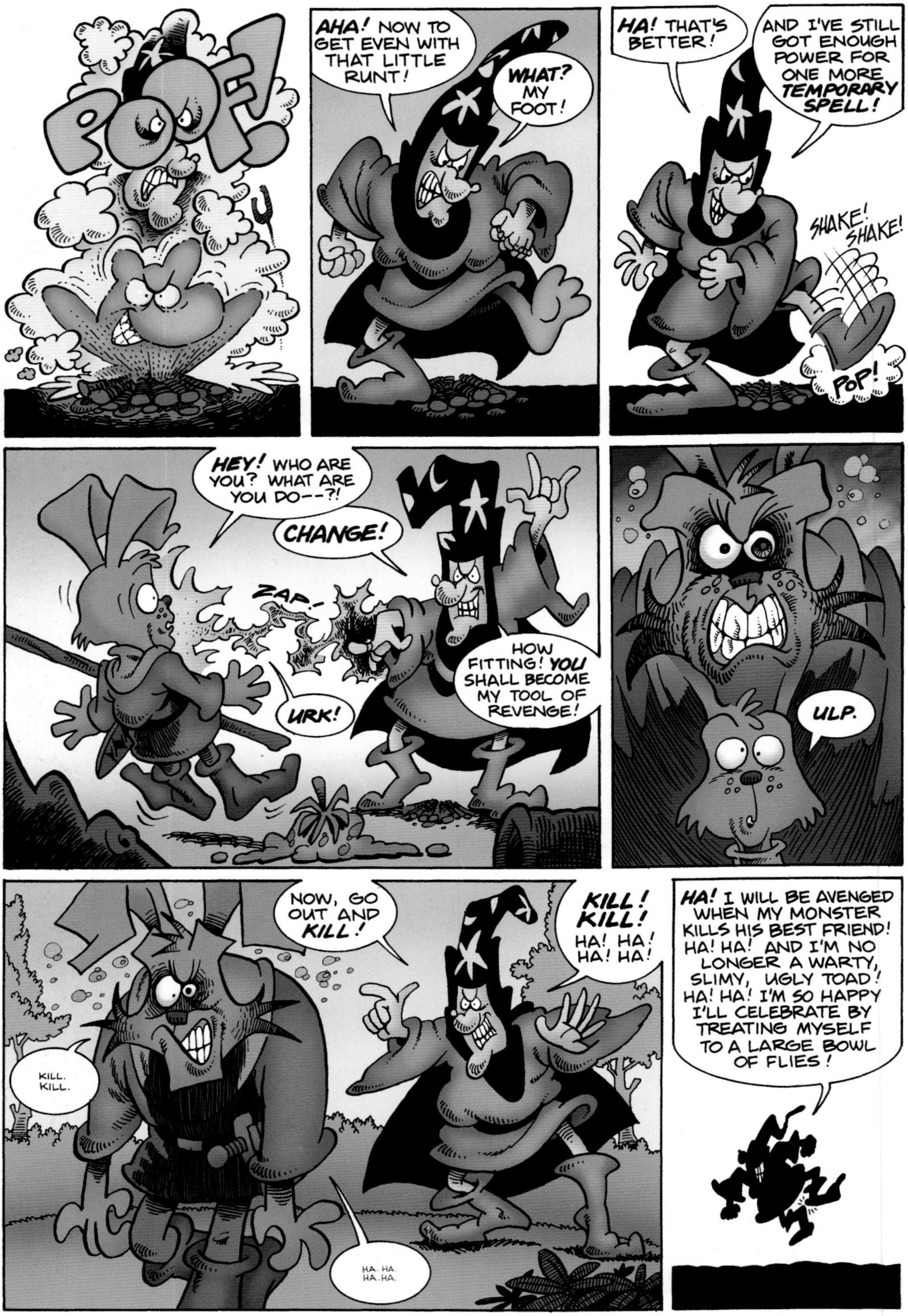
POOF!
AHA! NOW TO GET EVEN WITH THAT LITTLE RUNT!
WHAT? MY FOOT!
HA! THAT'S BETTER!
AND I'VE STILL GOT ENOUGH POWER FOR ONE MORE TEMPORARY SPELL!
SHAKE! SHAKE!
POP!
HEY! WHO ARE YOU? WHAT ARE YOU DO--?!
CHANGE!
ZAP-
URK!
HOW FITTING! YOU SHALL BECOME MY TOOL OF REVENGE!
ULP.
NOW, GO OUT AND KILL!
KILL! KILL! HA! HA! HA! HA!
KILL. KILL.
HA. HA. HA. HA.
HA! I WILL BE AVENGED WHEN MY MONSTER KILLS HIS BEST FRIEND! HA! HA! AND I'M NO LONGER A WARTY, SLIMY, UGLY TOAD! HA! HA! I'M SO HAPPY I'LL CELEBRATE BY TREATING MYSELF TO A LARGE BOWL OF FLIES!

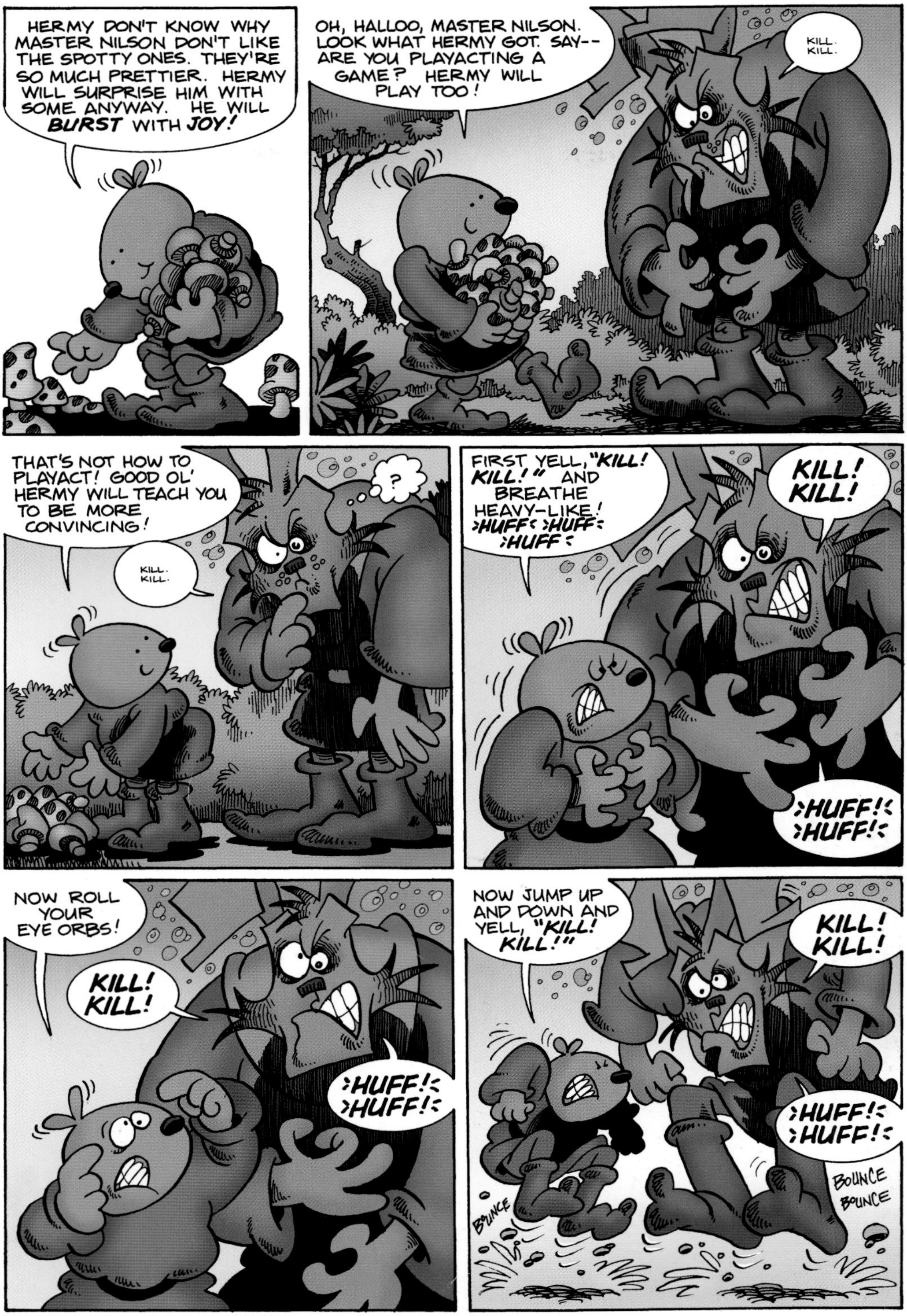

HERMY DON'T KNOW WHY MASTER NILSON DON'T LIKE THE SPOTTY ONES. THEY'RE SO MUCH PRETTIER. HERMY WILL SURPRISE HIM WITH SOME ANYWAY. HE WILL BURST WITH JOY!
OH, HALLOO, MASTER NILSON. LOOK WHAT HERMY GOT. SAY-- ARE YOU PLAYACTING A GAME? HERMY WILL PLAY TOO!
KILL. KILL.
THAT'S NOT HOW TO PLAYACT! GOOD OL' HERMY WILL TEACH YOU TO BE MORE CONVINCING!
?
KILL. KILL.
FIRST YELL, "KILL! KILL!" AND BREATHE HEAVY-LIKE! HUFF HUFF HUFF
KILL! KILL!
HUFF! HUFF!
NOW ROLL YOUR EYE ORBS!
KILL! KILL!
HUFF! HUFF!
NOW JUMP UP AND DOWN AND YELL, "KILL! KILL!"
KILL! KILL!
HUFF! HUFF!
BOUNCE
BOUNCE
BOUNCE

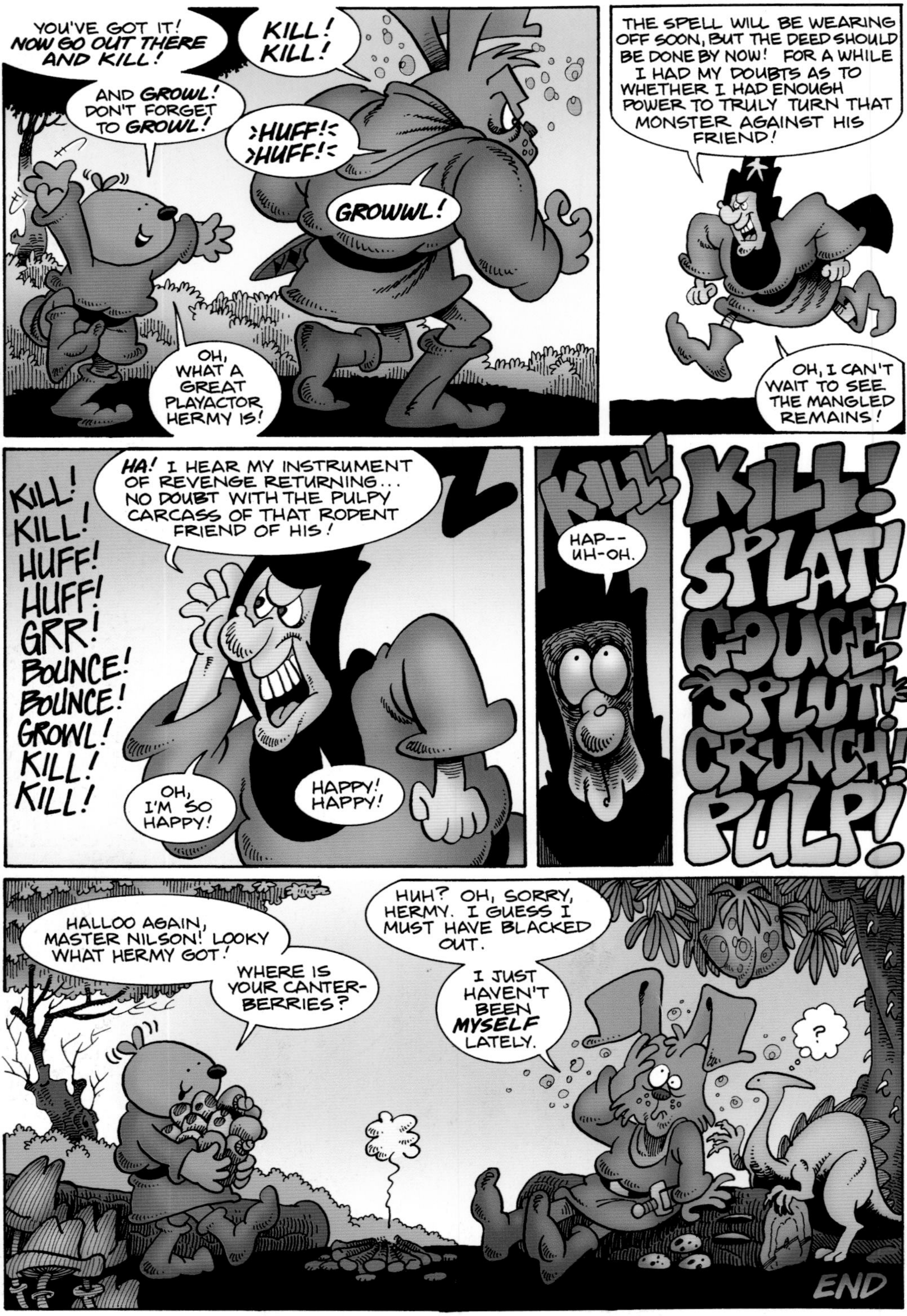

YOU'VE GOT IT! NOW GO OUT THERE AND KILL!
KILL! KILL!
AND GROWL! DON'T FORGET TO GROWL!
HUFF! HUFF!
GROWWL!
OH, WHAT A GREAT PLAYACTOR HERMY IS!
THE SPELL WILL BE WEARING OFF SOON, BUT THE DEED SHOULD BE DONE BY NOW! FOR A WHILE I HAD MY DOUBTS AS TO WHETHER I HAD ENOUGH POWER TO TRULY TURN THAT MONSTER AGAINST HIS FRIEND!
OH, I CAN'T WAIT TO SEE THE MANGLED REMAINS!
KILL! KILL! HUFF! HUFF! GRR! BOUNCE! BOUNCE! GROWL! KILL! KILL!
HA! I HEAR MY INSTRUMENT OF REVENGE RETURNING... NO DOUBT WITH THE PULPY CARCASS OF THAT RODENT FRIEND OF HIS!
OH, I'M SO HAPPY!
HAPPY! HAPPY!
KILL!
HAP-- UH-OH.
KILL! SPLAT! GOUGE! SPLUT! CRUNCH! PULP!
HALLOO AGAIN, MASTER NILSON! LOOKY WHAT HERMY GOT!
WHERE IS YOUR CANTER-BERRIES?
HUH? OH, SORRY, HERMY. I GUESS I MUST HAVE BLACKED OUT.
I JUST HAVEN'T BEEN MYSELF LATELY.
?
END

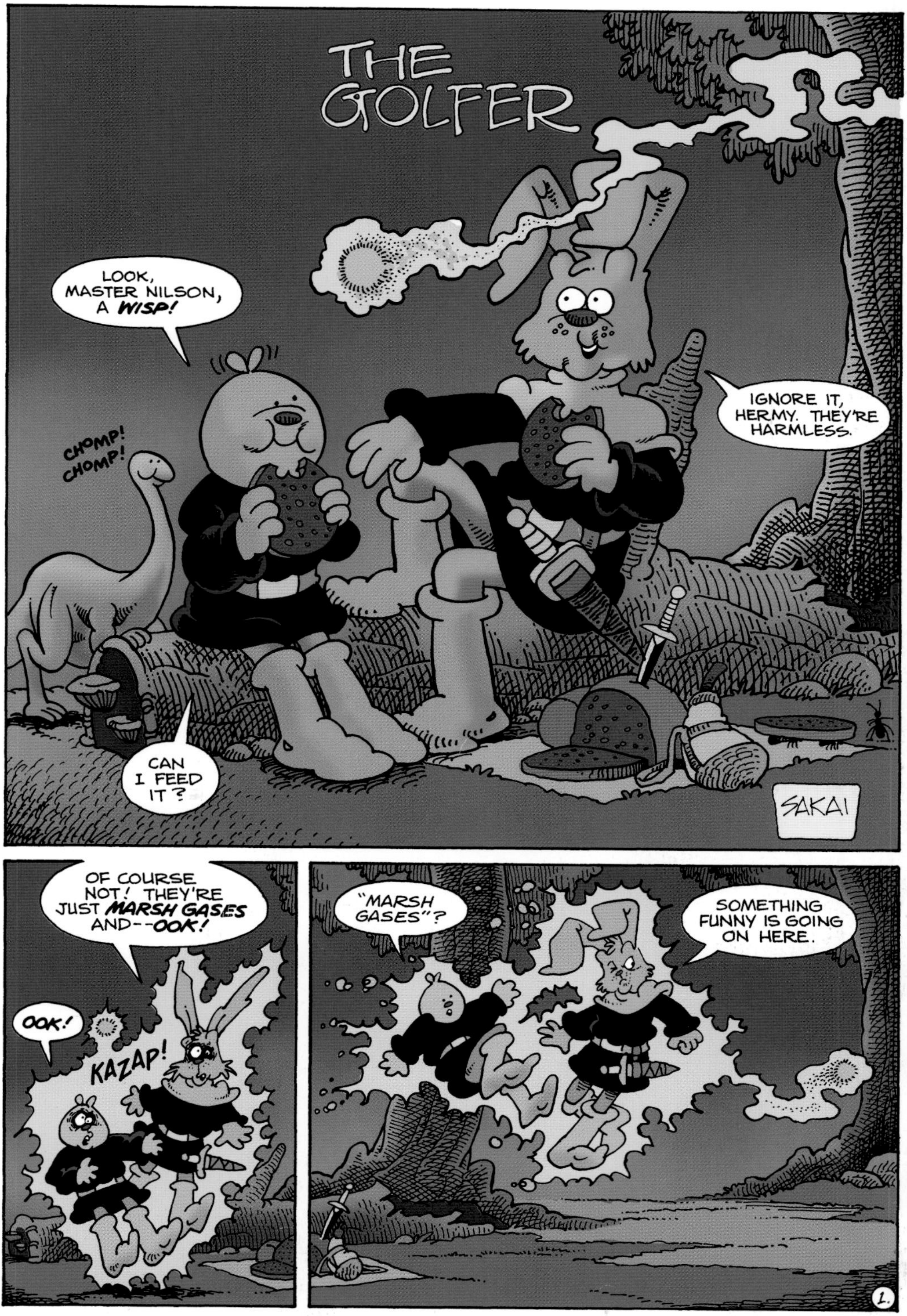
THE GOLFER
LOOK, MASTER NILSON, A WISP!
IGNORE IT, HERMY. THEY'RE HARMLESS.
CHOMP! CHOMP!
CAN I FEED IT?
SAKAI
OF COURSE NOT! THEY'RE JUST MARSH GASES AND--OOK!
OOK!
KAZAP!
"MARSH GASES"?
SOMETHING FUNNY IS GOING ON HERE.
1.

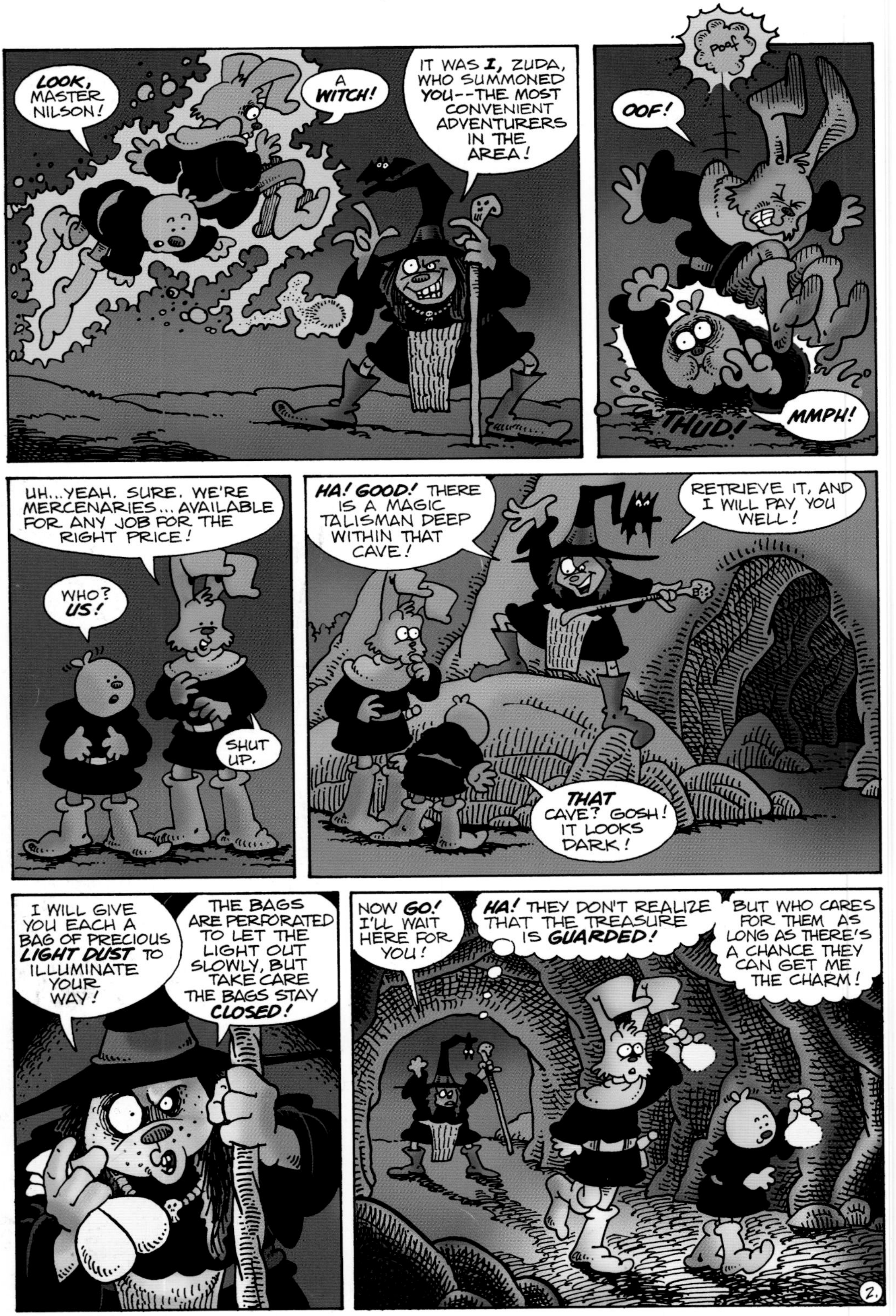

LOOK, MASTER NILSON!
A WITCH!
IT WAS I, ZUDA, WHO SUMMONED YOU--THE MOST CONVENIENT ADVENTURERS IN THE AREA!
Poof
OOF!
THUD!
MMPH!
UH...YEAH. SURE. WE'RE MERCENARIES... AVAILABLE FOR ANY JOB FOR THE RIGHT PRICE!
WHO? US!
SHUT UP.
HA! GOOD! THERE IS A MAGIC TALISMAN DEEP WITHIN THAT CAVE!
RETRIEVE IT, AND I WILL PAY YOU WELL!
THAT CAVE? GOSH! IT LOOKS DARK!
I WILL GIVE YOU EACH A BAG OF PRECIOUS LIGHT DUST TO ILLUMINATE YOUR WAY!
THE BAGS ARE PERFORATED TO LET THE LIGHT OUT SLOWLY, BUT TAKE CARE THE BAGS STAY CLOSED!
NOW GO! I'LL WAIT HERE FOR YOU!
HA! THEY DON'T REALIZE THAT THE TREASURE IS GUARDED!
BUT WHO CARES FOR THEM AS LONG AS THERE'S A CHANCE THEY CAN GET ME THE CHARM!
2.

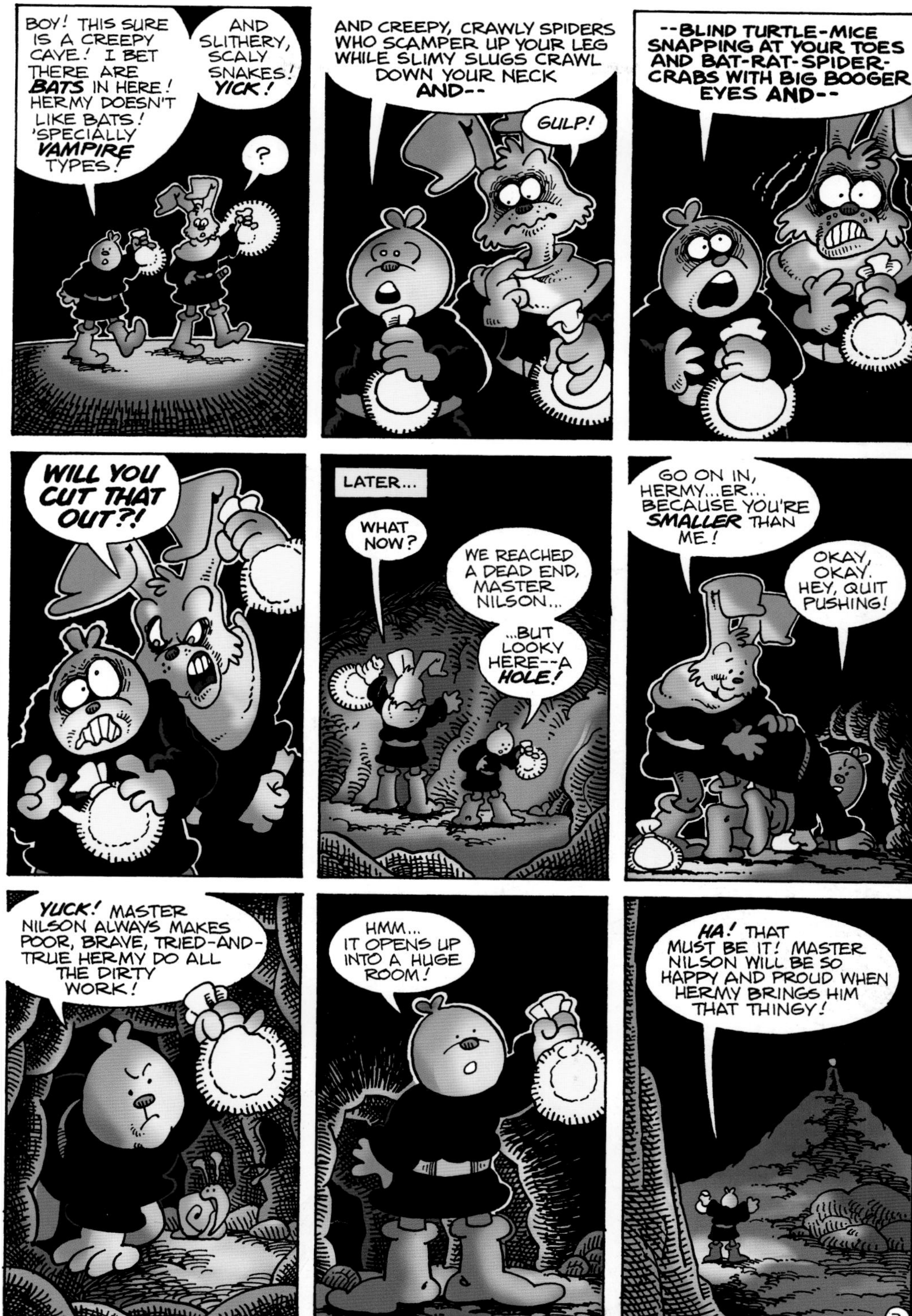
BOY! THIS SURE IS A CREEPY CAVE! I BET THERE ARE BATS IN HERE! HERMY DOESN'T LIKE BATS! 'SPECIALLY VAMPIRE TYPES!
AND SLITHERY, SCALY SNAKES! YICK!
?
AND CREEPY, CRAWLY SPIDERS WHO SCAMPER UP YOUR LEG WHILE SLIMY SLUGS CRAWL DOWN YOUR NECK AND--
GULP!
--BLIND TURTLE-MICE SNAPPING AT YOUR TOES AND BAT-RAT-SPIDER-CRABS WITH BIG BOOGER EYES AND--
WILL YOU CUT THAT OUT?!
LATER...
WHAT NOW?
WE REACHED A DEAD END, MASTER NILSON...
...BUT LOOKY HERE--A HOLE!
GO ON IN, HERMY...ER... BECAUSE YOU'RE SMALLER THAN ME!
OKAY, OKAY. HEY, QUIT PUSHING!
YUCK! MASTER NILSON ALWAYS MAKES POOR, BRAVE, TRIED-AND-TRUE HERMY DO ALL THE DIRTY WORK!
HMM... IT OPENS UP INTO A HUGE ROOM!
HA! THAT MUST BE IT! MASTER NILSON WILL BE SO HAPPY AND PROUD WHEN HERMY BRINGS HIM THAT THINGY!
3.

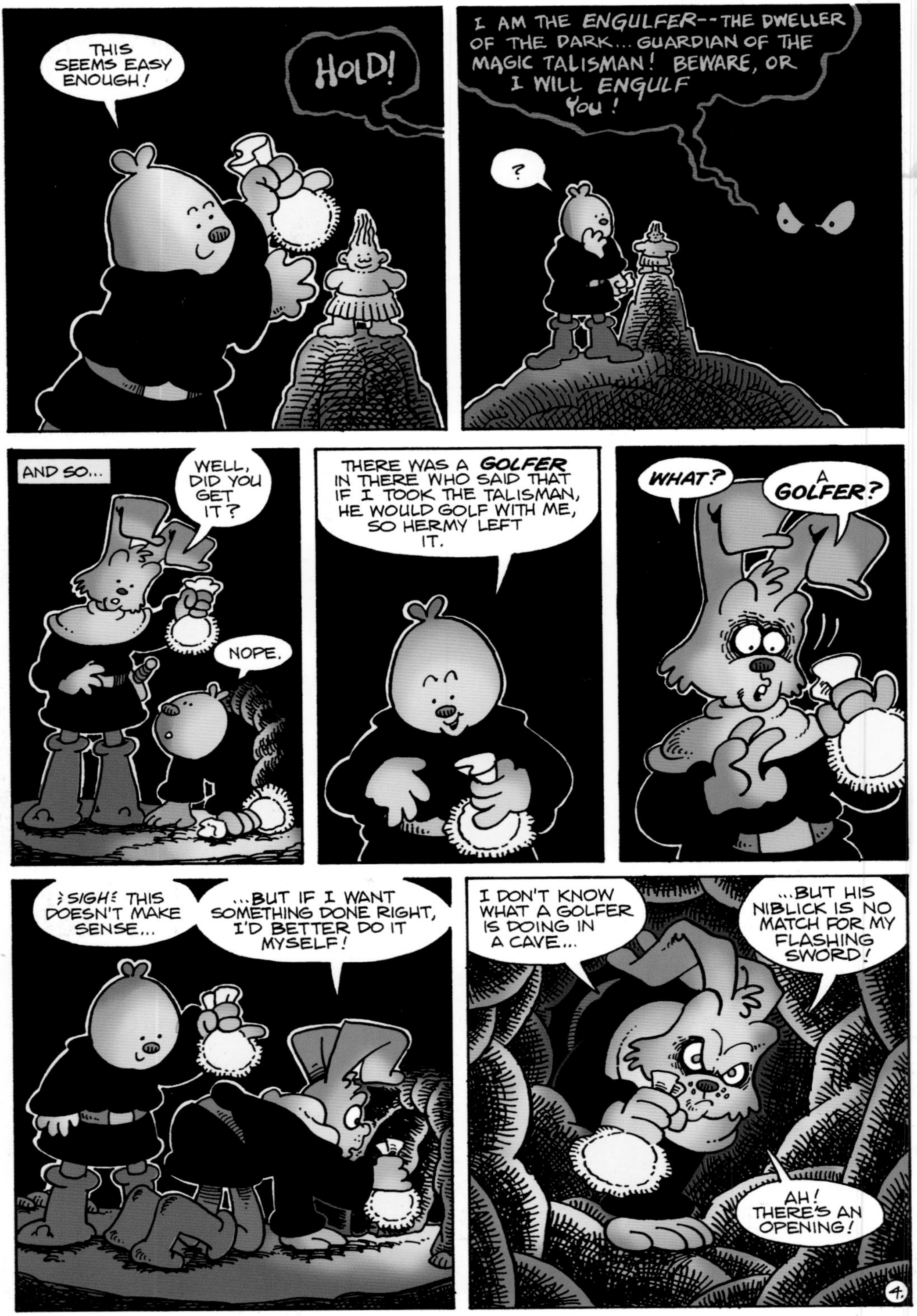
THIS SEEMS EASY ENOUGH!
HOLD!
I AM THE ENGULFER--THE DWELLER OF THE DARK... GUARDIAN OF THE MAGIC TALISMAN! BEWARE, OR I WILL ENGULF YOU!
?
AND SO...
WELL, DID YOU GET IT?
NOPE.
THERE WAS A GOLFER IN THERE WHO SAID THAT IF I TOOK THE TALISMAN, HE WOULD GOLF WITH ME, SO HERMY LEFT IT.
WHAT?
A GOLFER?
:SIGH: THIS DOESN'T MAKE SENSE...
...BUT IF I WANT SOMETHING DONE RIGHT, I'D BETTER DO IT MYSELF!
I DON'T KNOW WHAT A GOLFER IS DOING IN A CAVE...
...BUT HIS NIBLICK IS NO MATCH FOR MY FLASHING SWORD!
AH! THERE'S AN OPENING!
4.

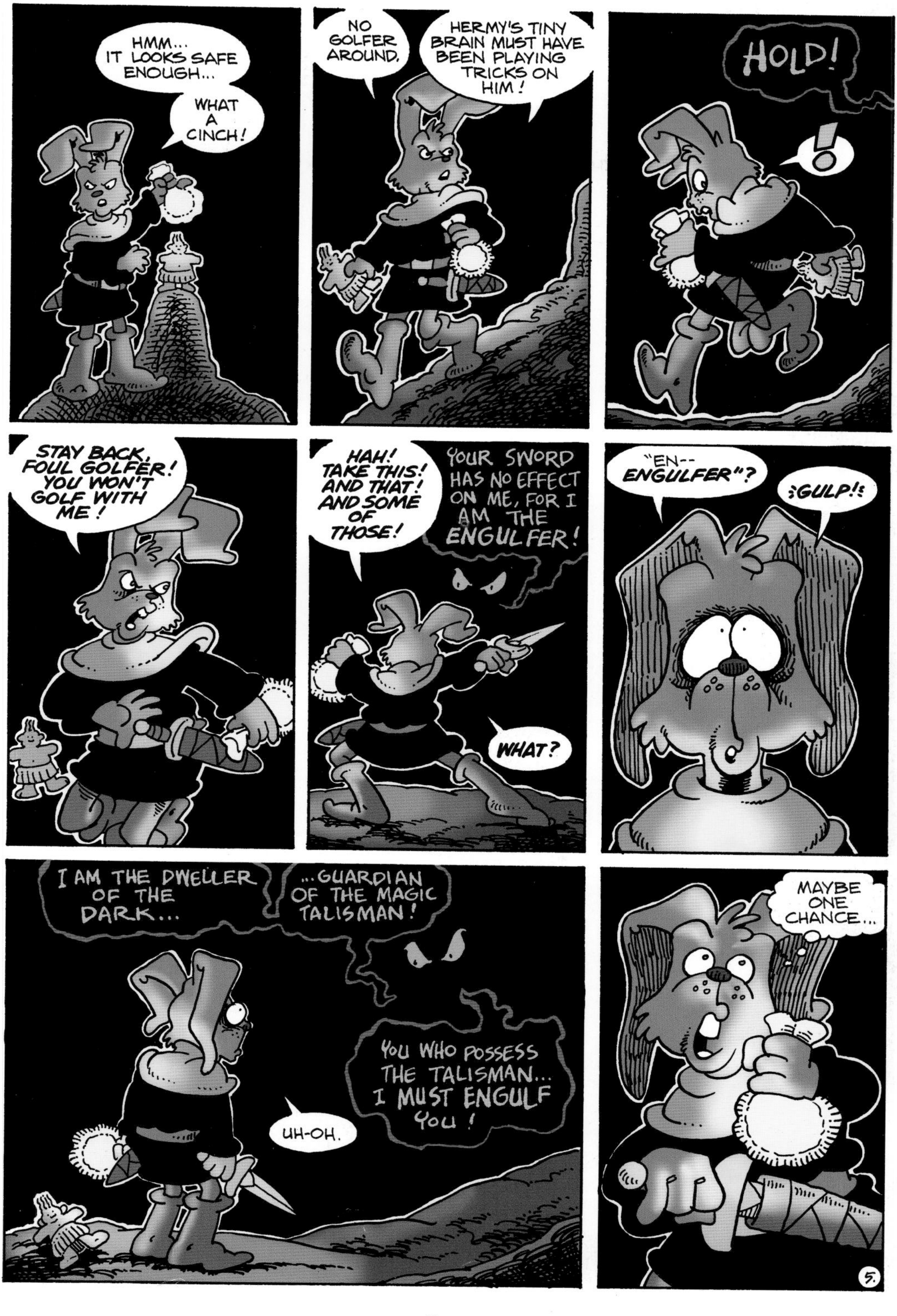
HMM... IT LOOKS SAFE ENOUGH...
WHAT A CINCH!
NO GOLFER AROUND.
HERMY'S TINY BRAIN MUST HAVE BEEN PLAYING TRICKS ON HIM!
HOLD!
!
STAY BACK, FOUL GOLFER! YOU WON'T GOLF WITH ME!
HAH! TAKE THIS! AND THAT! AND SOME OF THOSE!
YOUR SWORD HAS NO EFFECT ON ME, FOR I AM THE ENGULFER!
WHAT?
"EN-- ENGULFER"?
:GULP!:
I AM THE DWELLER OF THE DARK...
...GUARDIAN OF THE MAGIC TALISMAN!
YOU WHO POSSESS THE TALISMAN... I MUST ENGULF YOU!
UH-OH.
MAYBE ONE CHANCE...
5.

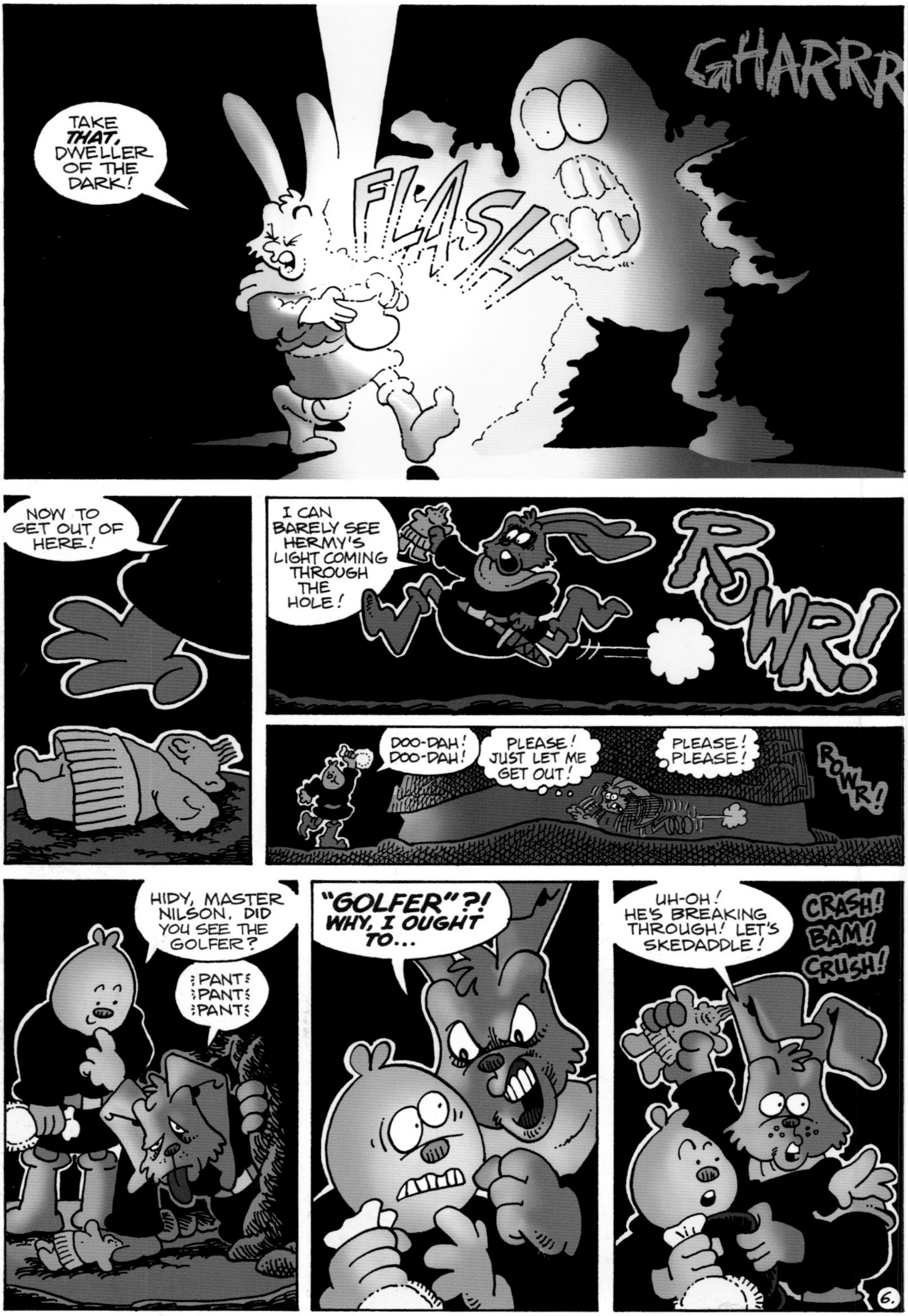
TAKE THAT, DWELLER OF THE DARK!
FLASH
GHARRR
NOW TO GET OUT OF HERE!
I CAN BARELY SEE HERMY'S LIGHT COMING THROUGH THE HOLE!
ROWR!
DOO-DAH! DOO-DAH!
PLEASE! JUST LET ME GET OUT!
PLEASE! PLEASE!
ROWR!
HIDY, MASTER NILSON. DID YOU SEE THE GOLFER?
PANT PANT PANT
"GOLFER"?! WHY, I OUGHT TO...
UH-OH! HE'S BREAKING THROUGH! LET'S SKEDADDLE!
CRASH! BAM! CRUSH!
6.

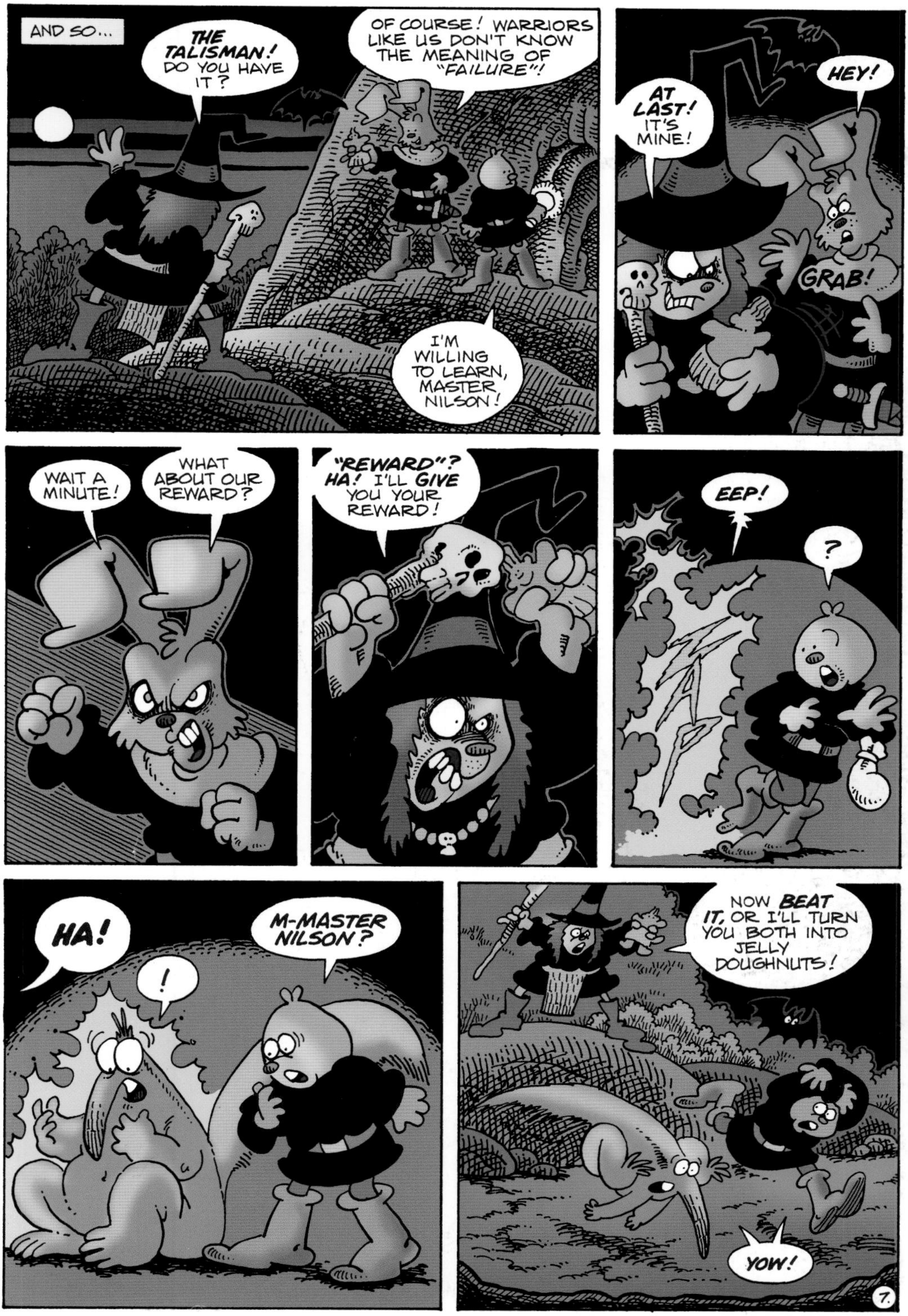
AND SO...
THE TALISMAN! DO YOU HAVE IT?
OF COURSE! WARRIORS LIKE US DON'T KNOW THE MEANING OF "FAILURE"!
I'M WILLING TO LEARN, MASTER NILSON!
AT LAST! IT'S MINE!
HEY!
GRAB!
WAIT A MINUTE!
WHAT ABOUT OUR REWARD?
"REWARD"? HA! I'LL GIVE YOU YOUR REWARD!
EEP!
?
HA!
!
M-MASTER NILSON?
NOW BEAT IT, OR I'LL TURN YOU BOTH INTO JELLY DOUGHNUTS!
YOW!
7.

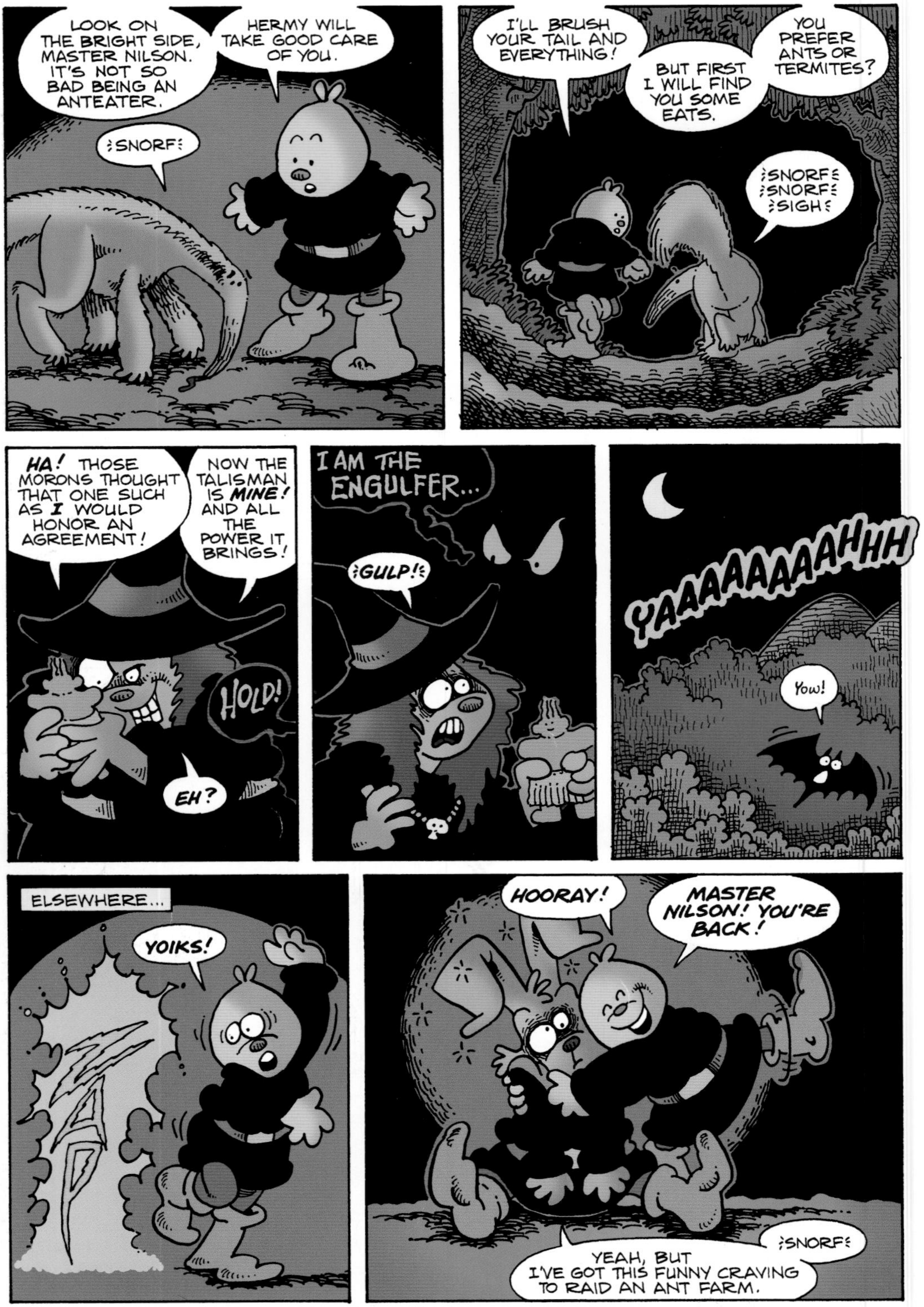
LOOK ON THE BRIGHT SIDE, MASTER NILSON. IT'S NOT SO BAD BEING AN ANTEATER.
HERMY WILL TAKE GOOD CARE OF YOU.
SNORF
I'LL BRUSH YOUR TAIL AND EVERYTHING!
BUT FIRST I WILL FIND YOU SOME EATS.
YOU PREFER ANTS OR TERMITES?
SNORF SNORF SIGH
HA! THOSE MORONS THOUGHT THAT ONE SUCH AS I WOULD HONOR AN AGREEMENT!
NOW THE TALISMAN IS MINE! AND ALL THE POWER IT BRINGS!
HOLD!
EH?
I AM THE ENGULFER...
GULP!
YAAAAAAAAAHHH
YOW!
ELSEWHERE...
YOIKS!
HOORAY!
MASTER NILSON! YOU'RE BACK!
YEAH, BUT I'VE GOT THIS FUNNY CRAVING TO RAID AN ANT FARM.
SNORF
END

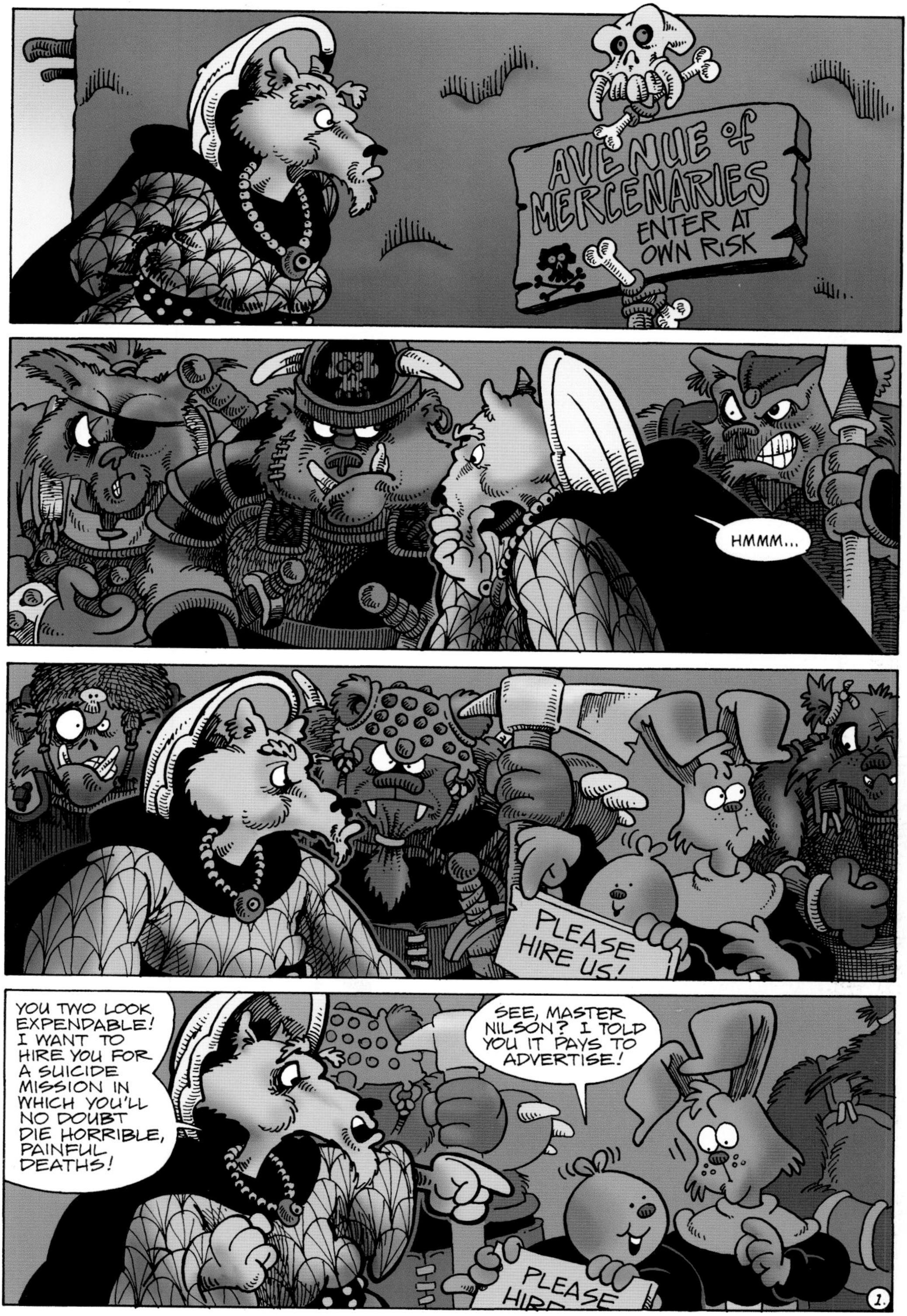
AVENUE of MERCENARIES
ENTER AT OWN RISK
HMMM...
PLEASE HIRE US!
YOU TWO LOOK EXPENDABLE! I WANT TO HIRE YOU FOR A SUICIDE MISSION IN WHICH YOU'LL NO DOUBT DIE HORRIBLE, PAINFUL DEATHS!
SEE, MASTER NILSON? I TOLD YOU IT PAYS TO ADVERTISE!
1.

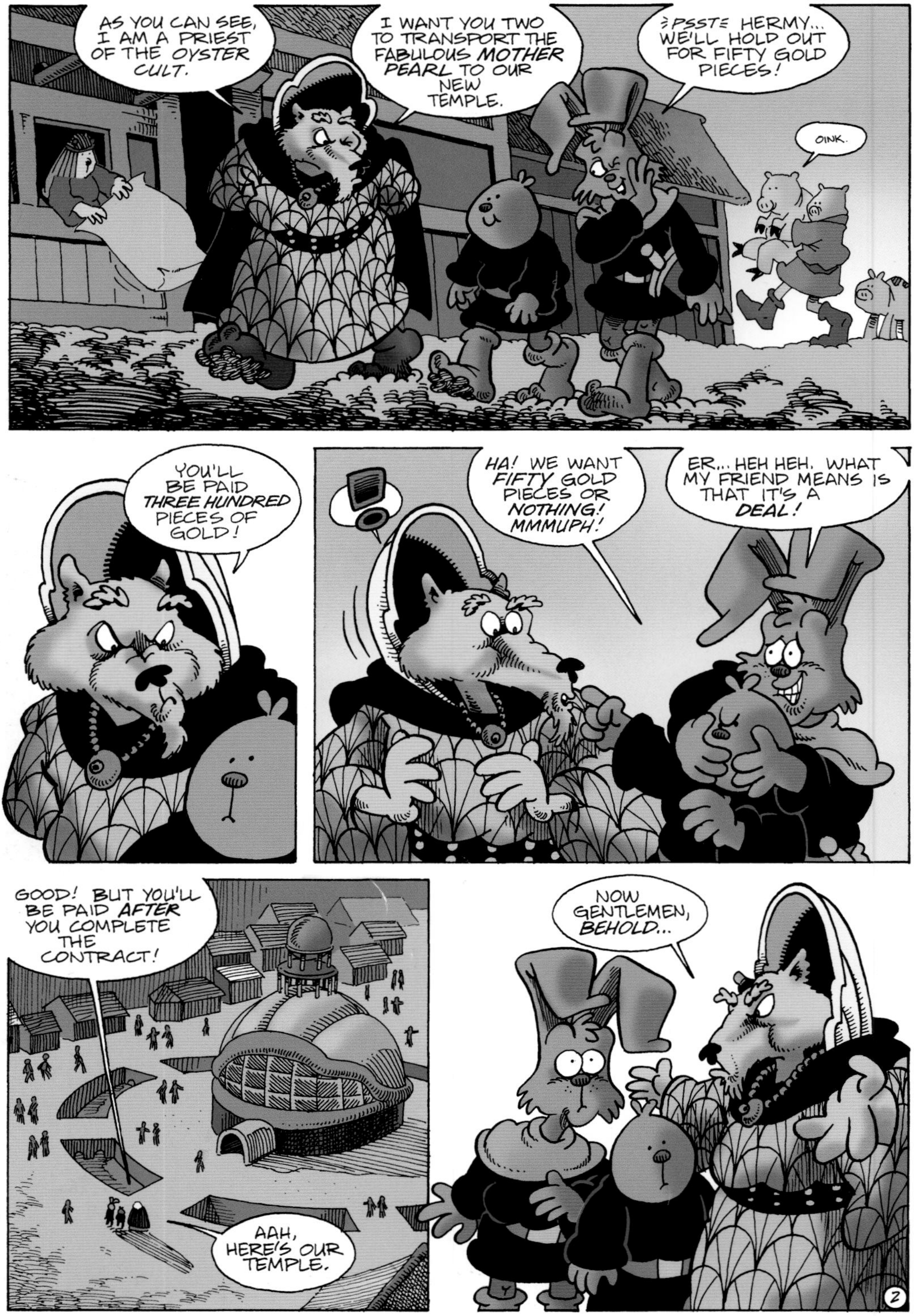
AS YOU CAN SEE, I AM A PRIEST OF THE OYSTER CULT.
I WANT YOU TWO TO TRANSPORT THE FABULOUS MOTHER PEARL TO OUR NEW TEMPLE.
=PSST= HERMY... WE'LL HOLD OUT FOR FIFTY GOLD PIECES!
OINK.
YOU'LL BE PAID THREE HUNDRED PIECES OF GOLD!
HA! WE WANT FIFTY GOLD PIECES OR NOTHING! MMMUPH!
ER... HEH HEH. WHAT MY FRIEND MEANS IS THAT IT'S A DEAL!
GOOD! BUT YOU'LL BE PAID AFTER YOU COMPLETE THE CONTRACT!
AAH, HERE'S OUR TEMPLE.
NOW GENTLEMEN, BEHOLD...
2

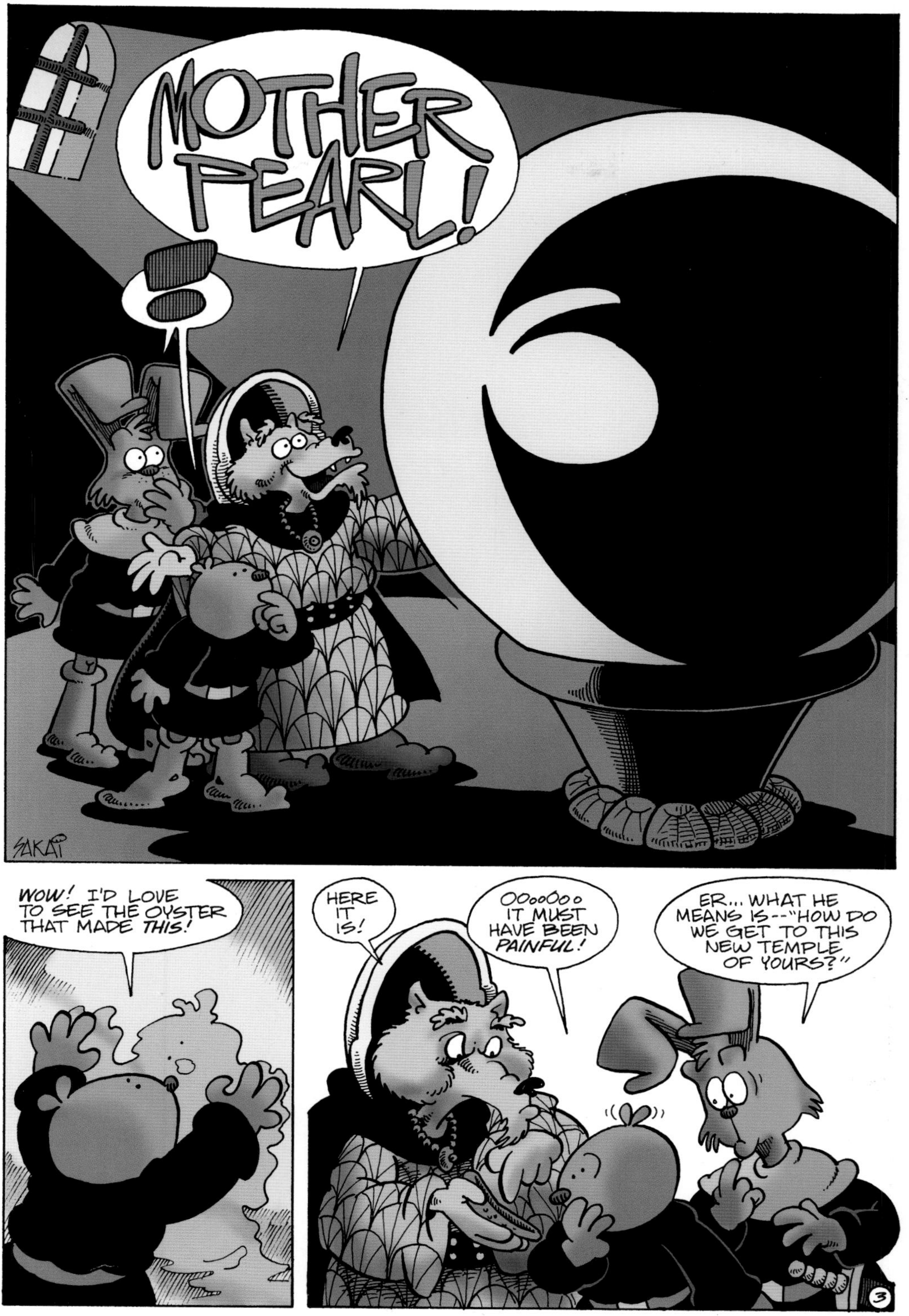
MOTHER PEARL!
SAKAI
WOW! I'D LOVE TO SEE THE OYSTER THAT MADE THIS!
HERE IT IS!
OOooOOo IT MUST HAVE BEEN PAINFUL!
ER... WHAT HE MEANS IS--"HOW DO WE GET TO THIS NEW TEMPLE OF YOURS?"
3

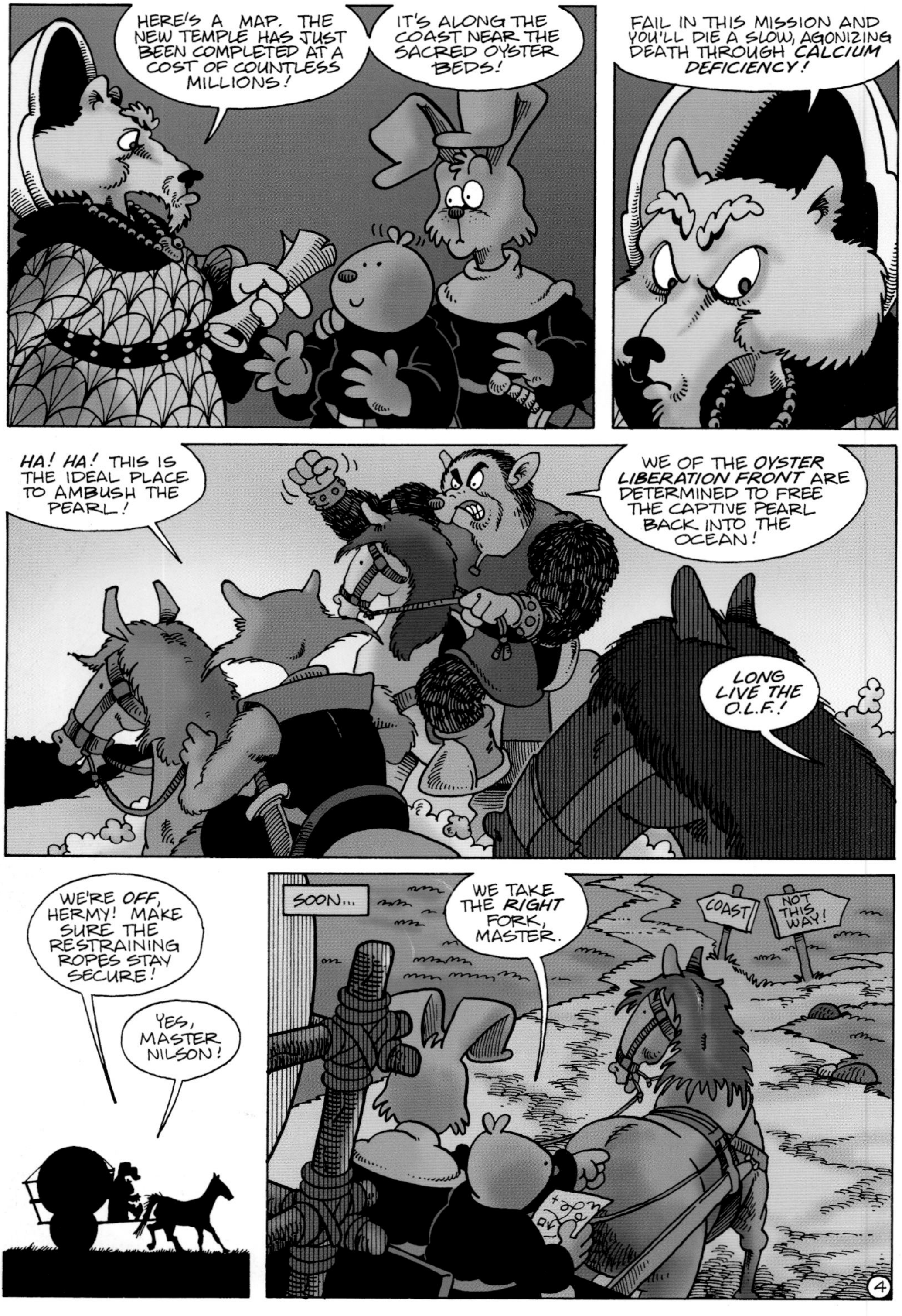

HERE'S A MAP. THE NEW TEMPLE HAS JUST BEEN COMPLETED AT A COST OF COUNTLESS MILLIONS!
IT'S ALONG THE COAST NEAR THE SACRED OYSTER BEDS!
FAIL IN THIS MISSION AND YOU'LL DIE A SLOW, AGONIZING DEATH THROUGH CALCIUM DEFICIENCY!
HA! HA! THIS IS THE IDEAL PLACE TO AMBUSH THE PEARL!
WE OF THE OYSTER LIBERATION FRONT ARE DETERMINED TO FREE THE CAPTIVE PEARL BACK INTO THE OCEAN!
LONG LIVE THE O.L.F.!
WE'RE OFF, HERMY! MAKE SURE THE RESTRAINING ROPES STAY SECURE!
YES, MASTER NILSON!
SOON...
WE TAKE THE RIGHT FORK, MASTER.
COAST
NOT THIS WAY!
4

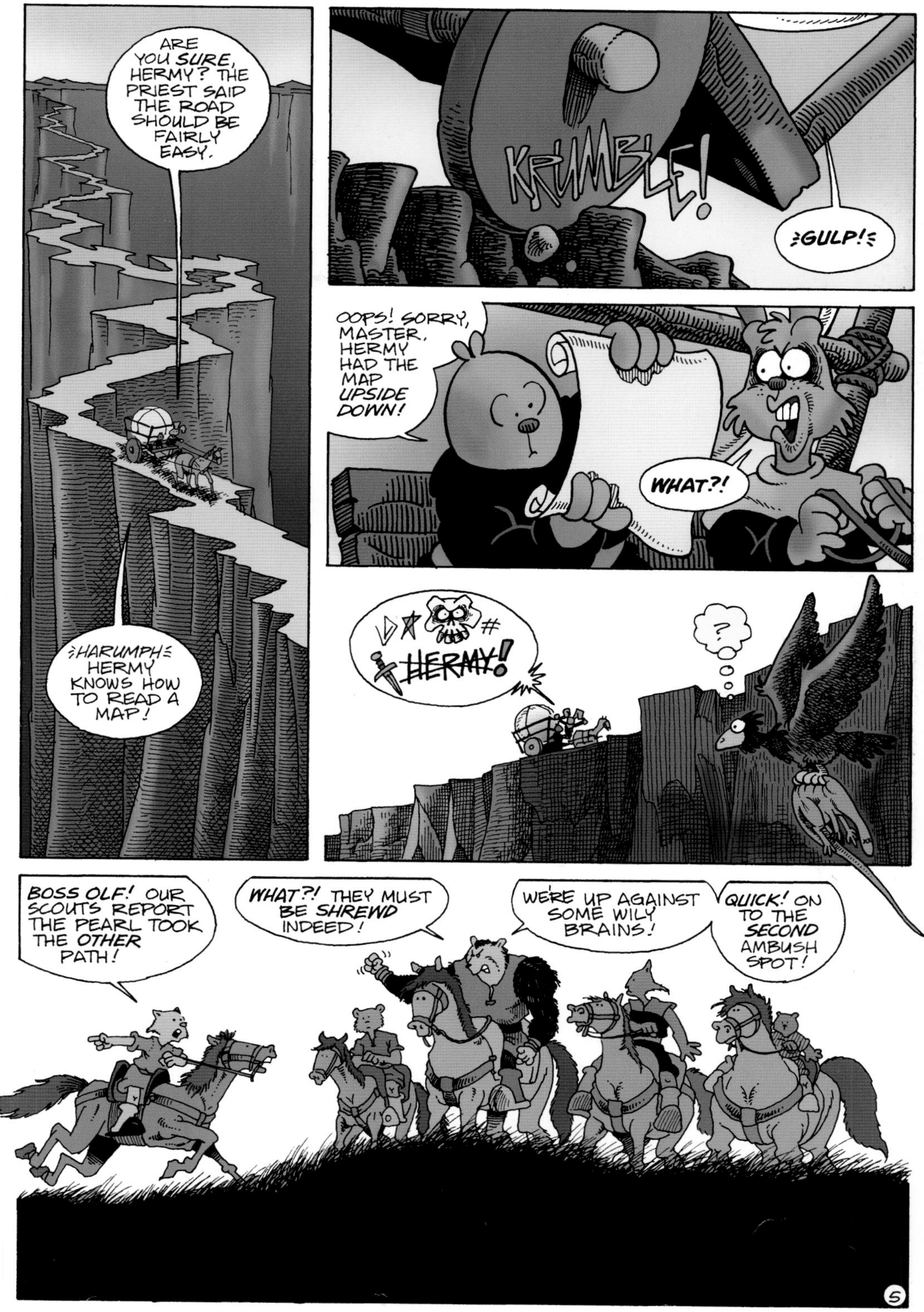
ARE YOU SURE, HERMY? THE PRIEST SAID THE ROAD SHOULD BE FAIRLY EASY.
KRUMBLE!
GULP!
HARUMPH HERMY KNOWS HOW TO READ A MAP!
OOPS! SORRY, MASTER. HERMY HAD THE MAP UPSIDE DOWN!
WHAT?!
HERMY!
?
BOSS OLF! OUR SCOUTS REPORT THE PEARL TOOK THE OTHER PATH!
WHAT?! THEY MUST BE SHREWD INDEED!
WE'RE UP AGAINST SOME WILY BRAINS!
QUICK! ON TO THE SECOND AMBUSH SPOT!
5

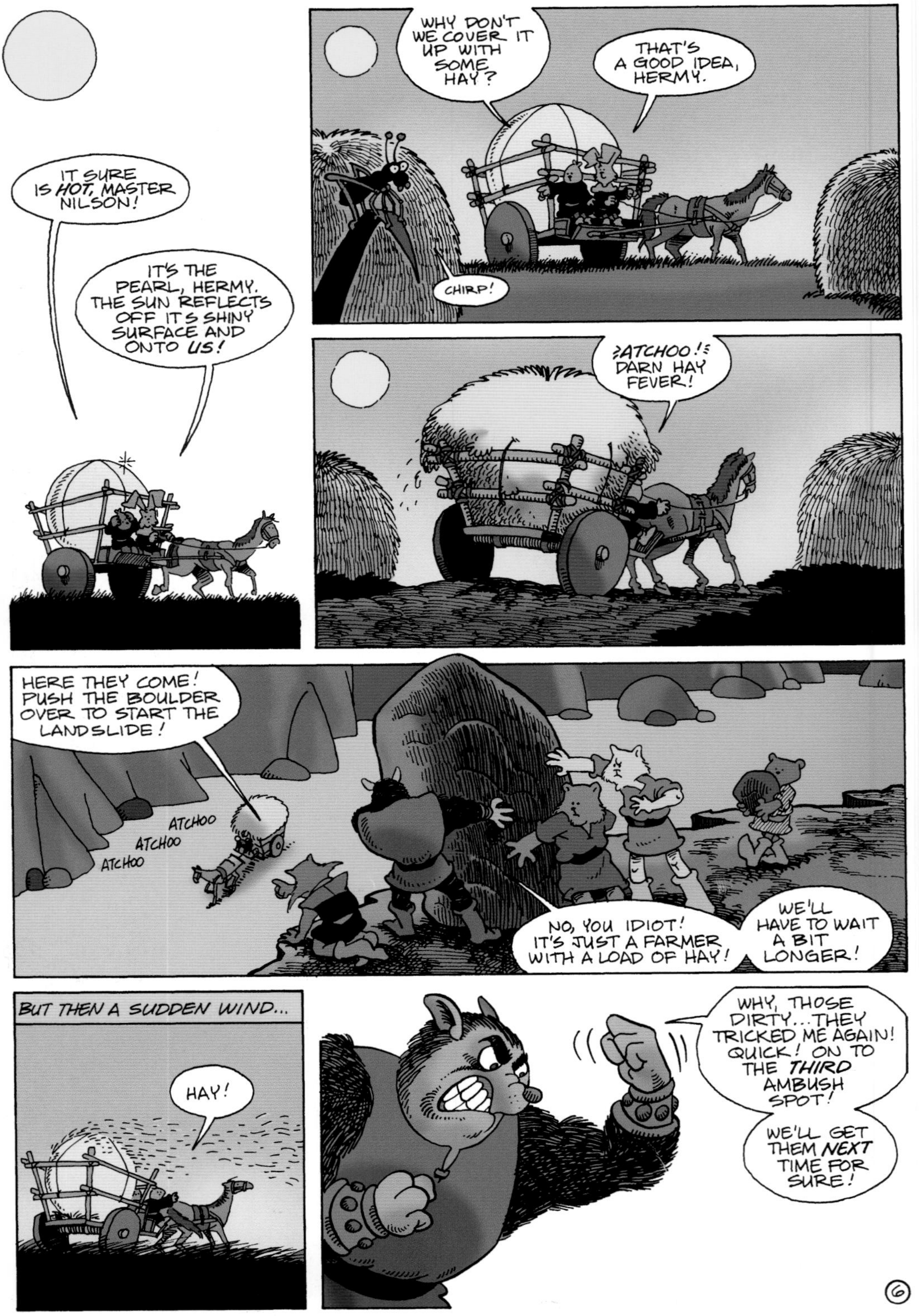
IT SURE IS HOT, MASTER NILSON!
IT'S THE PEARL, HERMY. THE SUN REFLECTS OFF IT'S SHINY SURFACE AND ONTO US!
WHY DON'T WE COVER IT UP WITH SOME HAY?
THAT'S A GOOD IDEA, HERMY.
CHIRP!
ATCHOO! DARN HAY FEVER!
HERE THEY COME! PUSH THE BOULDER OVER TO START THE LANDSLIDE!
ATCHOO
ATCHOO
ATCHOO
NO, YOU IDIOT! IT'S JUST A FARMER WITH A LOAD OF HAY!
WE'LL HAVE TO WAIT A BIT LONGER!
BUT THEN A SUDDEN WIND...
HAY!
WHY, THOSE DIRTY... THEY TRICKED ME AGAIN! QUICK! ON TO THE THIRD AMBUSH SPOT!
WE'LL GET THEM NEXT TIME FOR SURE!
6

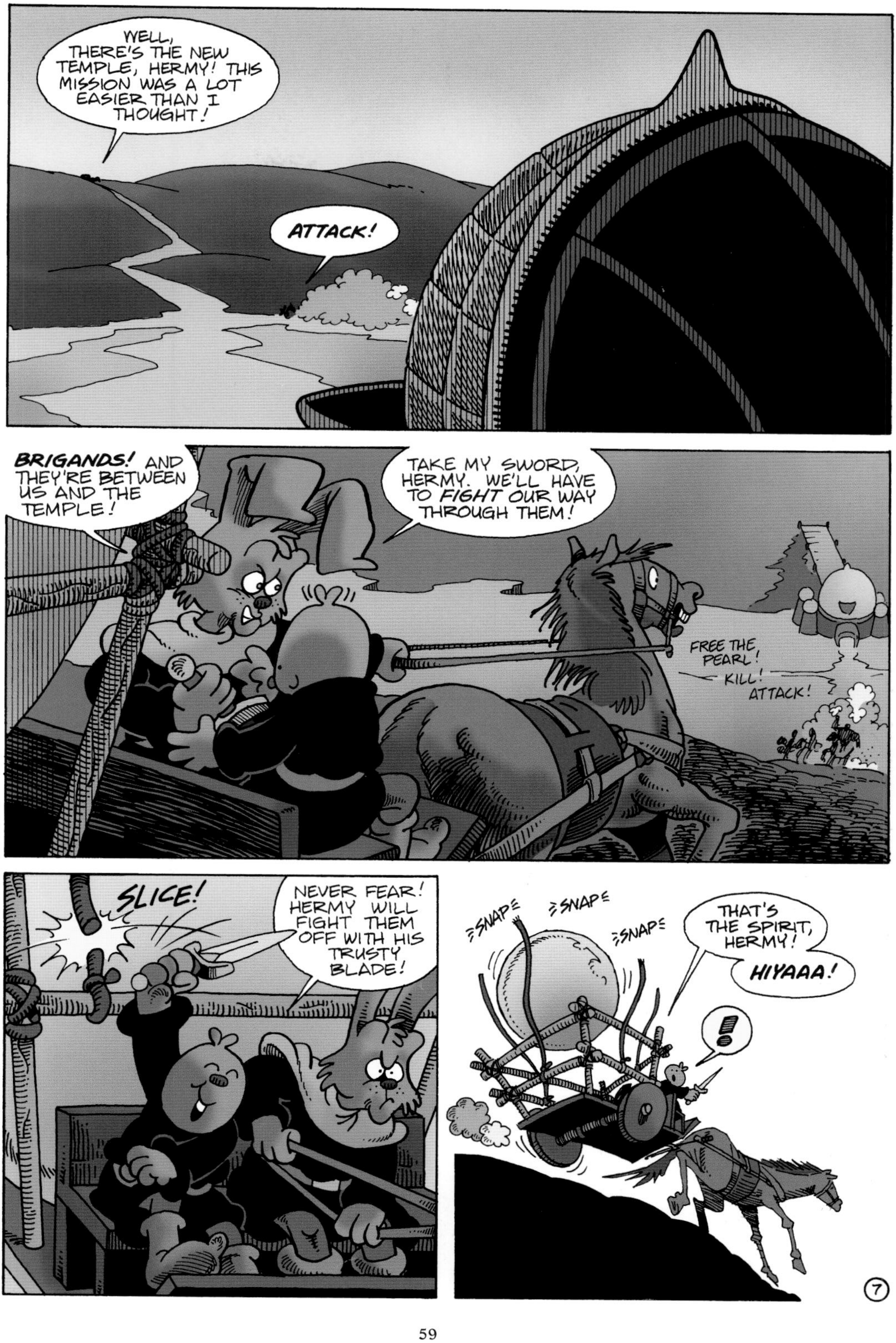
WELL, THERE'S THE NEW TEMPLE, HERMY! THIS MISSION WAS A LOT EASIER THAN I THOUGHT!
ATTACK!
BRIGANDS! AND THEY'RE BETWEEN US AND THE TEMPLE!
TAKE MY SWORD, HERMY. WE'LL HAVE TO FIGHT OUR WAY THROUGH THEM!
FREE THE PEARL!
KILL!
ATTACK!
SLICE!
NEVER FEAR! HERMY WILL FIGHT THEM OFF WITH HIS TRUSTY BLADE!
SNAP
SNAP
SNAP
THAT'S THE SPIRIT, HERMY!
HIYAAA!
!
7

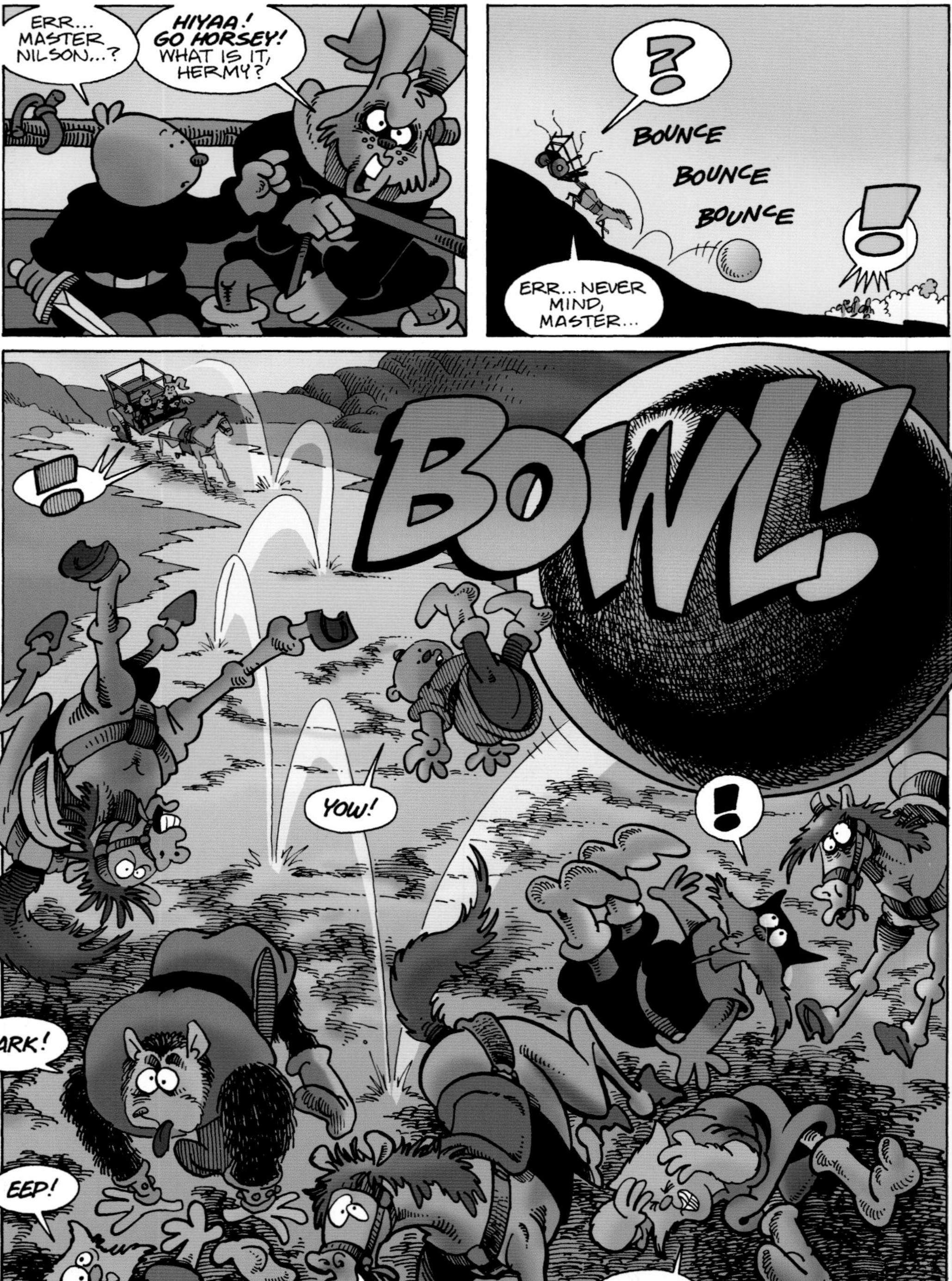
ERR... MASTER NILSON...?
HIYAA! GO HORSEY! WHAT IS IT, HERMY?
?
BOUNCE
BOUNCE
BOUNCE
ERR... NEVER MIND, MASTER...
!
BOWL!
YOW!
!
GARK!
EEP!
GURK!
8

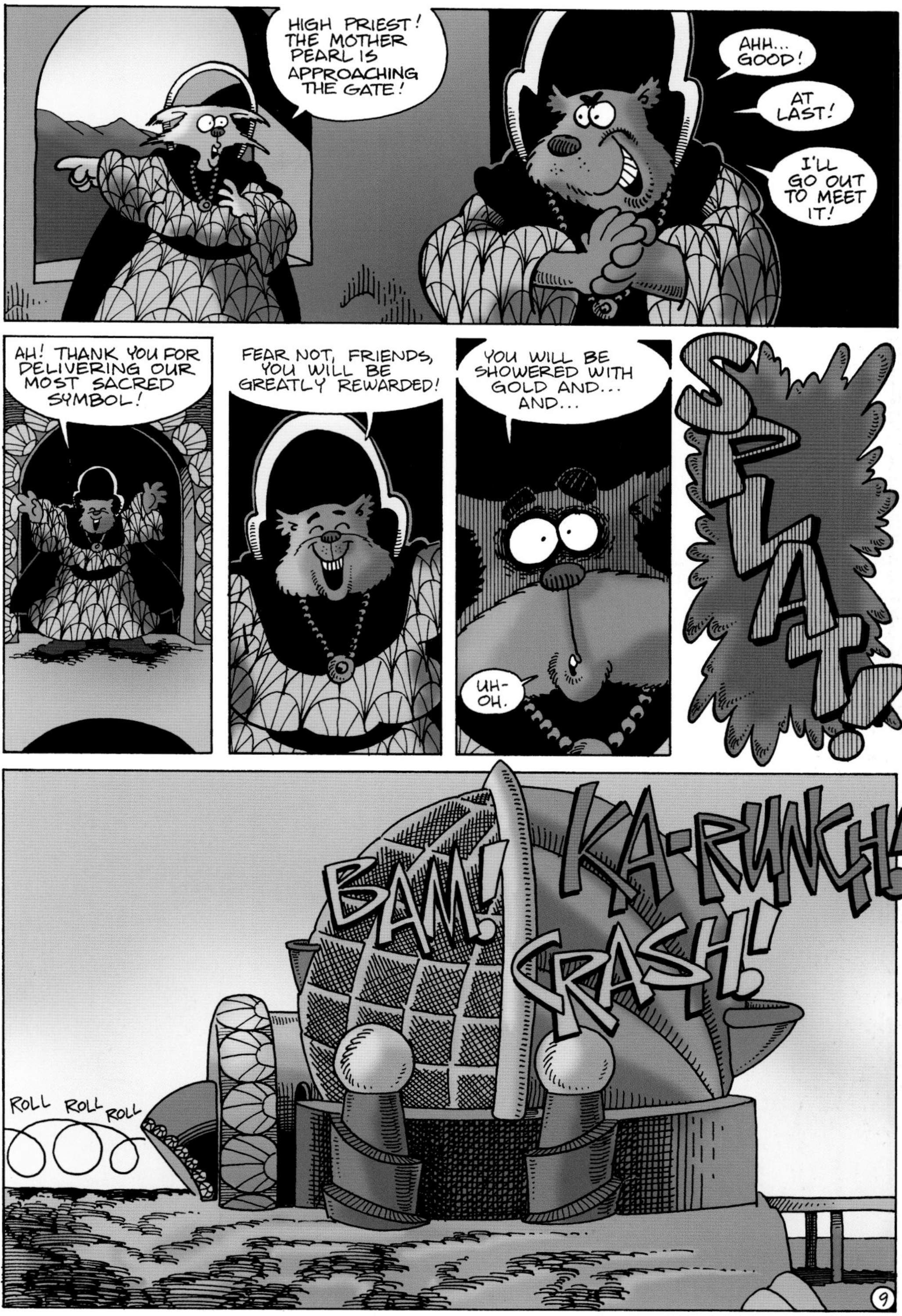
HIGH PRIEST! THE MOTHER PEARL IS APPROACHING THE GATE!
AHH... GOOD!
AT LAST!
I'LL GO OUT TO MEET IT!
AH! THANK YOU FOR DELIVERING OUR MOST SACRED SYMBOL!
FEAR NOT, FRIENDS, YOU WILL BE GREATLY REWARDED!
YOU WILL BE SHOWERED WITH GOLD AND... AND...
UH-OH.
SPLAT!
BAM!
KA-RUNCH!
CRASH!
ROLL ROLL ROLL
9

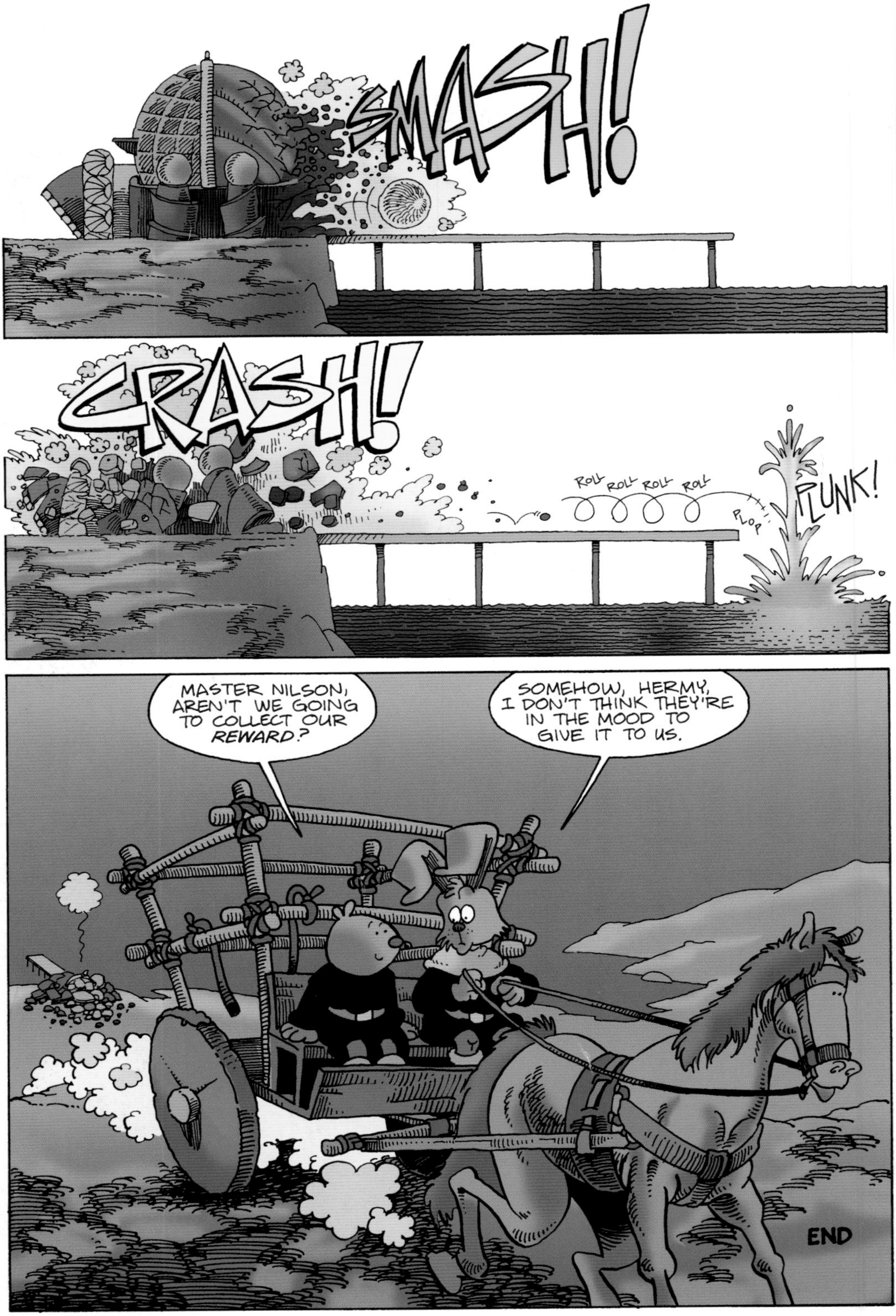
SMASH!
CRASH!
ROLL ROLL ROLL ROLL
PLOP
PLUNK!
MASTER NILSON, AREN'T WE GOING TO COLLECT OUR *REWARD*?
SOMEHOW, HERMY, I DON'T THINK THEY'RE IN THE MOOD TO GIVE IT TO US.
END

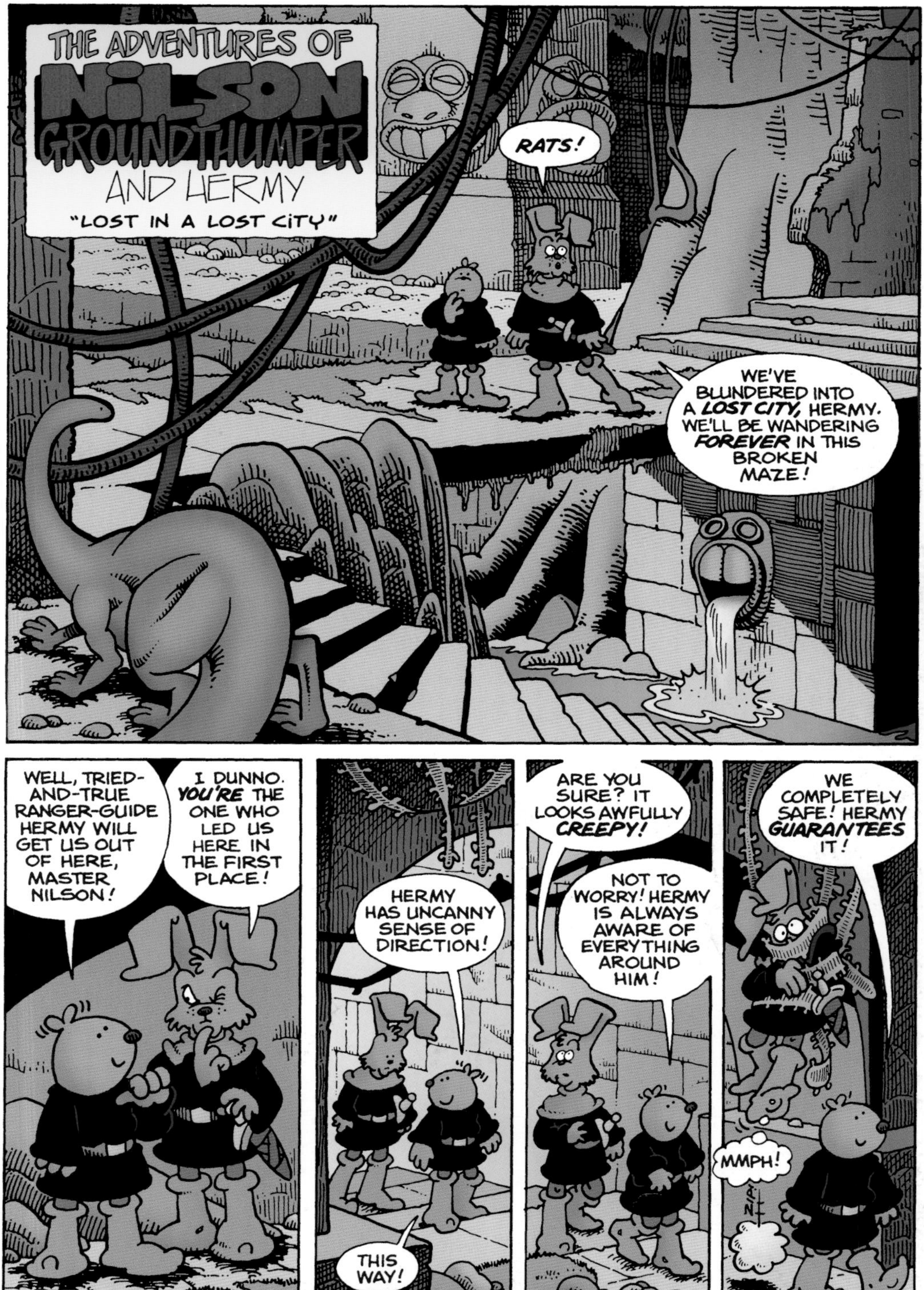
THE ADVENTURES OF
NILSON GROUNDTHUMPER
AND HERMY
"LOST IN A LOST CITY"
RATS!
WE'VE BLUNDERED INTO A LOST CITY, HERMY. WE'LL BE WANDERING FOREVER IN THIS BROKEN MAZE!
WELL, TRIED-AND-TRUE RANGER-GUIDE HERMY WILL GET US OUT OF HERE, MASTER NILSON!
I DUNNO. YOU'RE THE ONE WHO LED US HERE IN THE FIRST PLACE!
HERMY HAS UNCANNY SENSE OF DIRECTION!
THIS WAY!
ARE YOU SURE? IT LOOKS AWFULLY CREEPY!
NOT TO WORRY! HERMY IS ALWAYS AWARE OF EVERYTHING AROUND HIM!
WE COMPLETELY SAFE! HERMY GUARANTEES IT!
MMPH!
ZIP!
1.

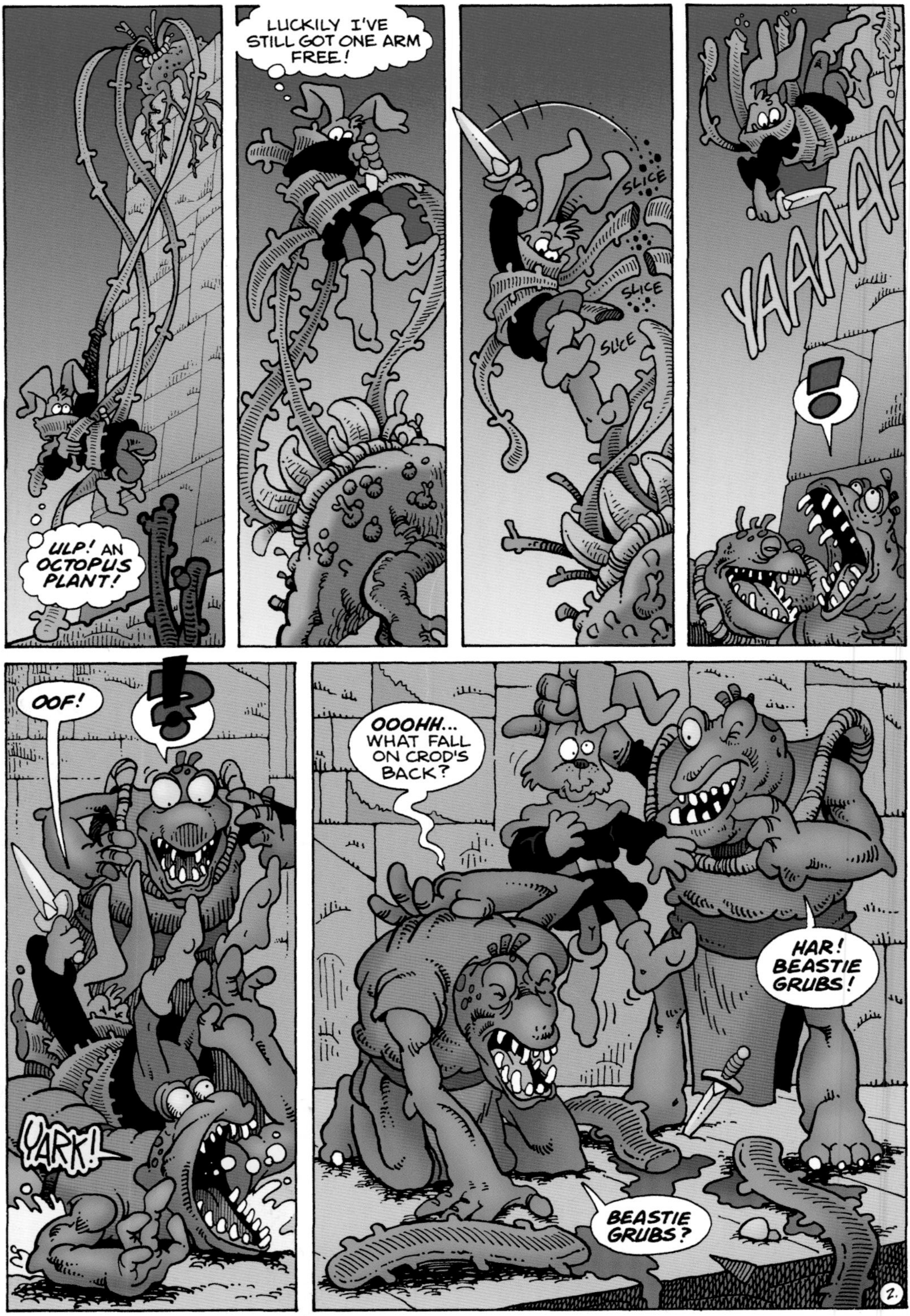
ULP! AN OCTOPUS PLANT!
LUCKILY I'VE STILL GOT ONE ARM FREE!
SLICE
SLICE
SLICE
YAAAAA
OOF!
YARK!
OOOHH... WHAT FALL ON CROD'S BACK?
HAR! BEASTIE GRUBS!
BEASTIE GRUBS?
2.

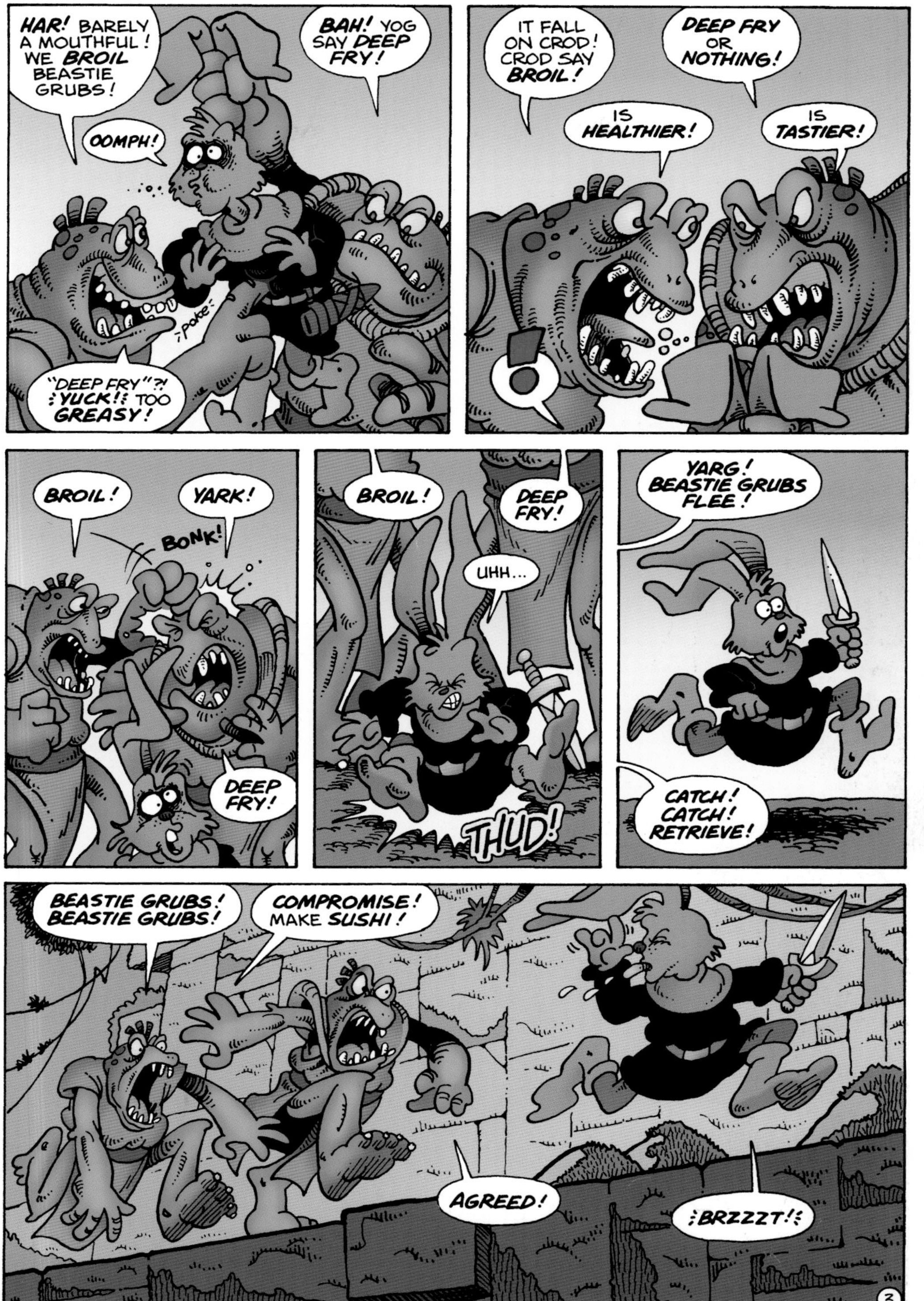
HAR! BARELY A MOUTHFUL! WE BROIL BEASTIE GRUBS!
BAH! YOG SAY DEEP FRY!
OOMPH!
¡poke!
"DEEP FRY"?! ¡YUCK!¡ TOO GREASY!
IT FALL ON CROD! CROD SAY BROIL!
DEEP FRY OR NOTHING!
IS HEALTHIER!
IS TASTIER!
BROIL!
YARK!
BONK!
DEEP FRY!
BROIL!
DEEP FRY!
UHH...
THUD!
YARG! BEASTIE GRUBS FLEE!
CATCH! CATCH! RETRIEVE!
BEASTIE GRUBS! BEASTIE GRUBS!
COMPROMISE! MAKE SUSHI!
AGREED!
¡BRZZZT!¡
3.

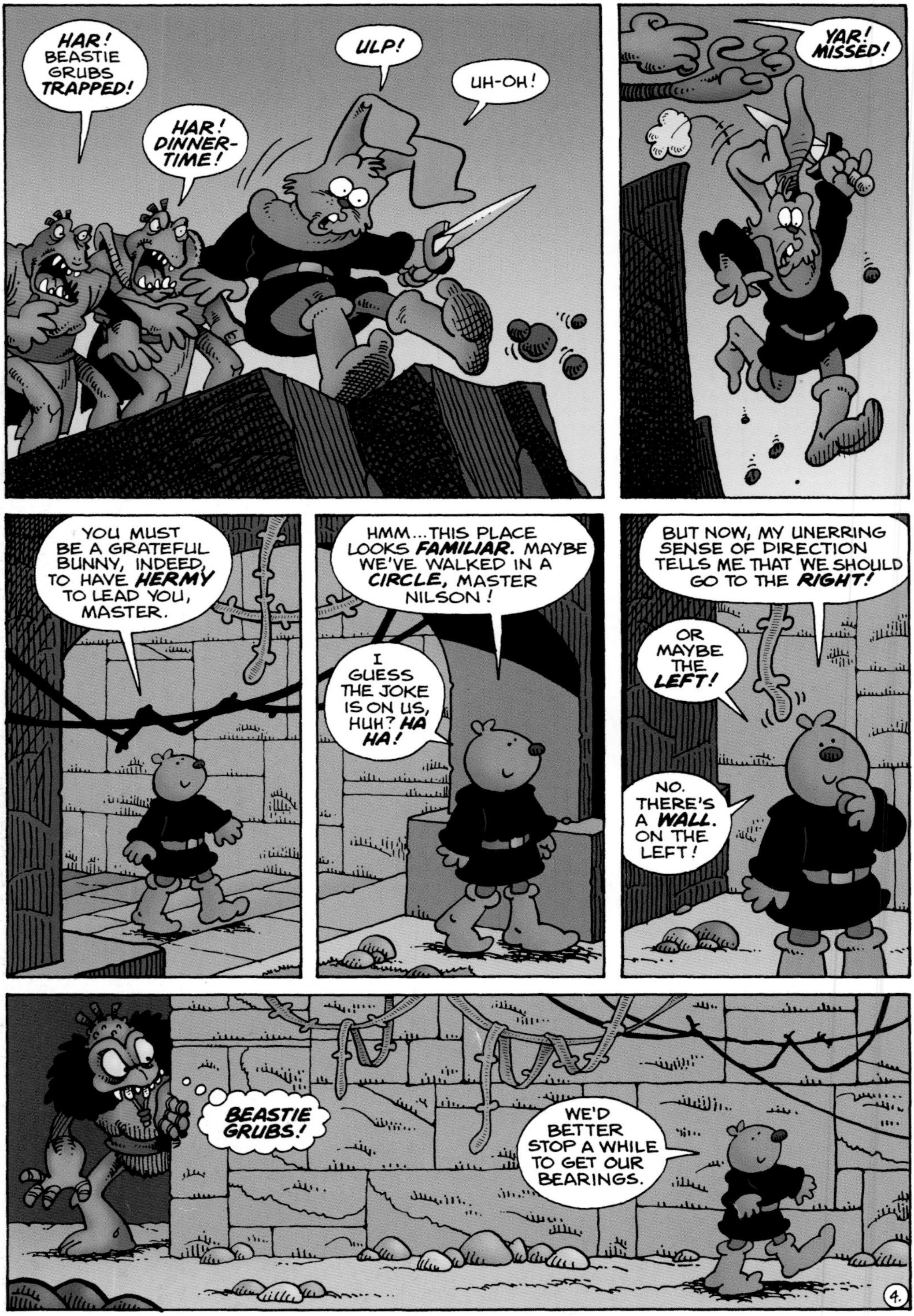
HAR! BEASTIE GRUBS TRAPPED!
ULP!
UH-OH!
HAR! DINNER-TIME!
YAR! MISSED!
YOU MUST BE A GRATEFUL BUNNY, INDEED, TO HAVE HERMY TO LEAD YOU, MASTER.
HMM... THIS PLACE LOOKS FAMILIAR. MAYBE WE'VE WALKED IN A CIRCLE, MASTER NILSON!
I GUESS THE JOKE IS ON US, HUH? HA HA!
BUT NOW, MY UNERRING SENSE OF DIRECTION TELLS ME THAT WE SHOULD GO TO THE RIGHT!
OR MAYBE THE LEFT!
NO. THERE'S A WALL. ON THE LEFT!
BEASTIE GRUBS!
WE'D BETTER STOP A WHILE TO GET OUR BEARINGS.
4.

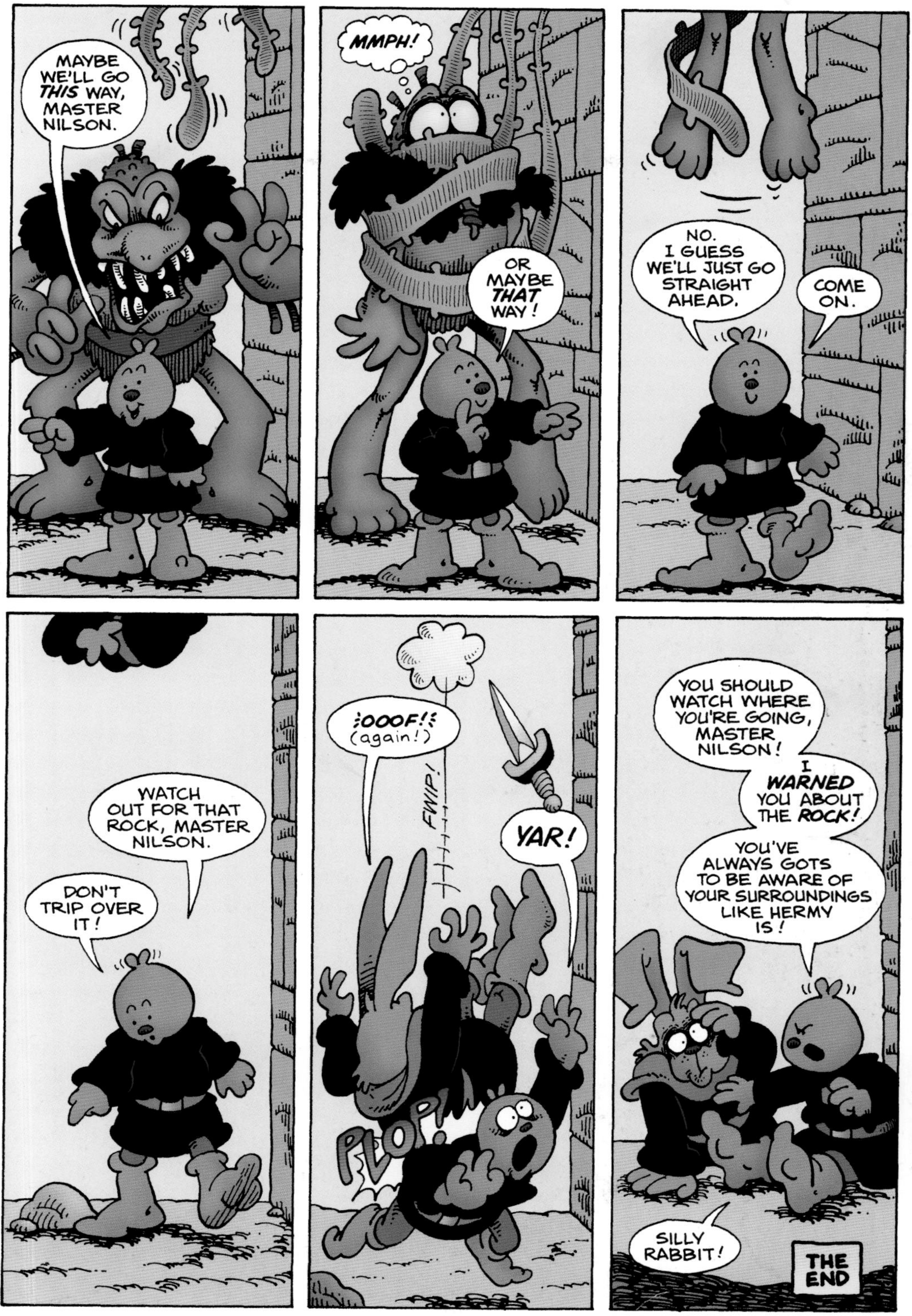
MAYBE WE'LL GO THIS WAY, MASTER NILSON.
MMPH!
OR MAYBE THAT WAY!
NO. I GUESS WE'LL JUST GO STRAIGHT AHEAD.
COME ON.
WATCH OUT FOR THAT ROCK, MASTER NILSON.
DON'T TRIP OVER IT!
OOOF! (again!)
FWIP!
YAR!
PLOP!
YOU SHOULD WATCH WHERE YOU'RE GOING, MASTER NILSON!
I WARNED YOU ABOUT THE ROCK!
YOU'VE ALWAYS GOTS TO BE AWARE OF YOUR SURROUNDINGS LIKE HERMY IS!
SILLY RABBIT!
THE END

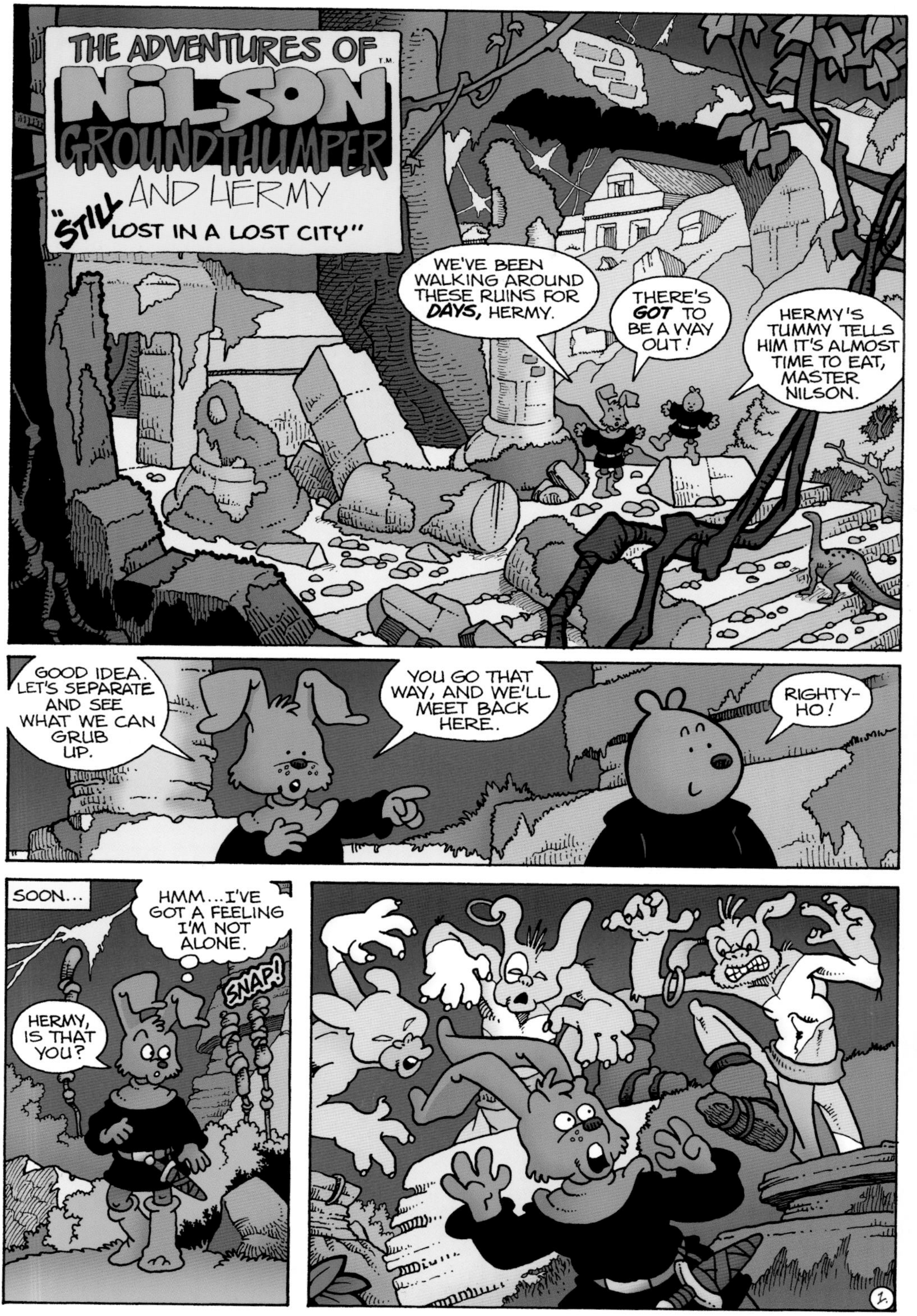

THE ADVENTURES OF NILSON GROUNDTHUMPER AND HERMY T.M.
"STILL LOST IN A LOST CITY"
WE'VE BEEN WALKING AROUND THESE RUINS FOR DAYS, HERMY.
THERE'S GOT TO BE A WAY OUT!
HERMY'S TUMMY TELLS HIM IT'S ALMOST TIME TO EAT, MASTER NILSON.
GOOD IDEA. LET'S SEPARATE AND SEE WHAT WE CAN GRUB UP.
YOU GO THAT WAY, AND WE'LL MEET BACK HERE.
RIGHTY-HO!
SOON...
HMM...I'VE GOT A FEELING I'M NOT ALONE.
SNAP!
HERMY, IS THAT YOU?
1.

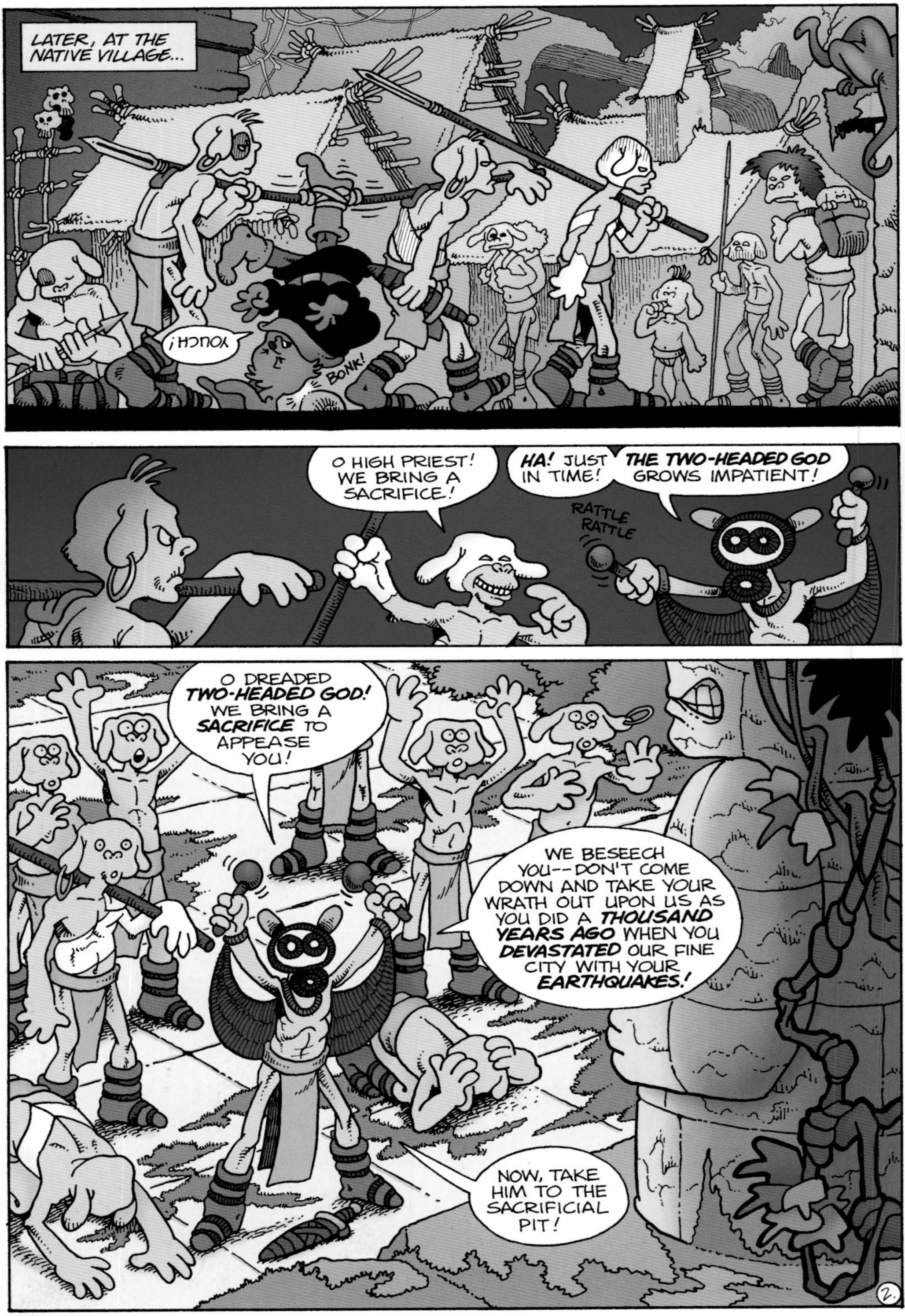

LATER, AT THE NATIVE VILLAGE...
YOUCH!
BONK!
O HIGH PRIEST! WE BRING A SACRIFICE!
HA! JUST IN TIME!
THE TWO-HEADED GOD GROWS IMPATIENT!
RATTLE RATTLE
O DREADED TWO-HEADED GOD! WE BRING A SACRIFICE TO APPEASE YOU!
WE BESEECH YOU--DON'T COME DOWN AND TAKE YOUR WRATH OUT UPON US AS YOU DID A THOUSAND YEARS AGO WHEN YOU DEVASTATED OUR FINE CITY WITH YOUR EARTHQUAKES!
NOW, TAKE HIM TO THE SACRIFICIAL PIT!

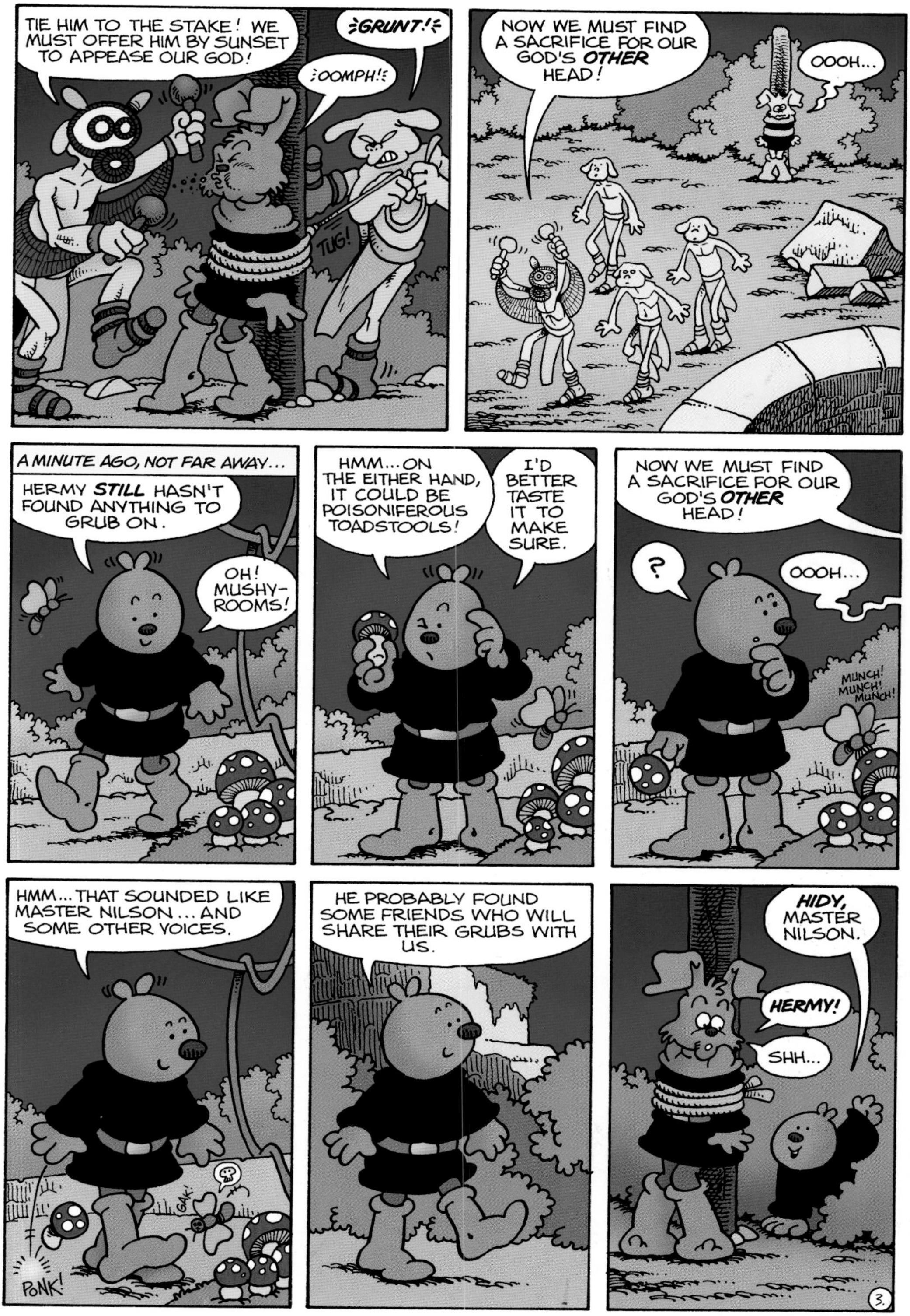
TIE HIM TO THE STAKE! WE MUST OFFER HIM BY SUNSET TO APPEASE OUR GOD!
GRUNT!
OOMPH!
TUG!
NOW WE MUST FIND A SACRIFICE FOR OUR GOD'S OTHER HEAD!
OOOH...
A MINUTE AGO, NOT FAR AWAY...
HERMY STILL HASN'T FOUND ANYTHING TO GRUB ON.
OH! MUSHY-ROOMS!
HMM... ON THE EITHER HAND, IT COULD BE POISONIFEROUS TOADSTOOLS!
I'D BETTER TASTE IT TO MAKE SURE.
NOW WE MUST FIND A SACRIFICE FOR OUR GOD'S OTHER HEAD!
?
OOOH...
MUNCH! MUNCH! MUNCH!
HMM... THAT SOUNDED LIKE MASTER NILSON... AND SOME OTHER VOICES.
PONK!
HE PROBABLY FOUND SOME FRIENDS WHO WILL SHARE THEIR GRUBS WITH US.
HIDY, MASTER NILSON.
HERMY!
SHH...
3.

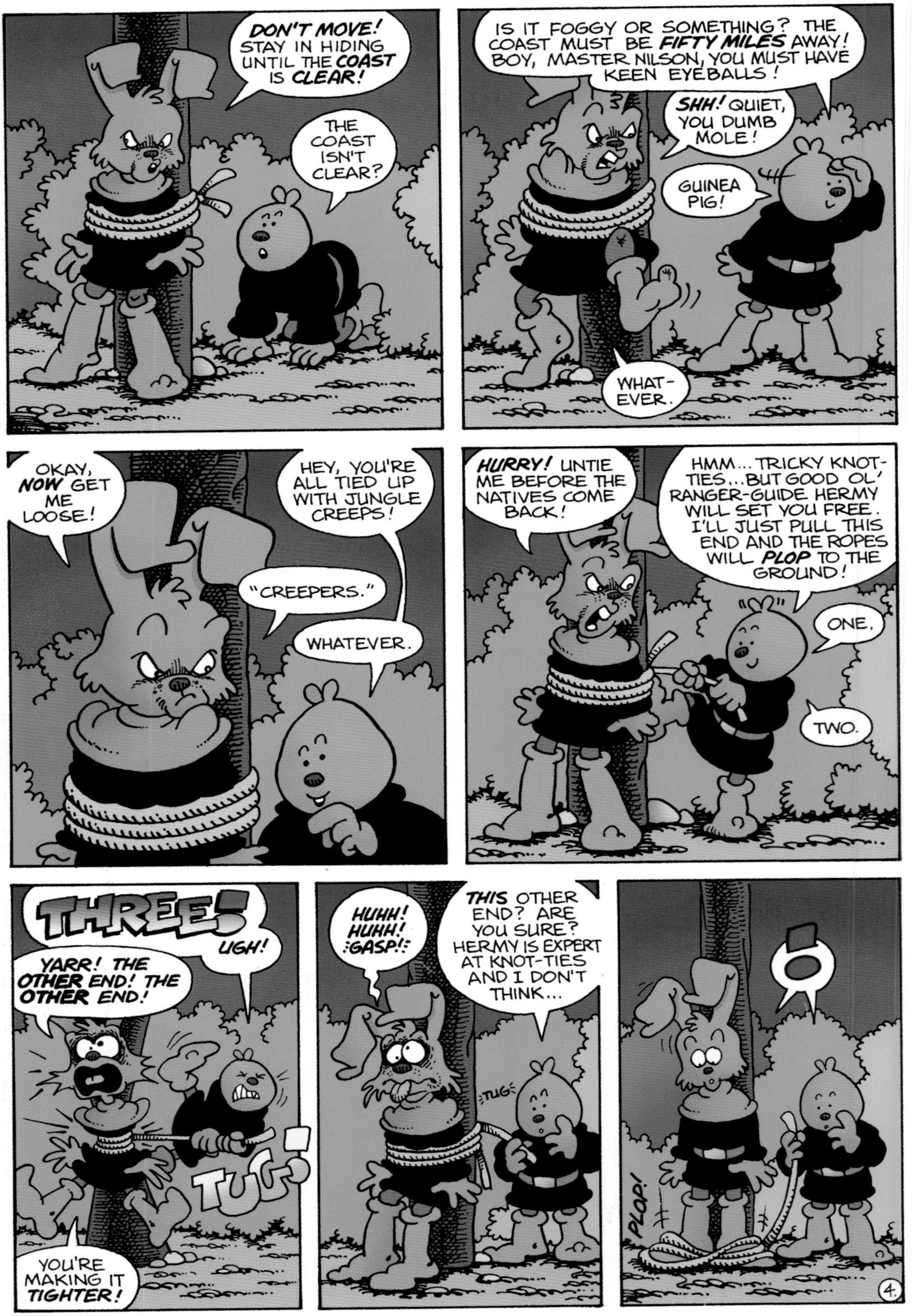
DON'T MOVE! STAY IN HIDING UNTIL THE COAST IS CLEAR!
THE COAST ISN'T CLEAR?
IS IT FOGGY OR SOMETHING? THE COAST MUST BE FIFTY MILES AWAY! BOY, MASTER NILSON, YOU MUST HAVE KEEN EYEBALLS!
SHH! QUIET, YOU DUMB MOLE!
GUINEA PIG!
WHAT-EVER.
OKAY, NOW GET ME LOOSE!
HEY, YOU'RE ALL TIED UP WITH JUNGLE CREEPS!
"CREEPERS."
WHATEVER.
HURRY! UNTIE ME BEFORE THE NATIVES COME BACK!
HMM... TRICKY KNOT-TIES...BUT GOOD OL' RANGER-GUIDE HERMY WILL SET YOU FREE. I'LL JUST PULL THIS END AND THE ROPES WILL PLOP TO THE GROUND!
ONE.
TWO.
THREE!
UGH!
YARR! THE OTHER END! THE OTHER END!
TUG
YOU'RE MAKING IT TIGHTER!
HUHH! HUHH! :GASP!:
THIS OTHER END? ARE YOU SURE? HERMY IS EXPERT AT KNOT-TIES AND I DON'T THINK...
TUG
PLOP!
4

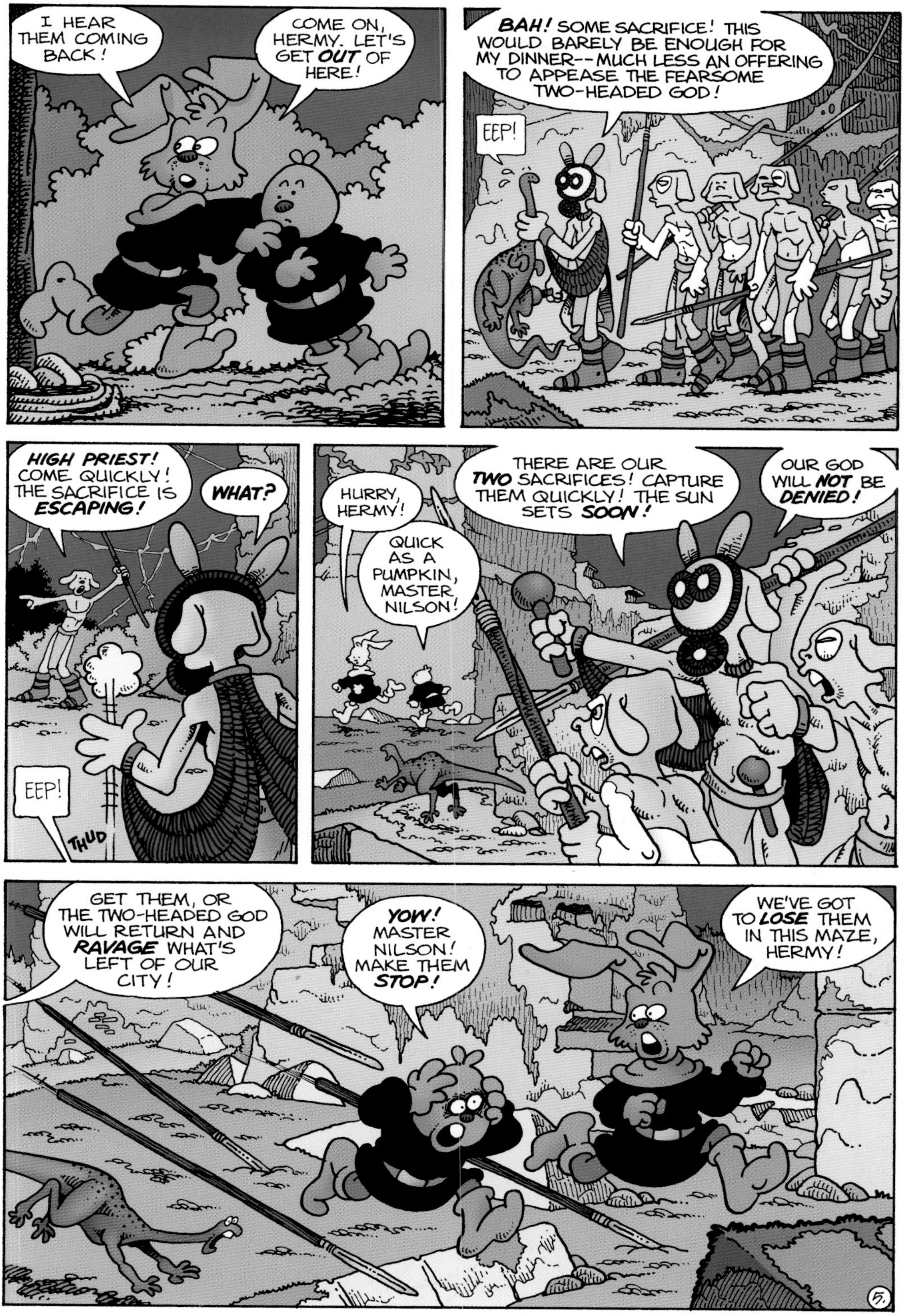

I HEAR THEM COMING BACK!
COME ON, HERMY. LET'S GET OUT OF HERE!
BAH! SOME SACRIFICE! THIS WOULD BARELY BE ENOUGH FOR MY DINNER--MUCH LESS AN OFFERING TO APPEASE THE FEARSOME TWO-HEADED GOD!
EEP!
HIGH PRIEST! COME QUICKLY! THE SACRIFICE IS ESCAPING!
WHAT?
EEP!
THUD
HURRY, HERMY!
QUICK AS A PUMPKIN, MASTER NILSON!
THERE ARE OUR TWO SACRIFICES! CAPTURE THEM QUICKLY! THE SUN SETS SOON!
OUR GOD WILL NOT BE DENIED!
GET THEM, OR THE TWO-HEADED GOD WILL RETURN AND RAVAGE WHAT'S LEFT OF OUR CITY!
YOW! MASTER NILSON! MAKE THEM STOP!
WE'VE GOT TO LOSE THEM IN THIS MAZE, HERMY!
5.

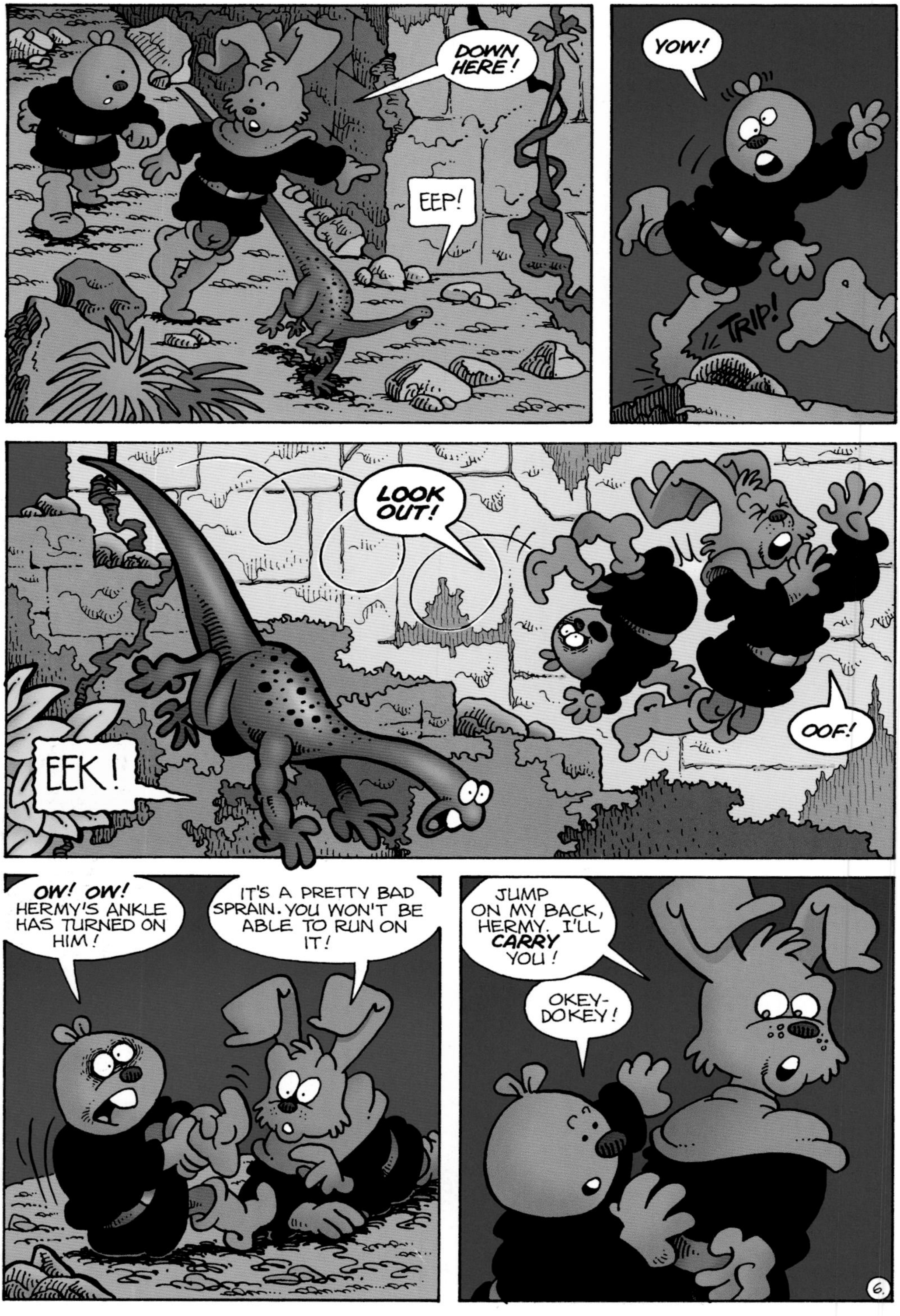

DOWN HERE!
EEP!
YOW!
TRIP!
LOOK OUT!
EEK!
OOF!
OW! OW! HERMY'S ANKLE HAS TURNED ON HIM!
IT'S A PRETTY BAD SPRAIN. YOU WON'T BE ABLE TO RUN ON IT!
JUMP ON MY BACK, HERMY. I'LL CARRY YOU!
OKEY-DOKEY!
6.

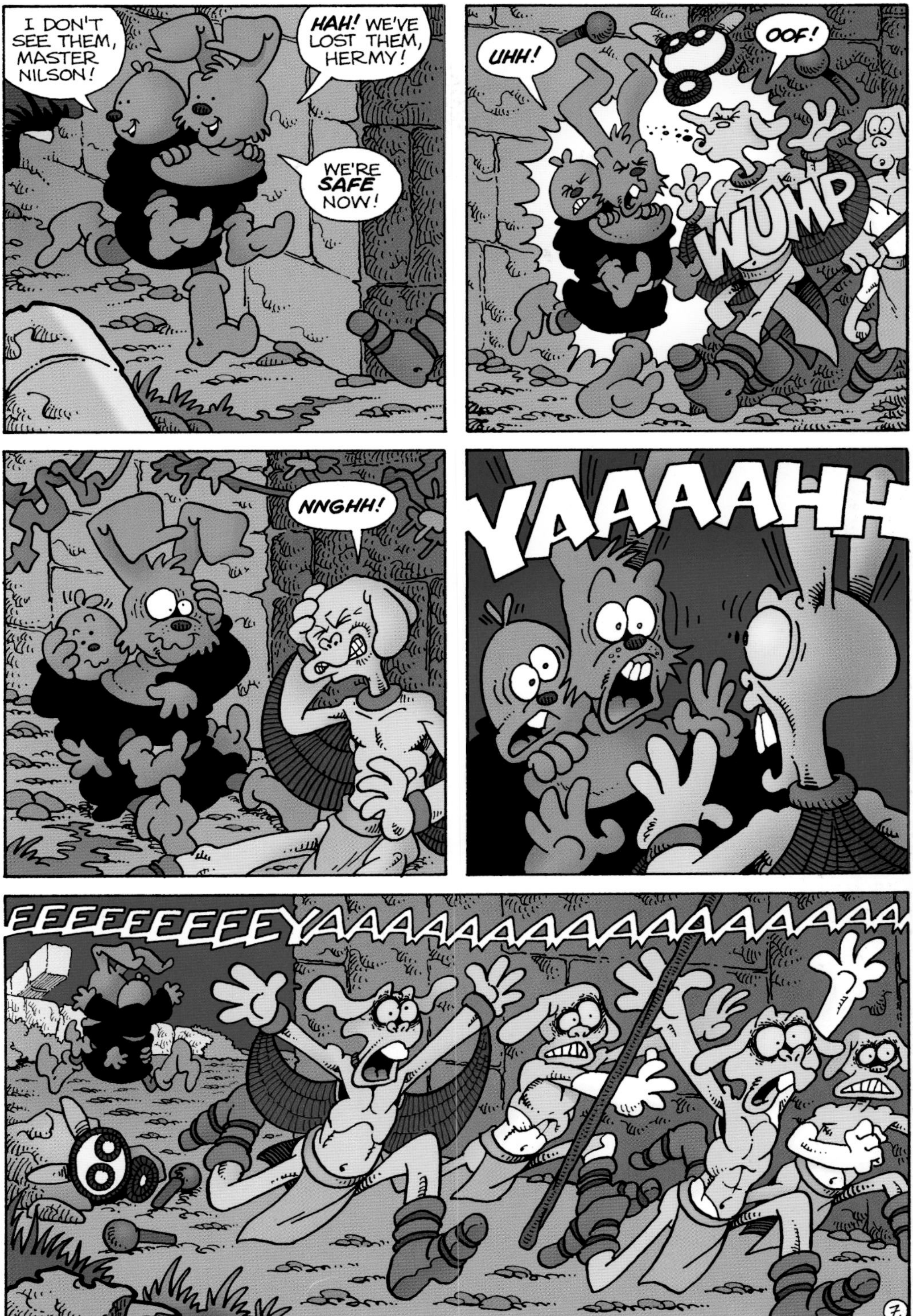
I DON'T SEE THEM, MASTER NILSON!
HAH! WE'VE LOST THEM, HERMY!
WE'RE SAFE NOW!
UHH!
OOF!
WUMP
NNGHH!
YAAAAHH
EEEEEEEEEEYAAAAAAAAAAAAAAAA
7.

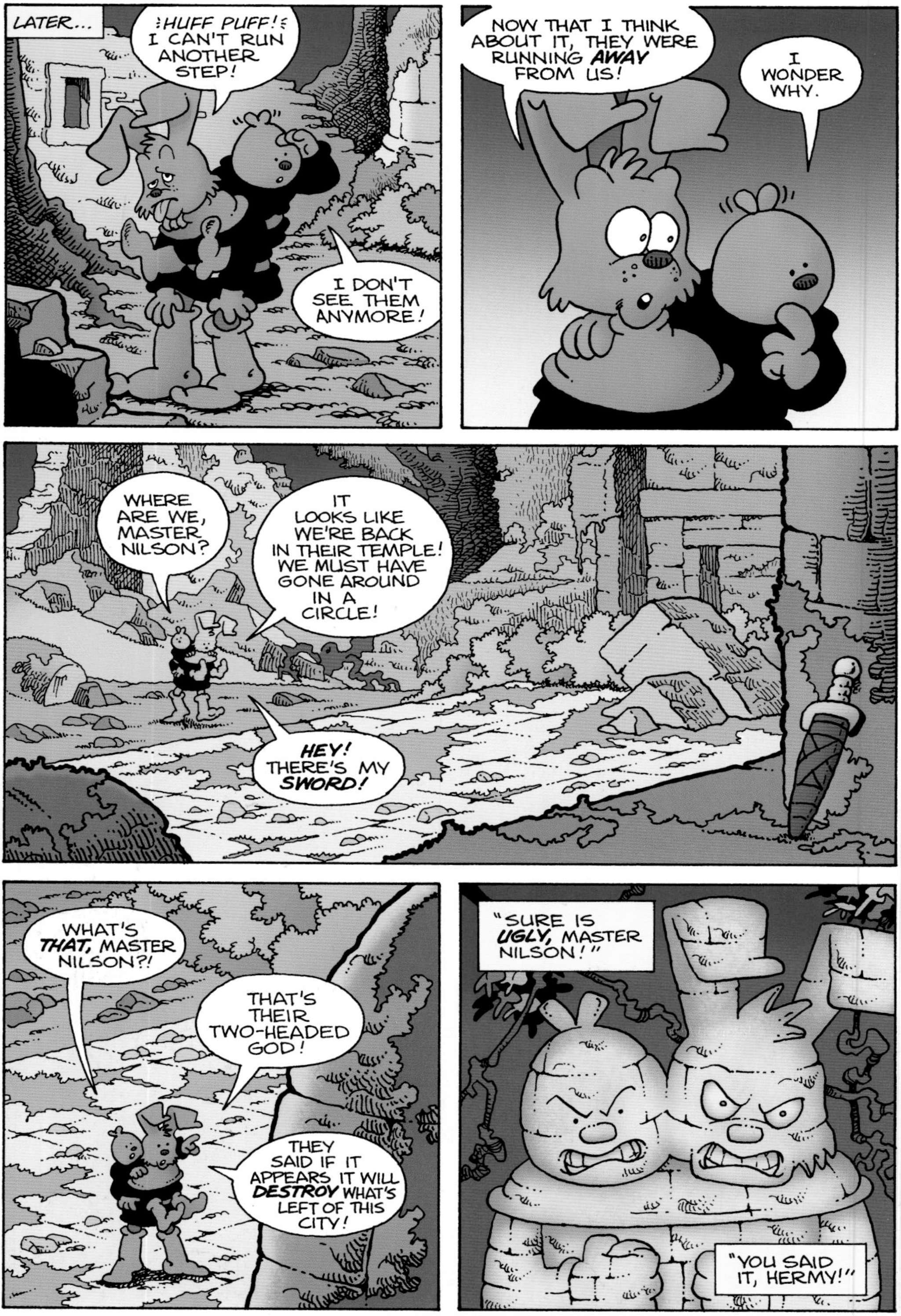
LATER...
HUFF PUFF! I CAN'T RUN ANOTHER STEP!
I DON'T SEE THEM ANYMORE!
NOW THAT I THINK ABOUT IT, THEY WERE RUNNING **AWAY** FROM US!
I WONDER WHY.
WHERE ARE WE, MASTER NILSON?
IT LOOKS LIKE WE'RE BACK IN THEIR TEMPLE! WE MUST HAVE GONE AROUND IN A CIRCLE!
HEY! THERE'S MY **SWORD!**
WHAT'S **THAT,** MASTER NILSON?!
THAT'S THEIR TWO-HEADED GOD!
THEY SAID IF IT APPEARS IT WILL **DESTROY** WHAT'S LEFT OF THIS CITY!
"SURE IS **UGLY,** MASTER NILSON!"
"YOU SAID IT, HERMY!"
END

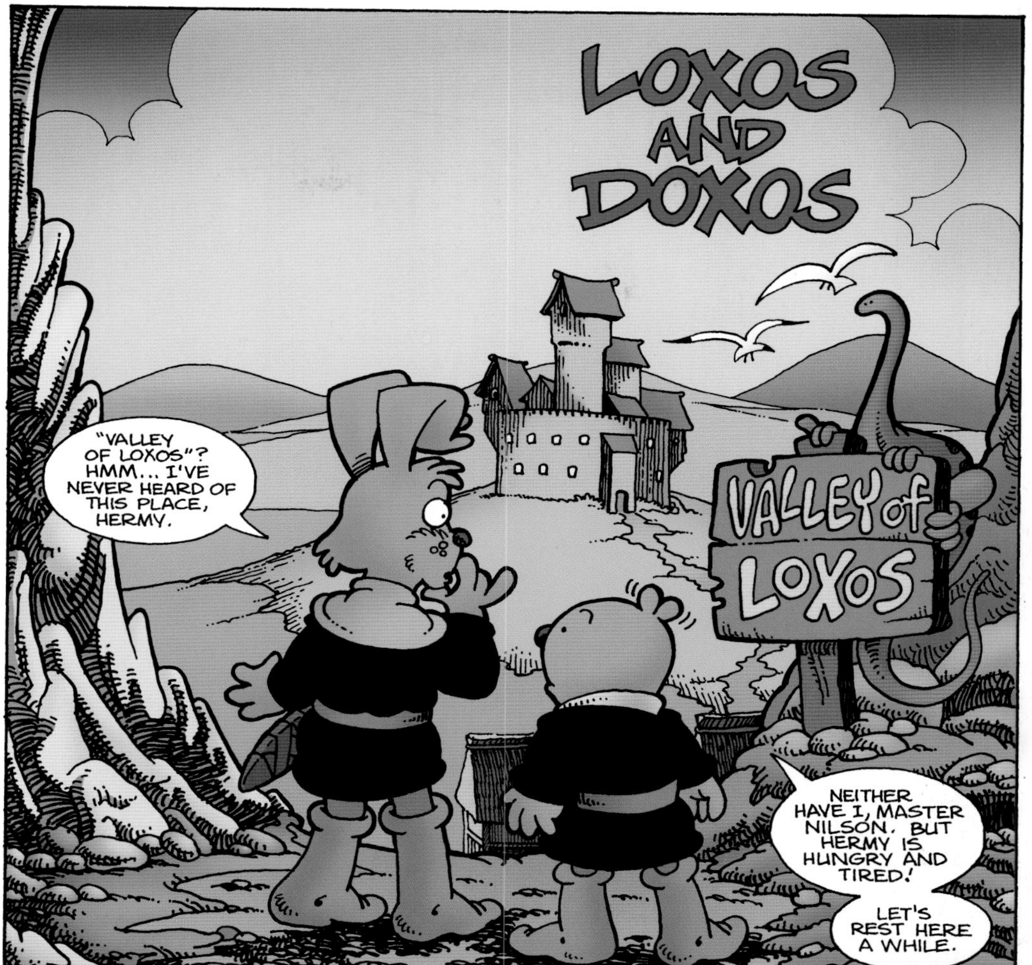
LOXOS AND DOXOS
"VALLEY OF LOXOS"? HMM... I'VE NEVER HEARD OF THIS PLACE, HERMY.
VALLEY of LOXOS
NEITHER HAVE I, MASTER NILSON. BUT HERMY IS HUNGRY AND TIRED!
LET'S REST HERE A WHILE.
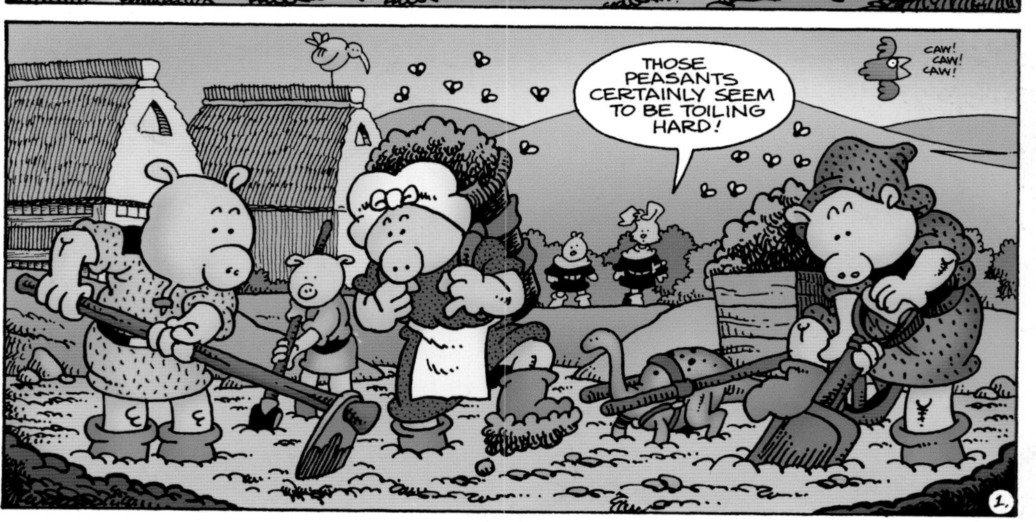
THOSE PEASANTS CERTAINLY SEEM TO BE TOILING HARD!
CAW! CAW! CAW!
1.

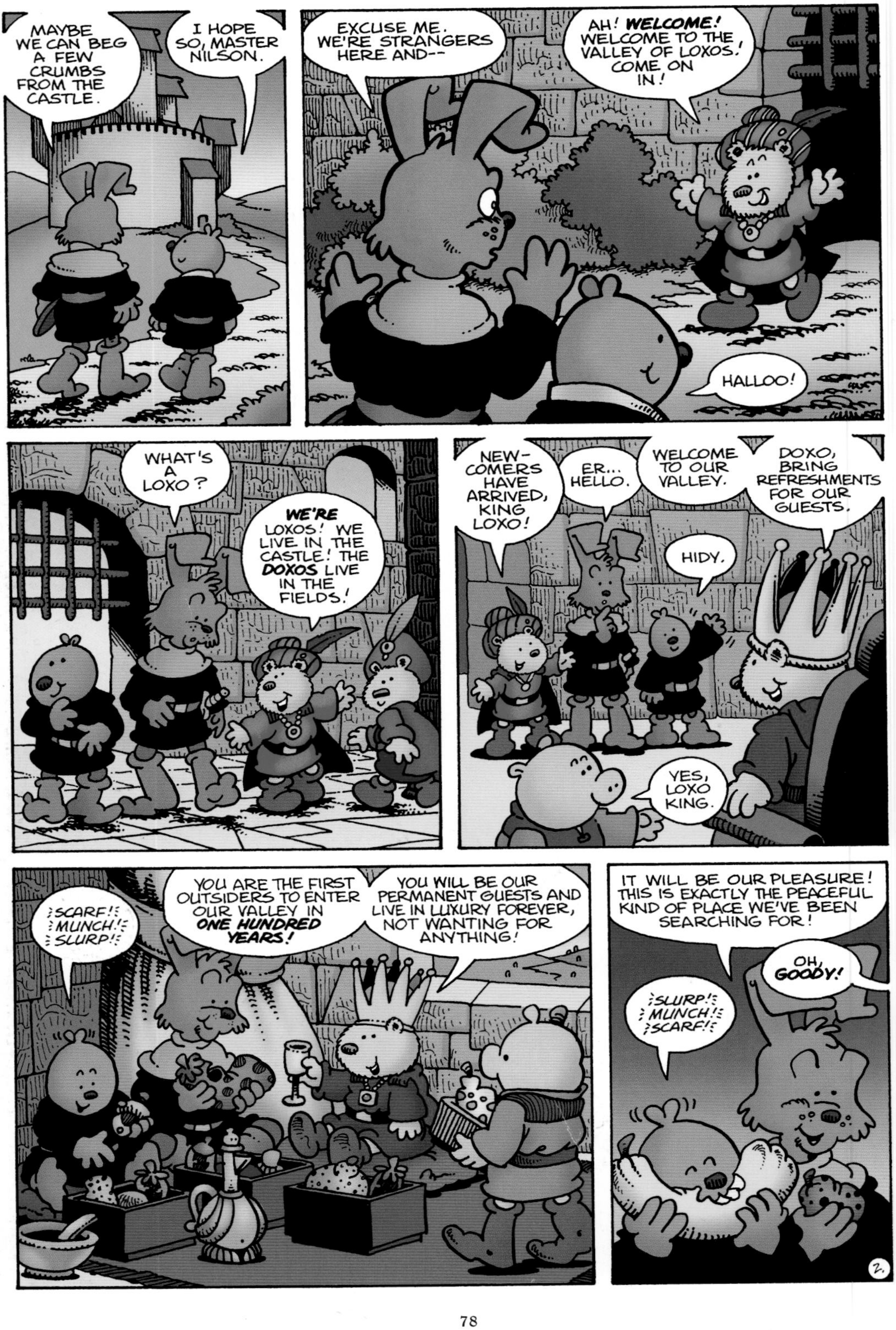
MAYBE WE CAN BEG A FEW CRUMBS FROM THE CASTLE.
I HOPE SO, MASTER NILSON.
EXCUSE ME. WE'RE STRANGERS HERE AND--
AH! WELCOME! WELCOME TO THE VALLEY OF LOXOS! COME ON IN!
HALLOO!
WHAT'S A LOXO?
WE'RE LOXOS! WE LIVE IN THE CASTLE! THE DOXOS LIVE IN THE FIELDS!
NEW-COMERS HAVE ARRIVED, KING LOXO!
ER... HELLO.
WELCOME TO OUR VALLEY.
DOXO, BRING REFRESHMENTS FOR OUR GUESTS.
HIDY.
YES, LOXO KING.
SCARF! MUNCH! SLURP!
YOU ARE THE FIRST OUTSIDERS TO ENTER OUR VALLEY IN ONE HUNDRED YEARS!
YOU WILL BE OUR PERMANENT GUESTS AND LIVE IN LUXURY FOREVER, NOT WANTING FOR ANYTHING!
IT WILL BE OUR PLEASURE! THIS IS EXACTLY THE PEACEFUL KIND OF PLACE WE'VE BEEN SEARCHING FOR!
OH, GOODY!
SLURP! MUNCH! SCARF!
2.

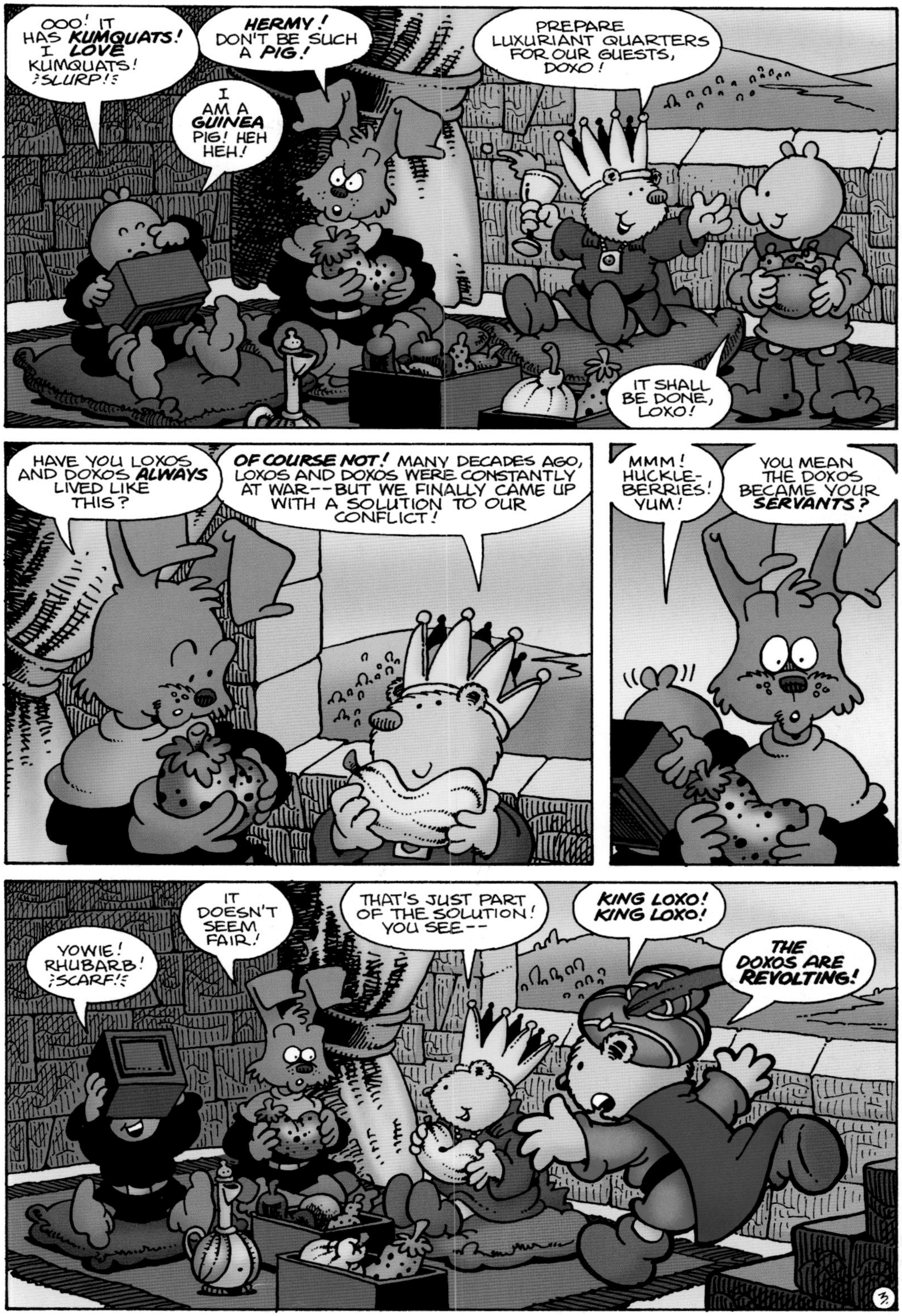
OOO! IT HAS **KUMQUATS!** I **LOVE** KUMQUATS! ¡SLURP!¡
HERMY! DON'T BE SUCH A **PIG!**
I AM A **GUINEA** PIG! HEH HEH!
PREPARE LUXURIANT QUARTERS FOR OUR GUESTS, DOXO!
IT SHALL BE DONE, LOXO!
HAVE YOU LOXOS AND DOXOS **ALWAYS** LIVED LIKE THIS?
OF COURSE NOT! MANY DECADES AGO, LOXOS AND DOXOS WERE CONSTANTLY AT WAR--BUT WE FINALLY CAME UP WITH A SOLUTION TO OUR CONFLICT!
MMM! HUCKLE-BERRIES! YUM!
YOU MEAN THE DOXOS BECAME YOUR **SERVANTS?**
YOWIE! RHUBARB! ¡SCARF!¡
IT DOESN'T SEEM FAIR!
THAT'S JUST PART OF THE SOLUTION! YOU SEE--
KING LOXO! KING LOXO!
THE DOXOS ARE REVOLTING!
3

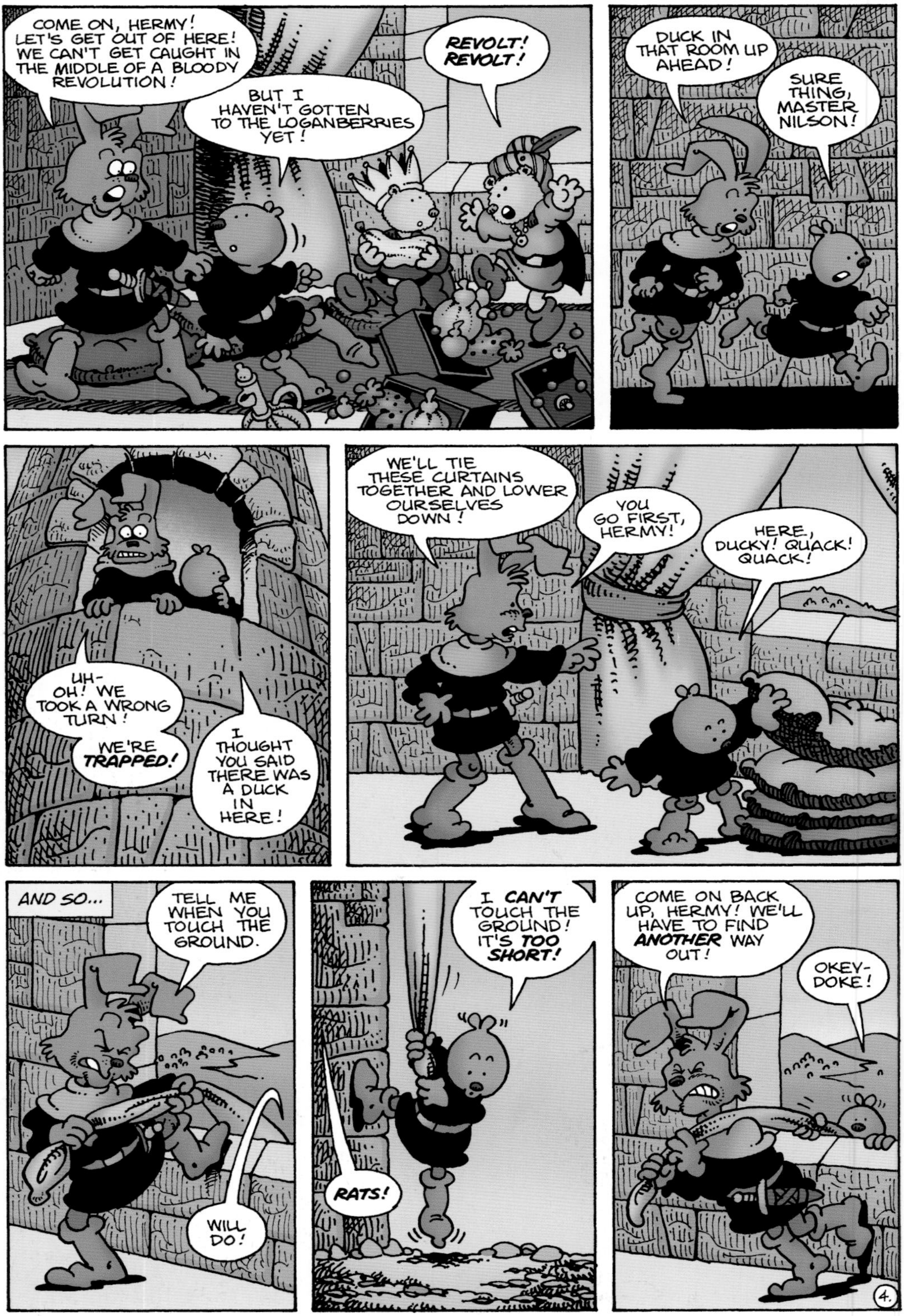
COME ON, HERMY! LET'S GET OUT OF HERE! WE CAN'T GET CAUGHT IN THE MIDDLE OF A BLOODY REVOLUTION!
BUT I HAVEN'T GOTTEN TO THE LOGANBERRIES YET!
REVOLT! REVOLT!
DUCK IN THAT ROOM UP AHEAD!
SURE THING, MASTER NILSON!
UH-OH! WE TOOK A WRONG TURN!
WE'RE TRAPPED!
I THOUGHT YOU SAID THERE WAS A DUCK IN HERE!
WE'LL TIE THESE CURTAINS TOGETHER AND LOWER OURSELVES DOWN!
YOU GO FIRST, HERMY!
HERE, DUCKY! QUACK! QUACK!
AND SO...
TELL ME WHEN YOU TOUCH THE GROUND.
WILL DO!
I CAN'T TOUCH THE GROUND! IT'S TOO SHORT!
RATS!
COME ON BACK UP, HERMY! WE'LL HAVE TO FIND ANOTHER WAY OUT!
OKEY-DOKE!
4.

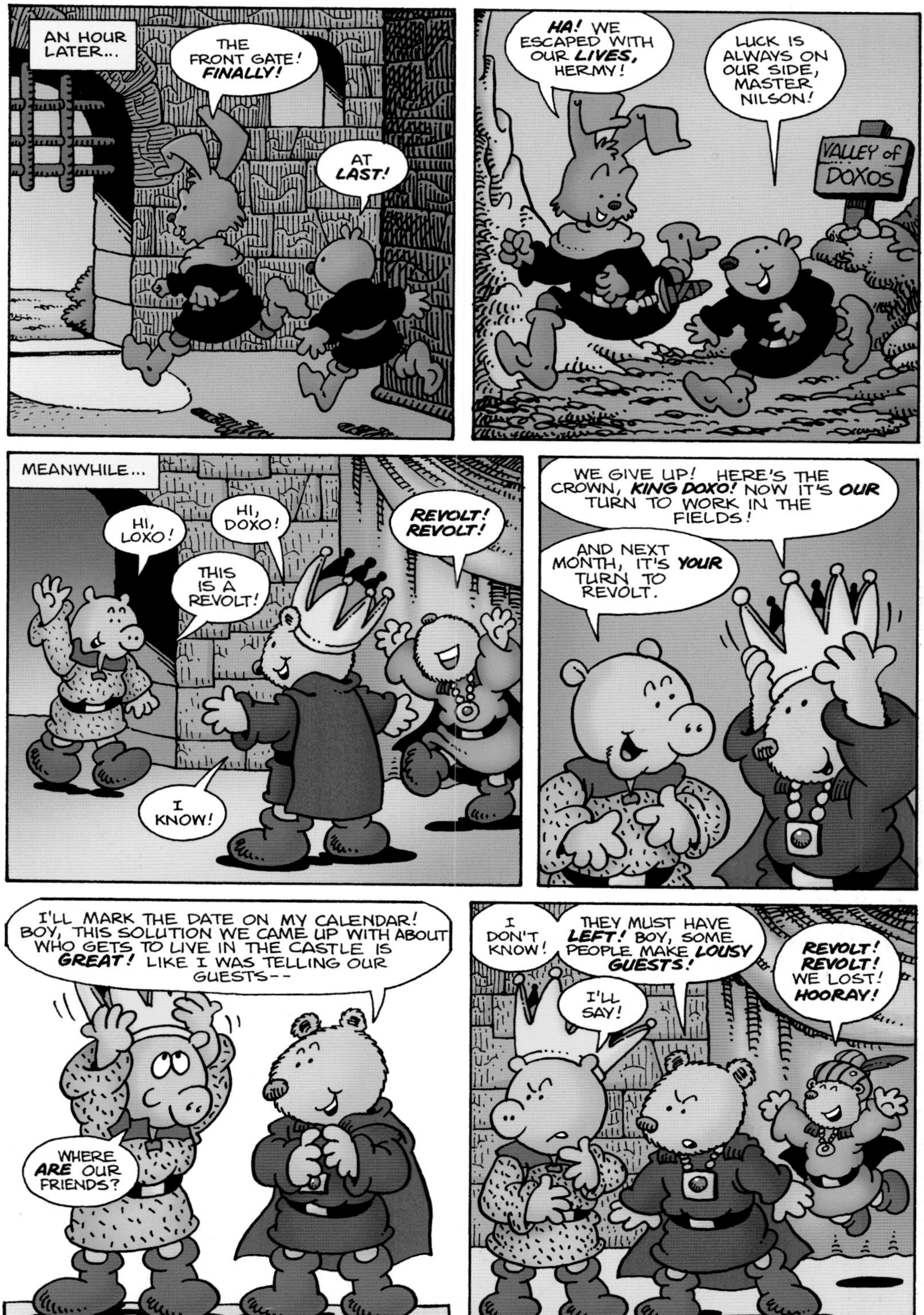
AN HOUR LATER...
THE FRONT GATE! FINALLY!
AT LAST!
HA! WE ESCAPED WITH OUR LIVES, HERMY!
LUCK IS ALWAYS ON OUR SIDE, MASTER NILSON!
VALLEY of DOXOS
MEANWHILE...
HI, LOXO!
HI, DOXO!
THIS IS A REVOLT!
REVOLT! REVOLT!
I KNOW!
WE GIVE UP! HERE'S THE CROWN, KING DOXO! NOW IT'S OUR TURN TO WORK IN THE FIELDS!
AND NEXT MONTH, IT'S YOUR TURN TO REVOLT.
I'LL MARK THE DATE ON MY CALENDAR! BOY, THIS SOLUTION WE CAME UP WITH ABOUT WHO GETS TO LIVE IN THE CASTLE IS GREAT! LIKE I WAS TELLING OUR GUESTS--
WHERE ARE OUR FRIENDS?
I DON'T KNOW!
THEY MUST HAVE LEFT! BOY, SOME PEOPLE MAKE LOUSY GUESTS!
I'LL SAY!
REVOLT! REVOLT! WE LOST! HOORAY!
END

THE RE-RETURN of the WIZARD

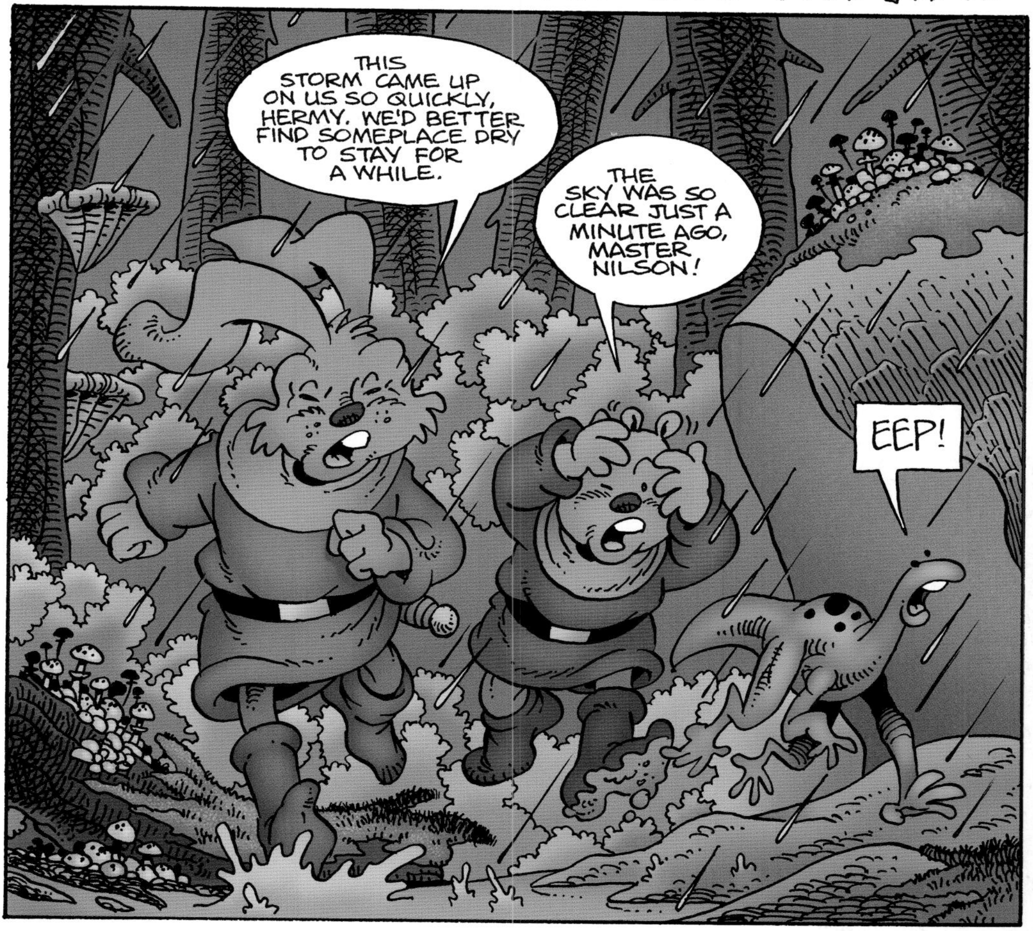
THIS STORM CAME UP ON US SO QUICKLY, HERMY. WE'D BETTER FIND SOMEPLACE DRY TO STAY FOR A WHILE.
THE SKY WAS SO CLEAR JUST A MINUTE AGO, MASTER NILSON!
EEP!

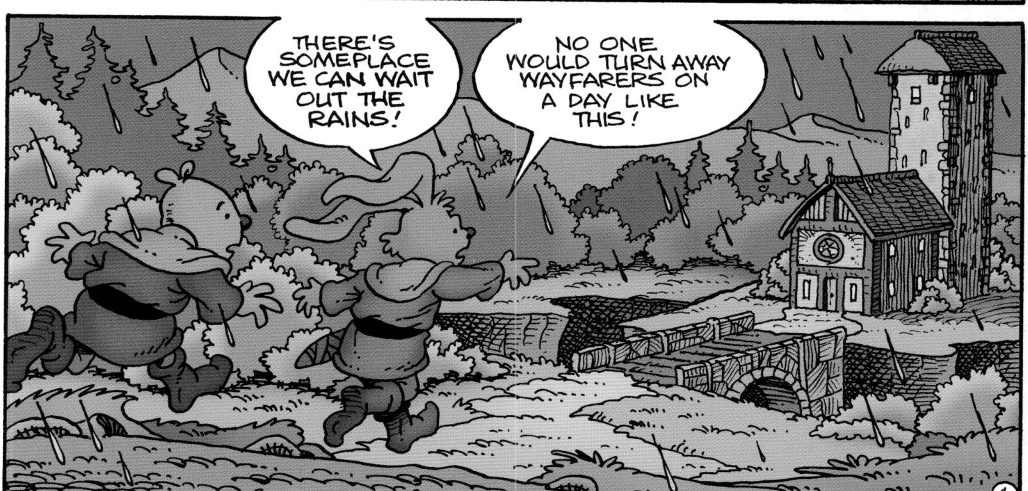
THERE'S SOMEPLACE WE CAN WAIT OUT THE RAINS!
NO ONE WOULD TURN AWAY WAYFARERS ON A DAY LIKE THIS!
1

AT LAST!
AT LAST!
AT LAST!

I FINALLY POSSESS WIZARD REINAVE'S AMULET OF POWER!

BUT IT IS ENCASED WITHIN THIS CRYSTAL SPHERE.

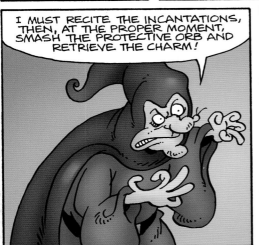

I MUST RECITE THE INCANTATIONS, THEN, AT THE PROPER MOMENT, SMASH THE PROTECTIVE ORB AND RETRIEVE THE CHARM!

BUT THERE IS A *TRAP*--THE AMULET IS PROTECTED BY THE *VAPORS OF HUBBELL*. THEY WILL ATTACK AND DESTROY HE WHO DARES BREAK THE SPHERE.

I MUST FIND SOME FOOL TO BREAK THE ORB FOR ME, THEN I CAN SAFELY CLAIM THE AMULET.

SO I CREATED THIS STORM TO LURE AN UNSUSPECTING TRAVELER TO SEEK SHELTER HERE.

AH! HERE COMES SOMEONE NOW!

HA HA HA HA HA! I AM HAPPY! SO HAPPY!

SOON I WILL HAVE MORE POWER THAN EVEN I CAN IMAGINE!

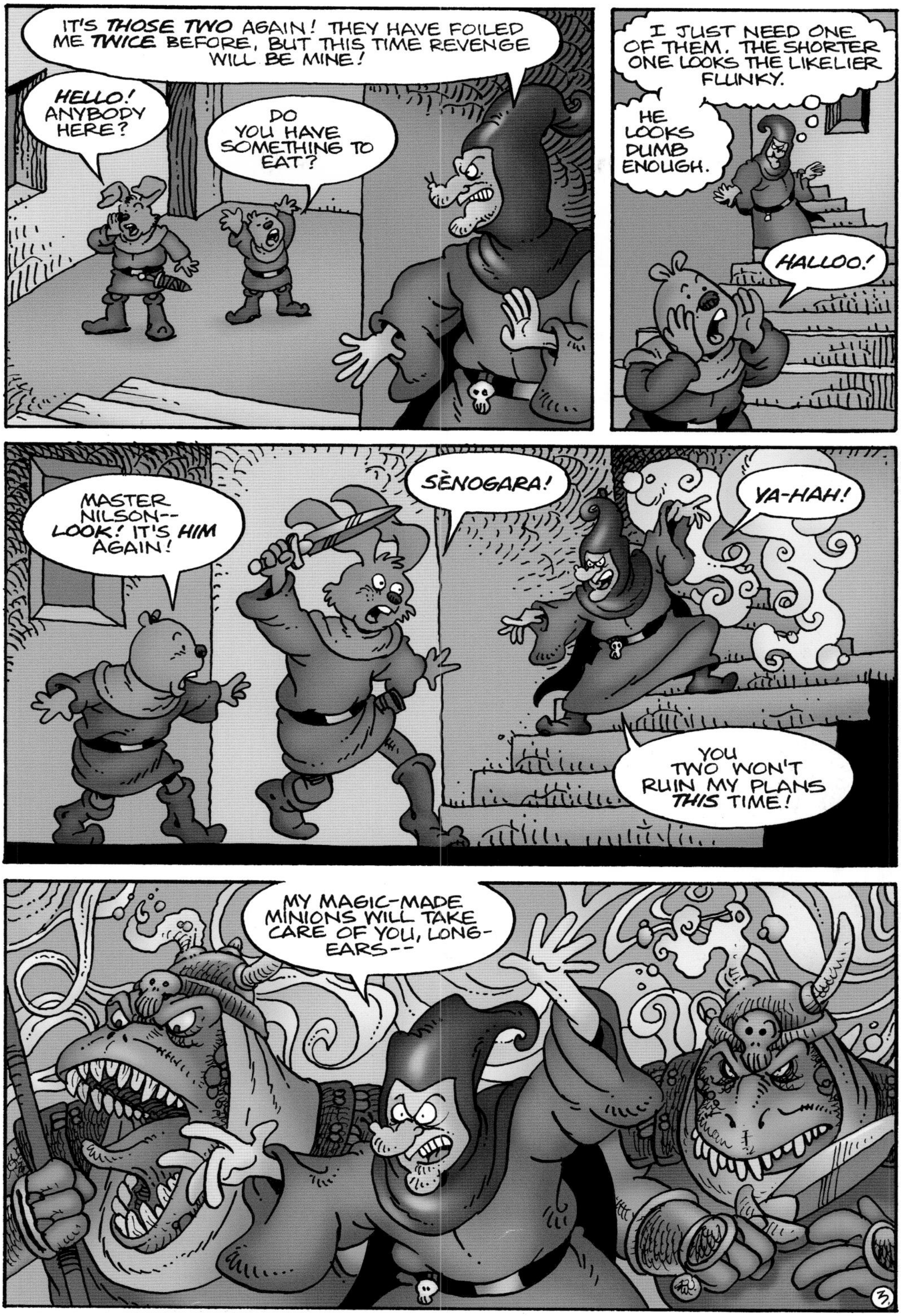
IT'S THOSE TWO AGAIN! THEY HAVE FOILED ME TWICE BEFORE, BUT THIS TIME REVENGE WILL BE MINE!
HELLO! ANYBODY HERE?
DO YOU HAVE SOMETHING TO EAT?
I JUST NEED ONE OF THEM. THE SHORTER ONE LOOKS THE LIKELIER FLUNKY.
HE LOOKS DUMB ENOUGH.
HALLOO!
MASTER NILSON-- LOOK! IT'S HIM AGAIN!
SÈNOGARA!
YA-HAH!
YOU TWO WON'T RUIN MY PLANS THIS TIME!
MY MAGIC-MADE MINIONS WILL TAKE CARE OF YOU, LONG-EARS--
3

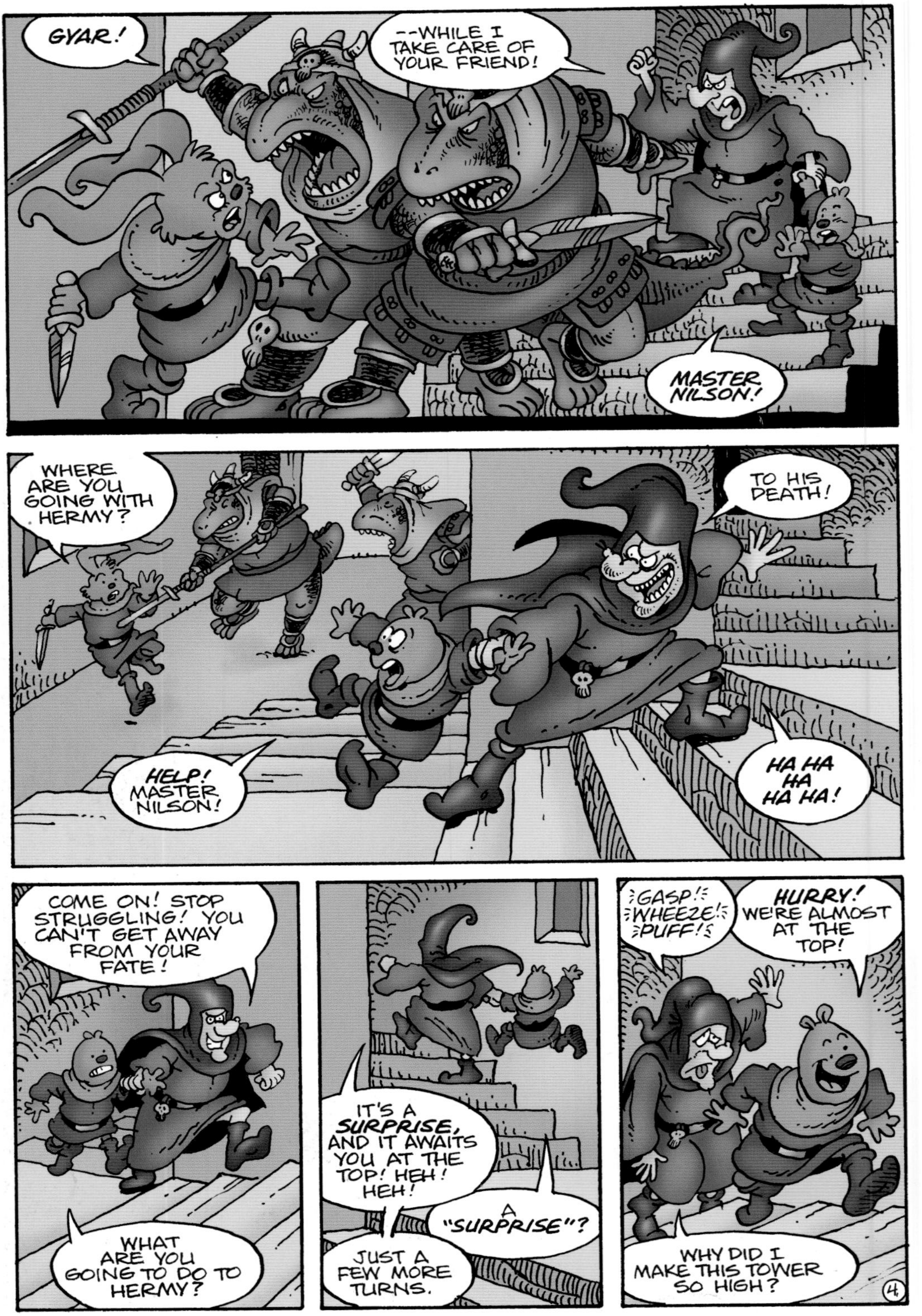
GYAR!
--WHILE I TAKE CARE OF YOUR FRIEND!
MASTER NILSON!
WHERE ARE YOU GOING WITH HERMY?
TO HIS DEATH!
HELP! MASTER NILSON!
HA HA HA HA HA!
COME ON! STOP STRUGGLING! YOU CAN'T GET AWAY FROM YOUR FATE!
WHAT ARE YOU GOING TO DO TO HERMY?
IT'S A SURPRISE, AND IT AWAITS YOU AT THE TOP! HEH! HEH! HEH!
A "SURPRISE"?
JUST A FEW MORE TURNS.
GASP! WHEEZE! PUFF!
HURRY! WE'RE ALMOST AT THE TOP!
WHY DID I MAKE THIS TOWER SO HIGH?
4

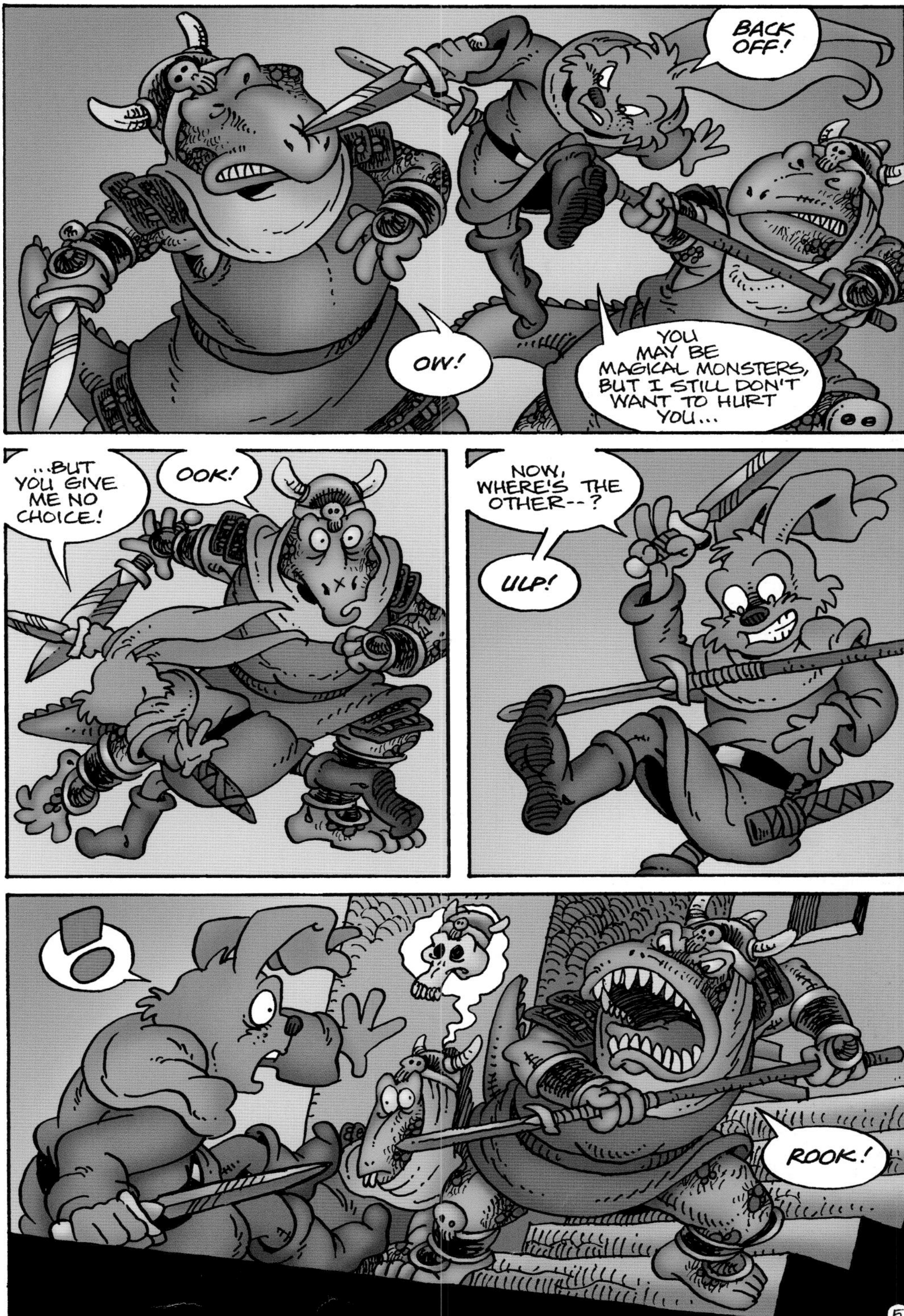
BACK OFF!
OW!
YOU MAY BE MAGICAL MONSTERS, BUT I STILL DON'T WANT TO HURT YOU...
...BUT YOU GIVE ME NO CHOICE!
OOK!
NOW, WHERE'S THE OTHER--?
ULP!
ROOK!
5.

DO YOU SEE THAT IN FRONT OF YOU?

OF COURSE HERMY SEES IT!

THIS ISN'T MUCH OF A SURPRISE!

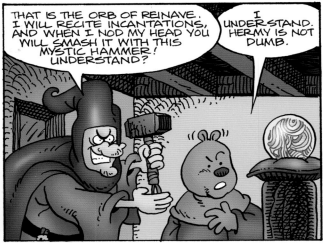

THAT IS THE ORB OF REINAVE. I WILL RECITE INCANTATIONS, AND WHEN I NOD MY HEAD YOU WILL SMASH IT WITH THIS MYSTIC HAMMER! UNDERSTAND?

I UNDERSTAND. HERMY IS NOT DUMB.

GOOD! NOW PREPARE YOURSELF!

MAKA LEONID GAFFEY PATORIKKU MAICHAN JENS TOOKIE TOOKI!

SQUA TRON! SQUA TRON! KLAATU!

NOW! NOW! NOW!

HIT IT! SMASH IT!

6.

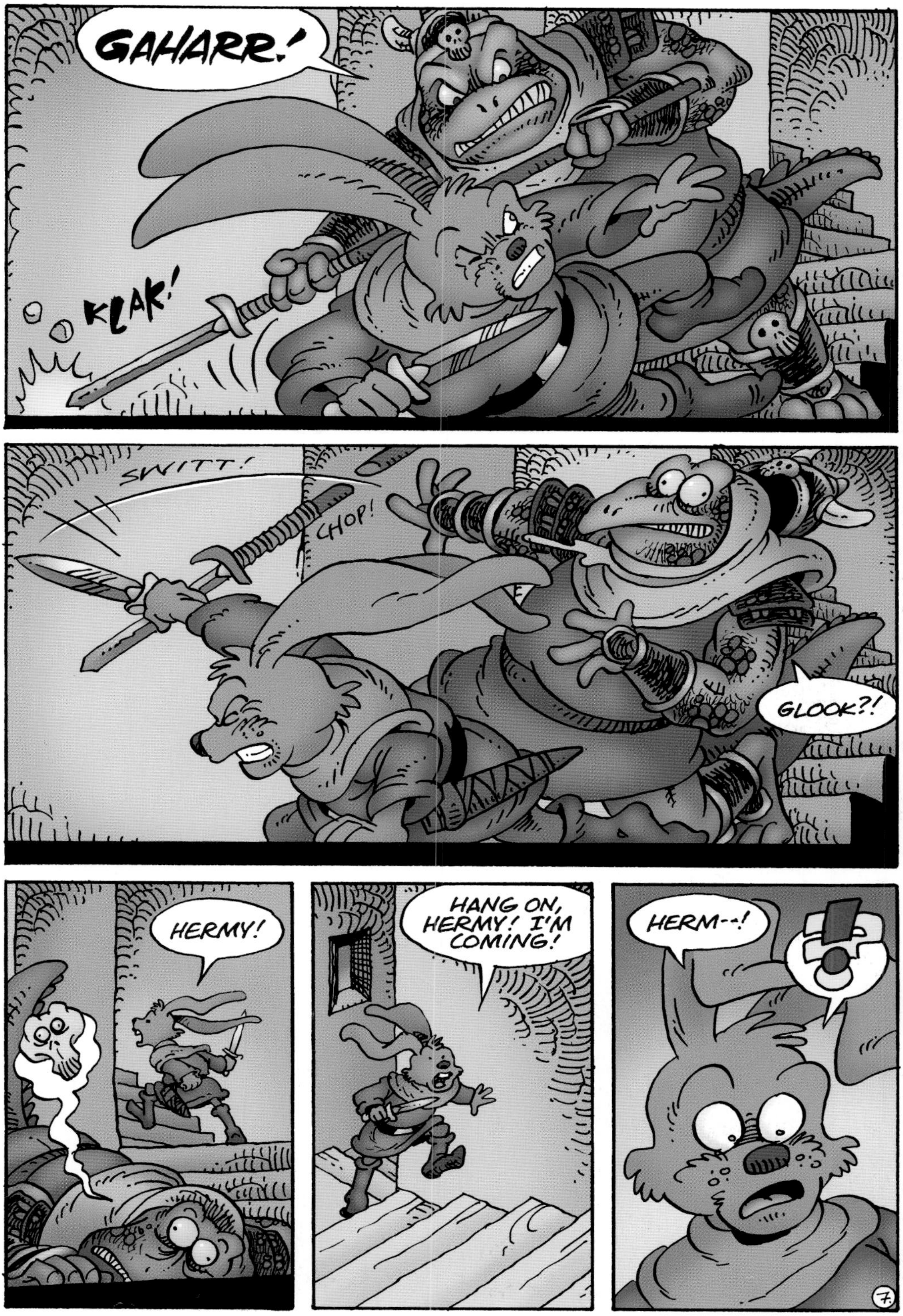
GAHARR!
KLAK!
SWITT!
CHOP!
GLOOK?!
HERMY!
HANG ON, HERMY! I'M COMING!
HERM--!
7

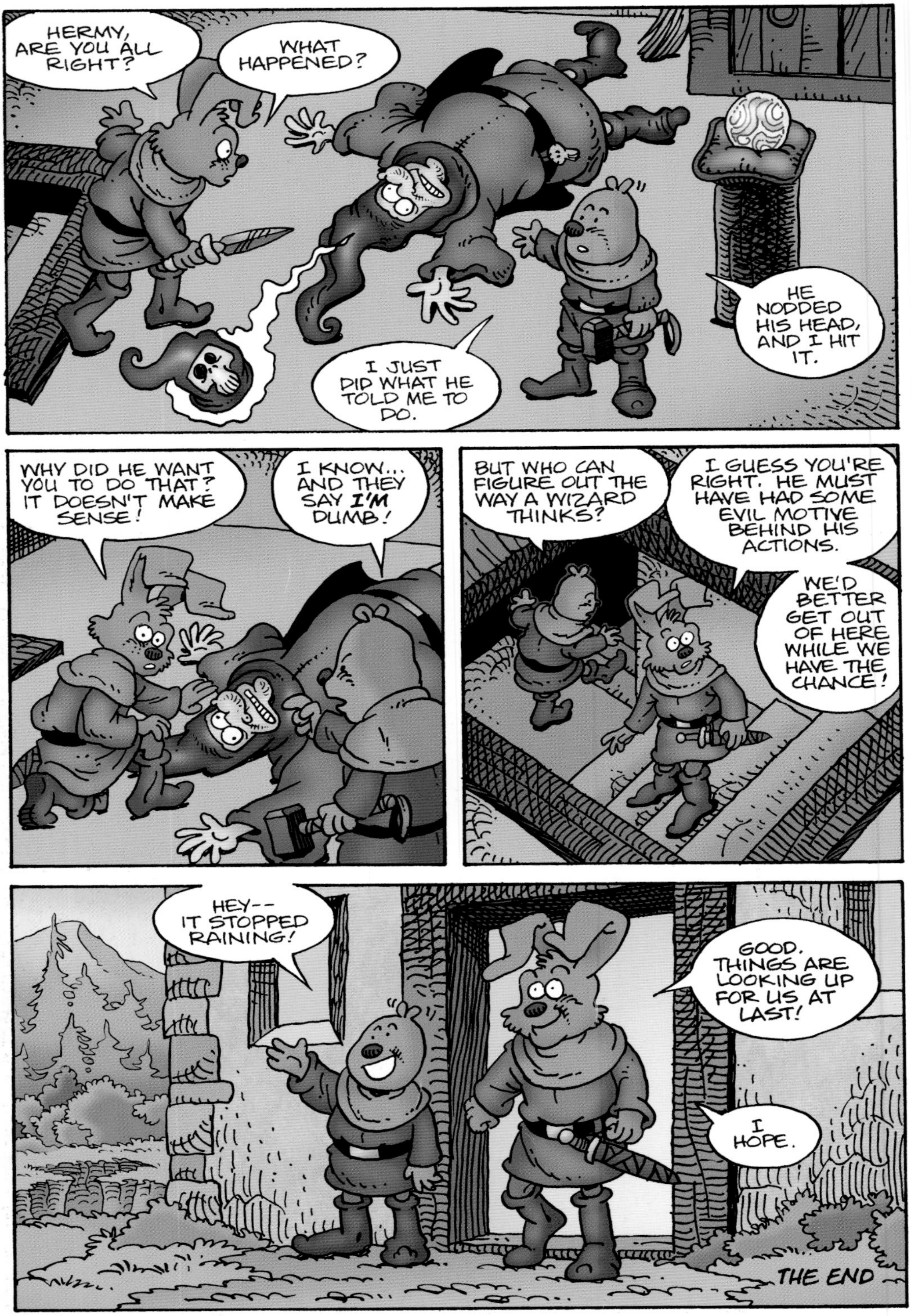
HERMY, ARE YOU ALL RIGHT?
WHAT HAPPENED?
I JUST DID WHAT HE TOLD ME TO DO.
HE NODDED HIS HEAD, AND I HIT IT.
WHY DID HE WANT YOU TO DO THAT? IT DOESN'T MAKE SENSE!
I KNOW... AND THEY SAY I'M DUMB!
BUT WHO CAN FIGURE OUT THE WAY A WIZARD THINKS?
I GUESS YOU'RE RIGHT. HE MUST HAVE HAD SOME EVIL MOTIVE BEHIND HIS ACTIONS.
WE'D BETTER GET OUT OF HERE WHILE WE HAVE THE CHANCE!
HEY-- IT STOPPED RAINING!
GOOD. THINGS ARE LOOKING UP FOR US AT LAST!
I HOPE.
THE END

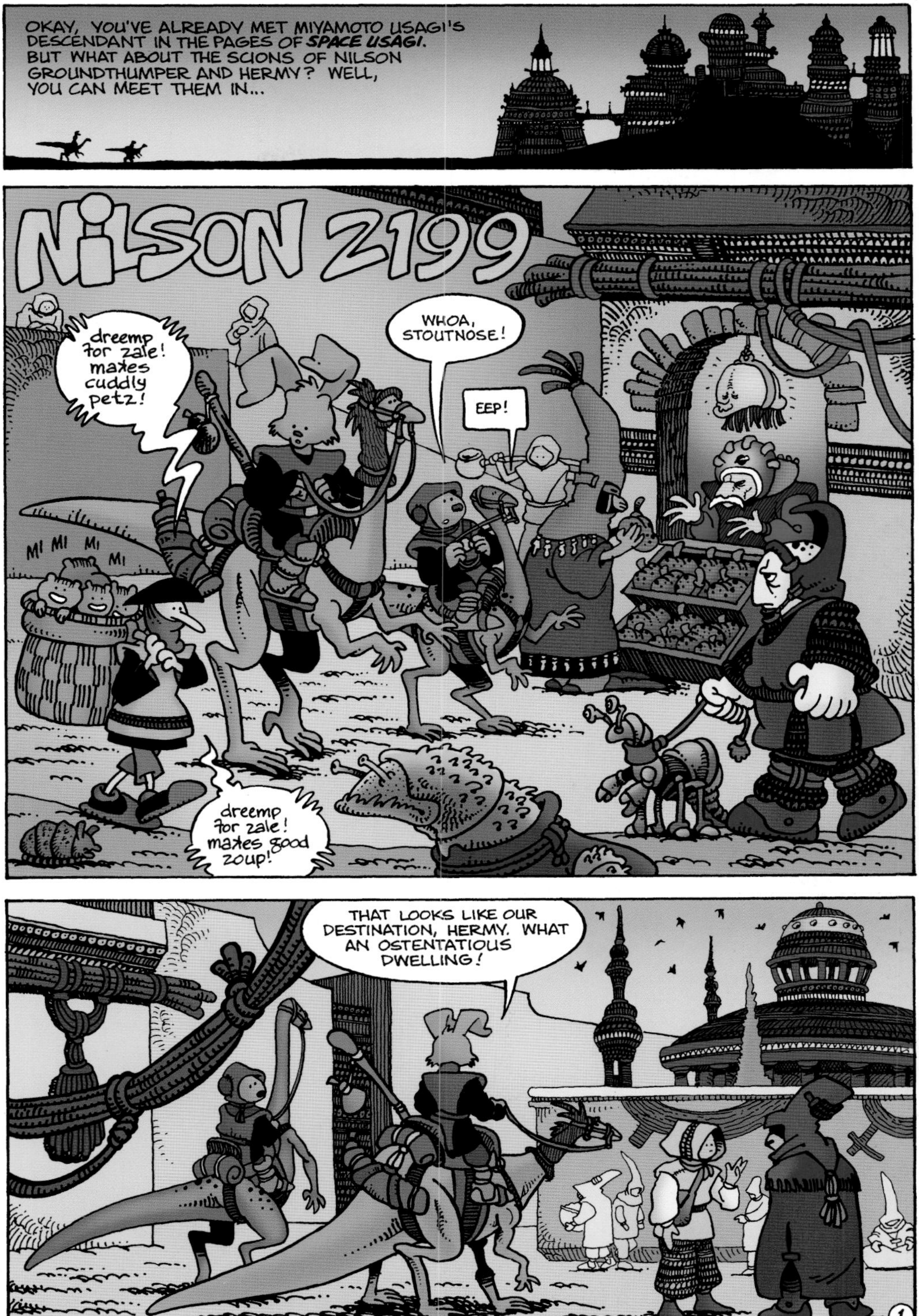
OKAY, YOU'VE ALREADY MET MIYAMOTO USAGI'S DESCENDANT IN THE PAGES OF SPACE USAGI. BUT WHAT ABOUT THE SCIONS OF NILSON GROUNDTHUMPER AND HERMY? WELL, YOU CAN MEET THEM IN...
NILSON 2199
dreemp for zale! makes cuddly petz!
WHOA, STOUTNOSE!
EEP!
MI MI MI MI
dreemp for zale! makes good zoup!
THAT LOOKS LIKE OUR DESTINATION, HERMY. WHAT AN OSTENTATIOUS DWELLING!
1.

AMBASSADOR MARTIOPHEROUS?

YEAH?! WHO WANTS TO KNOW?

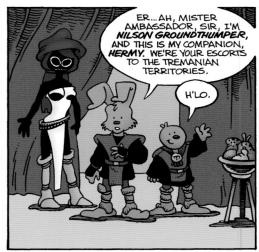

ER...AH, MISTER AMBASSADOR, SIR, I'M *NILSON GROUNDTHUMPER*, AND THIS IS MY COMPANION, *HERMY*. WE'RE YOUR ESCORTS TO THE TREMANIAN TERRITORIES.

H'LO.

IT'S ABOUT TIME! MY RETINUE AND TWO THOUSAND GUARDS HAVE BEEN READY FOR *FIVE HOURS*!

ER...BUT OUR ORDERS ARE TO TAKE ONLY *YOU*!

YUMMERS!

WHAT?! HOW CAN A PERSON OF MY IMPORTANCE GO ANYWHERE WITHOUT AN ENTOURAGE?!

WELL, WE'RE A LOT MORE THAN WE APPEAR, YOUR AMBASSADORSHIP! YOU SEE, I'M A RANGER FIRST CLASS, AND HERMY IS A --

:SLURP!:
:MUNCH!:
:SLOBBER!:

BAH! I *REFUSE* TO LEAVE MY CONVOY BEHIND! ARE WE GOING TO *FLY?!* IS THAT IT?

ER...NO. THE DEADLY SKIDHAWKS ARE STARTING THEIR MATING PERIOD NOW, AND IT WOULD BE DISASTROUS FOR ANY VEHICLE TO BE OUT IN THE SKIES.

ER......

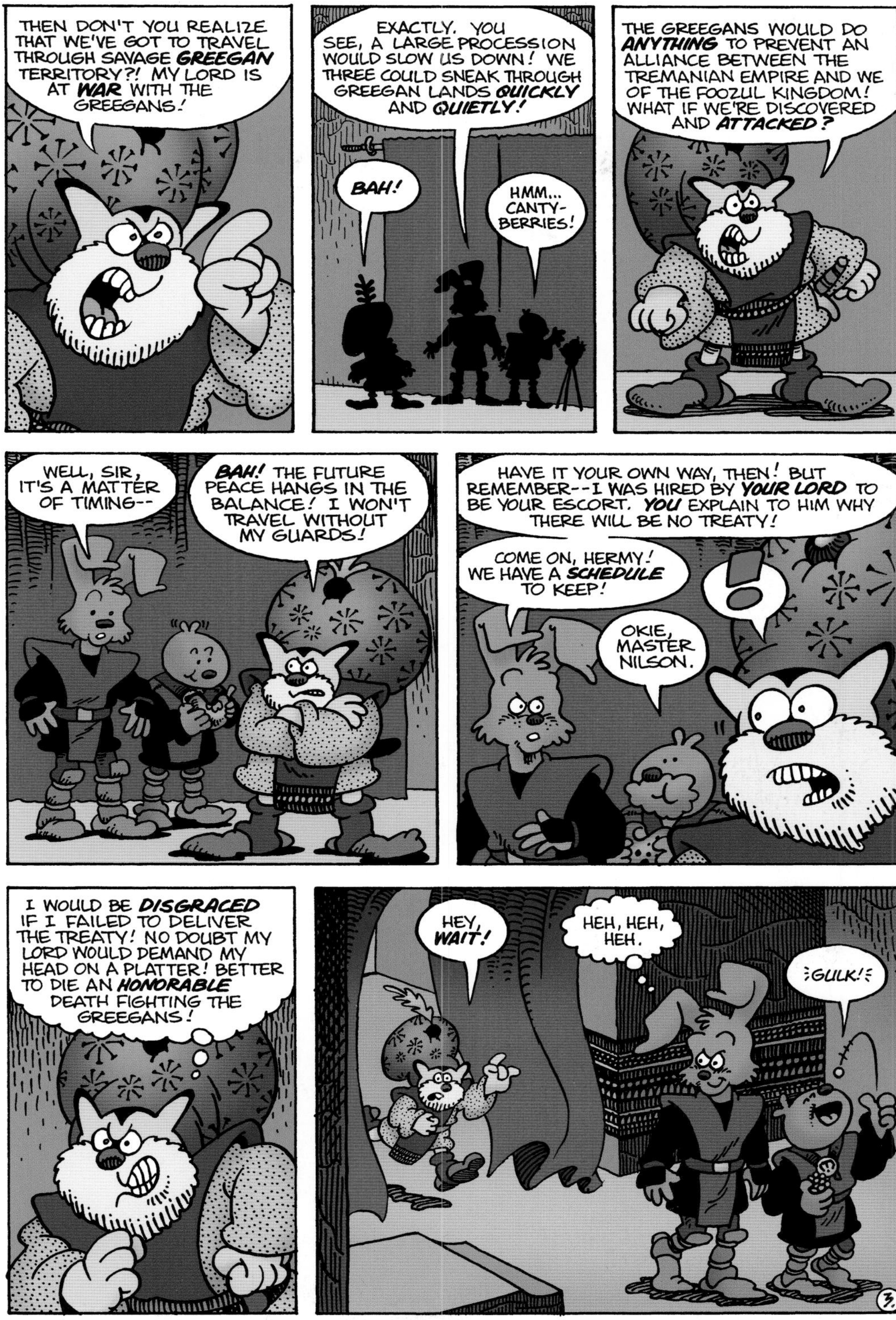
THEN DON'T YOU REALIZE THAT WE'VE GOT TO TRAVEL THROUGH SAVAGE **GREEGAN** TERRITORY?! MY LORD IS AT **WAR** WITH THE GREEGANS!
EXACTLY. YOU SEE, A LARGE PROCESSION WOULD SLOW US DOWN! WE THREE COULD SNEAK THROUGH GREEGAN LANDS **QUICKLY** AND **QUIETLY**!
BAH!
HMM... CANTY-BERRIES!
THE GREEGANS WOULD DO **ANYTHING** TO PREVENT AN ALLIANCE BETWEEN THE TREMANIAN EMPIRE AND WE OF THE FOOZUL KINGDOM! WHAT IF WE'RE DISCOVERED AND **ATTACKED**?
WELL, SIR, IT'S A MATTER OF TIMING--
BAH! THE FUTURE PEACE HANGS IN THE BALANCE! I WON'T TRAVEL WITHOUT MY GUARDS!
HAVE IT YOUR OWN WAY, THEN! BUT REMEMBER--I WAS HIRED BY **YOUR LORD** TO BE YOUR ESCORT. **YOU** EXPLAIN TO HIM WHY THERE WILL BE NO TREATY!
COME ON, HERMY! WE HAVE A **SCHEDULE** TO KEEP!
!
OKIE, MASTER NILSON.
I WOULD BE **DISGRACED** IF I FAILED TO DELIVER THE TREATY! NO DOUBT MY LORD WOULD DEMAND MY HEAD ON A PLATTER! BETTER TO DIE AN **HONORABLE** DEATH FIGHTING THE GREEGANS!
HEY, **WAIT**!
HEH, HEH, HEH.
GULK!
3.

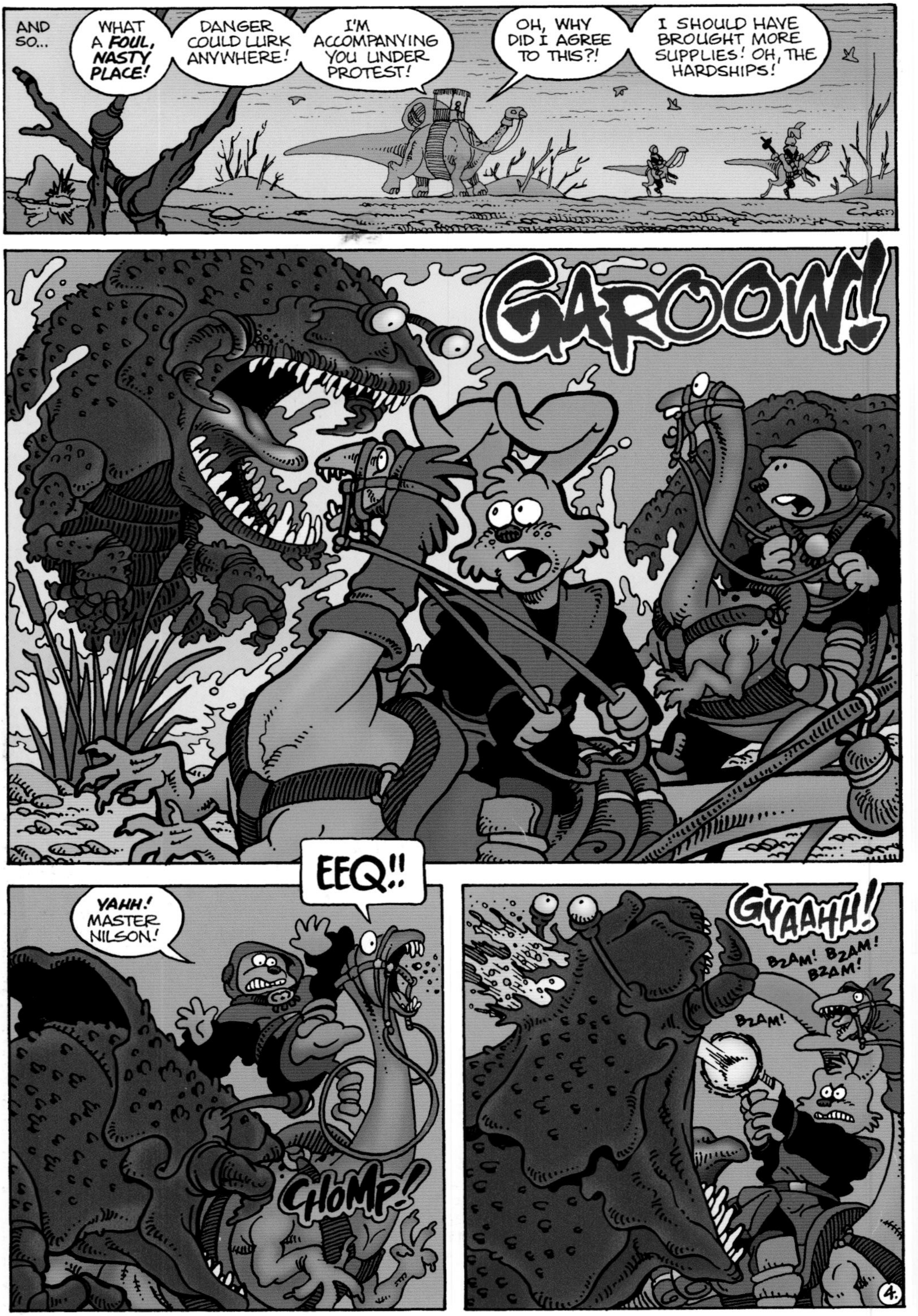

AND SO...
WHAT A FOUL, NASTY PLACE!
DANGER COULD LURK ANYWHERE!
I'M ACCOMPANYING YOU UNDER PROTEST!
OH, WHY DID I AGREE TO THIS?!
I SHOULD HAVE BROUGHT MORE SUPPLIES! OH, THE HARDSHIPS!
GAROOW!
YAHH! MASTER NILSON!
EEQ!!
CHOMP!
GYAAHH!
BZAM! BZAM! BZAM!
BZAM!
4.

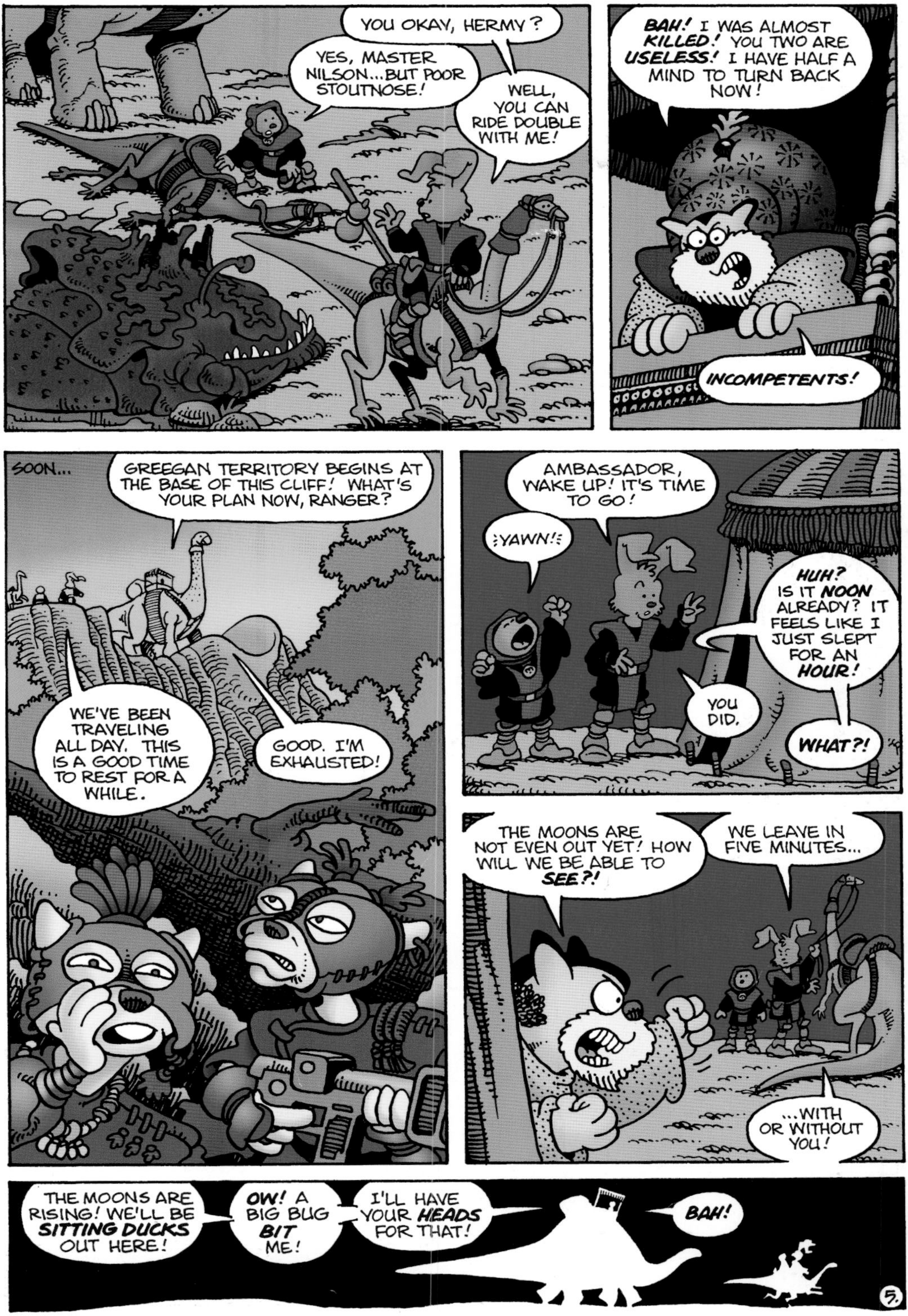
YOU OKAY, HERMY?
YES, MASTER NILSON...BUT POOR STOUTNOSE!
WELL, YOU CAN RIDE DOUBLE WITH ME!
BAH! I WAS ALMOST KILLED! YOU TWO ARE USELESS! I HAVE HALF A MIND TO TURN BACK NOW!
INCOMPETENTS!
SOON...
GREEGAN TERRITORY BEGINS AT THE BASE OF THIS CLIFF! WHAT'S YOUR PLAN NOW, RANGER?
WE'VE BEEN TRAVELING ALL DAY. THIS IS A GOOD TIME TO REST FOR A WHILE.
GOOD. I'M EXHAUSTED!
AMBASSADOR, WAKE UP! IT'S TIME TO GO!
YAWN!
HUH? IS IT NOON ALREADY? IT FEELS LIKE I JUST SLEPT FOR AN HOUR!
YOU DID.
WHAT?!
THE MOONS ARE NOT EVEN OUT YET! HOW WILL WE BE ABLE TO SEE?!
WE LEAVE IN FIVE MINUTES...
...WITH OR WITHOUT YOU!
THE MOONS ARE RISING! WE'LL BE SITTING DUCKS OUT HERE!
OW! A BIG BUG BIT ME!
I'LL HAVE YOUR HEADS FOR THAT!
BAH!
5.

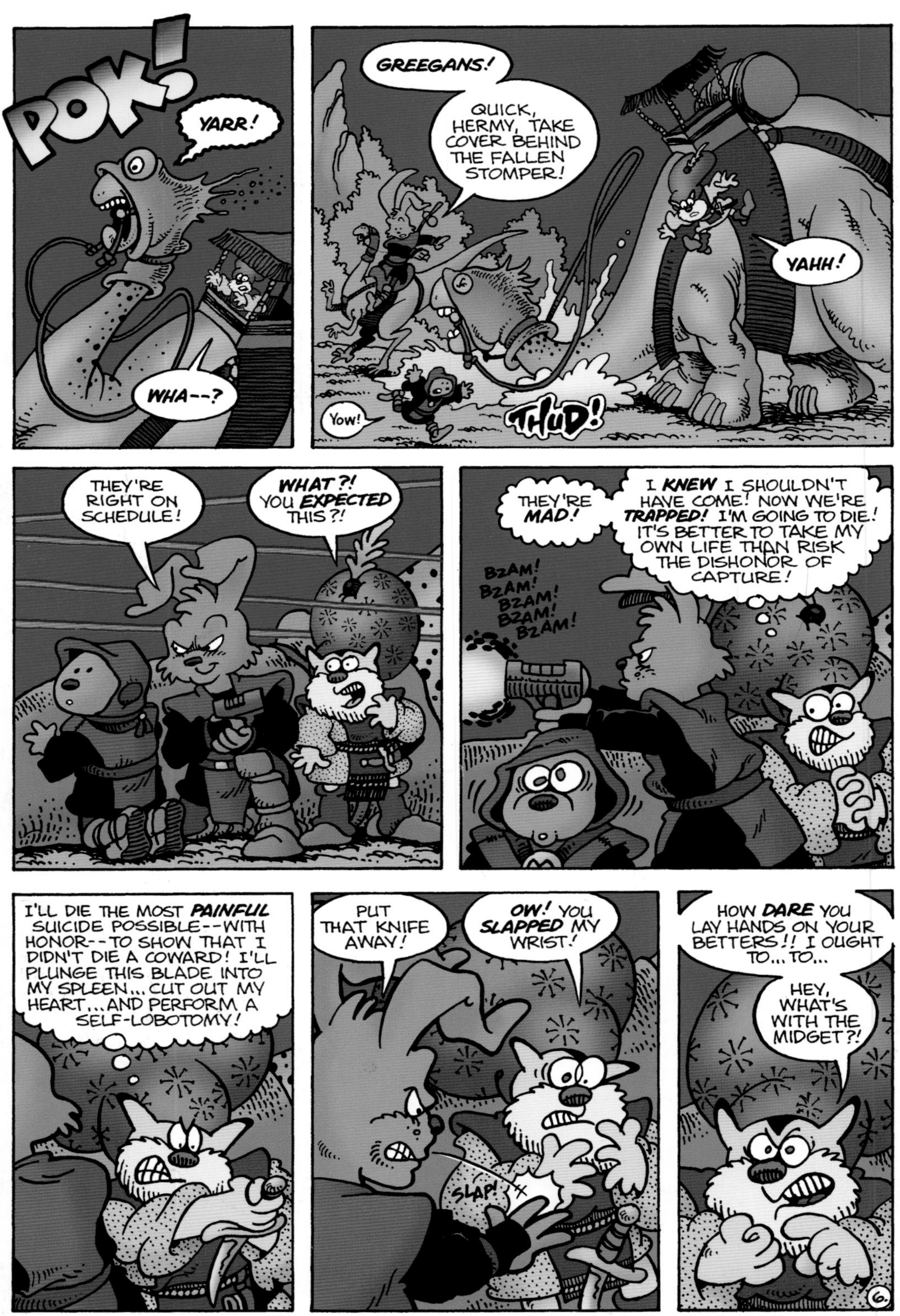

POK!
YARR!
WHA--?
GREEGANS!
QUICK, HERMY, TAKE COVER BEHIND THE FALLEN STOMPER!
YAHH!
YOW!
THUD!
THEY'RE RIGHT ON SCHEDULE!
WHAT?! YOU EXPECTED THIS?!
THEY'RE MAD!
I KNEW I SHOULDN'T HAVE COME! NOW WE'RE TRAPPED! I'M GOING TO DIE! IT'S BETTER TO TAKE MY OWN LIFE THAN RISK THE DISHONOR OF CAPTURE!
BZAM! BZAM! BZAM! BZAM! BZAM!
I'LL DIE THE MOST PAINFUL SUICIDE POSSIBLE--WITH HONOR--TO SHOW THAT I DIDN'T DIE A COWARD! I'LL PLUNGE THIS BLADE INTO MY SPLEEN... CUT OUT MY HEART... AND PERFORM A SELF-LOBOTOMY!
PUT THAT KNIFE AWAY!
OW! YOU SLAPPED MY WRIST!
SLAP!
HOW DARE YOU LAY HANDS ON YOUR BETTERS!! I OUGHT TO... TO...
HEY, WHAT'S WITH THE MIDGET?!
6.

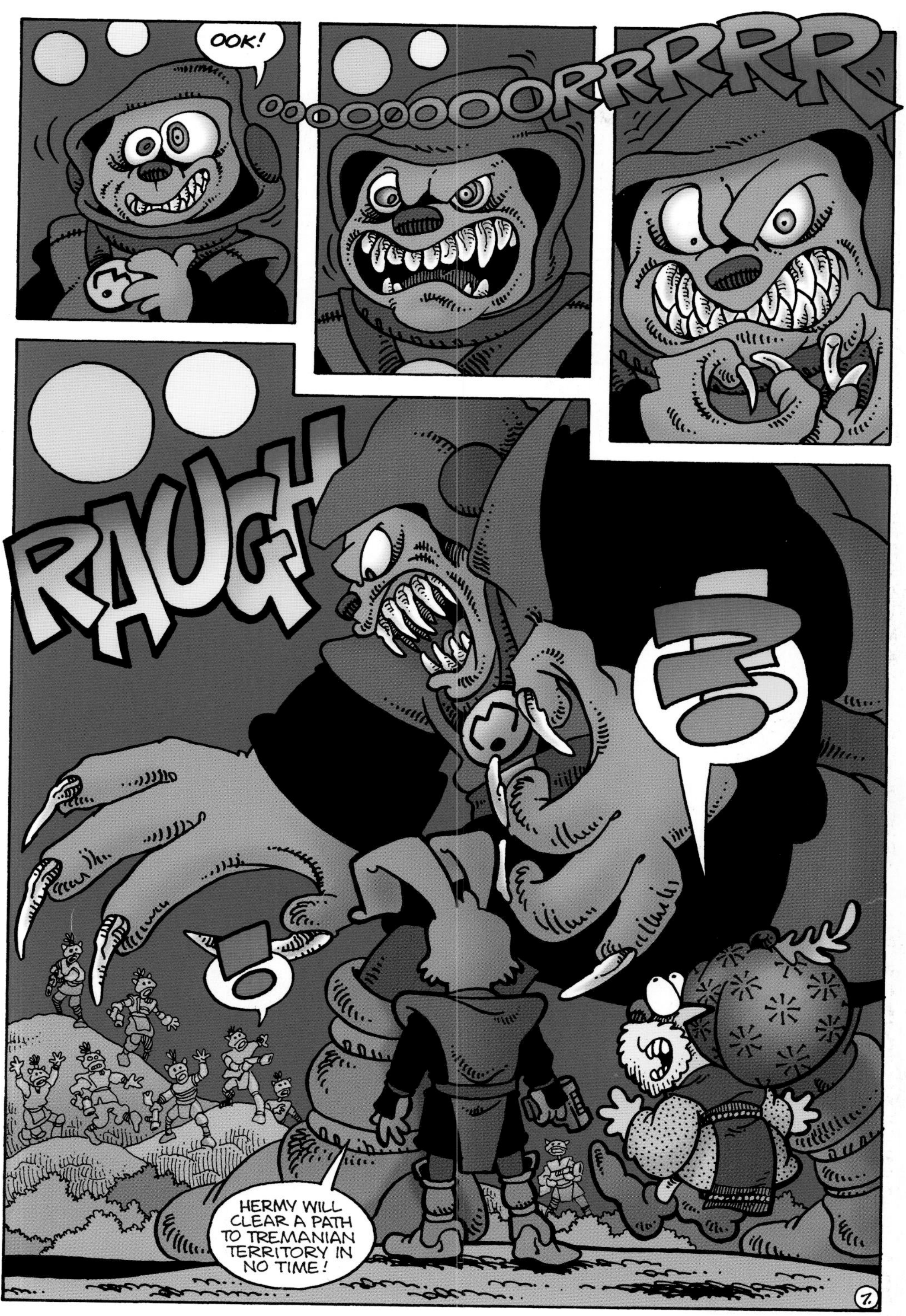
OOK!
OOOOOOOOORRRRRR
RAUGH
HERMY WILL CLEAR A PATH TO TREMANIAN TERRITORY IN NO TIME!
7.

AS I TOLD YOU EARLIER--IT'S ALL A MATTER OF TIMING. WE HAD TO GET TO THE BORDER OF GREEGAN TERRITORY TONIGHT...
...THE NIGHT OF THE DOUBLE FULL MOON!
HOMINA-HOMINA-HOMINA!
FUNNY THING. ONE OF HERMY'S ANCESTORS FELL IN A VAT OF A MAD SCIENTIST'S WERE-BEAST TONIC. THE TRAIT HAS BEEN PASSED DOWN OVER THE GENERATIONS.
HERMY MAY NOT BE TOO BRIGHT, BUT HE CAN BE USEFUL ON NIGHTS LIKE THIS.
UH...
WE'LL HAVE TO RIDE DOUBLE ON MY TOKAGESAURUS.
WELL, YOU COMING?
THERE'S A TREATY TO NEGOTIATE.
ER... AH...YES, SIR!
UH... THANK YOU.

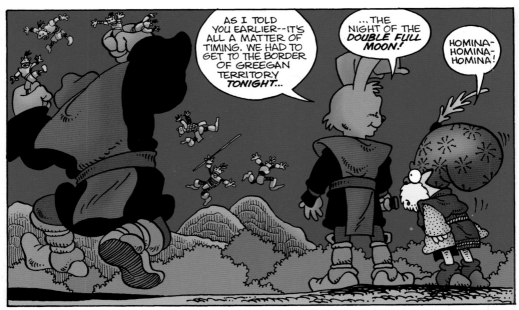

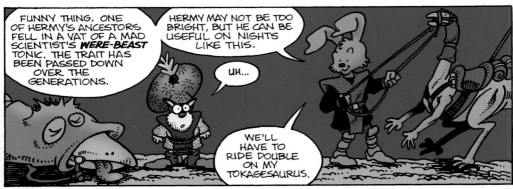

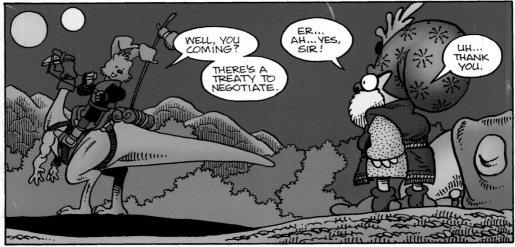

END

GALLERY

And so Nilson and Hermy, having established themselves as heroes (sort of), strode off into the annals of history. The preceding stories make up their complete adventures, which began in the pages of Thoughts & Image's *Albedo Anthropomorphics* and Fantagraphics's *Critters*, before the pair received their own special issue (facing page) in 1988. Stan's *Usagi Yojimbo*, which would become his life's work, had developed into a series the year before, and Nilson and Hermy's remaining deeds popped up occasionally in backup stories in *Usagi* through 1993, with one final adventure ("The Re-Return of the Wizard") appearing in *Dark Horse Presents* in 2013. However, Stan did illustrate the duo in a handful of other places throughout the years, and the following pages feature miscellaneous Nilson and Hermy covers, pinups, and convention sketches, as well as unused pages from an early version of their saga and previously unpublished artwork.

Cover art from *Critters Special* #1, published January 1988.

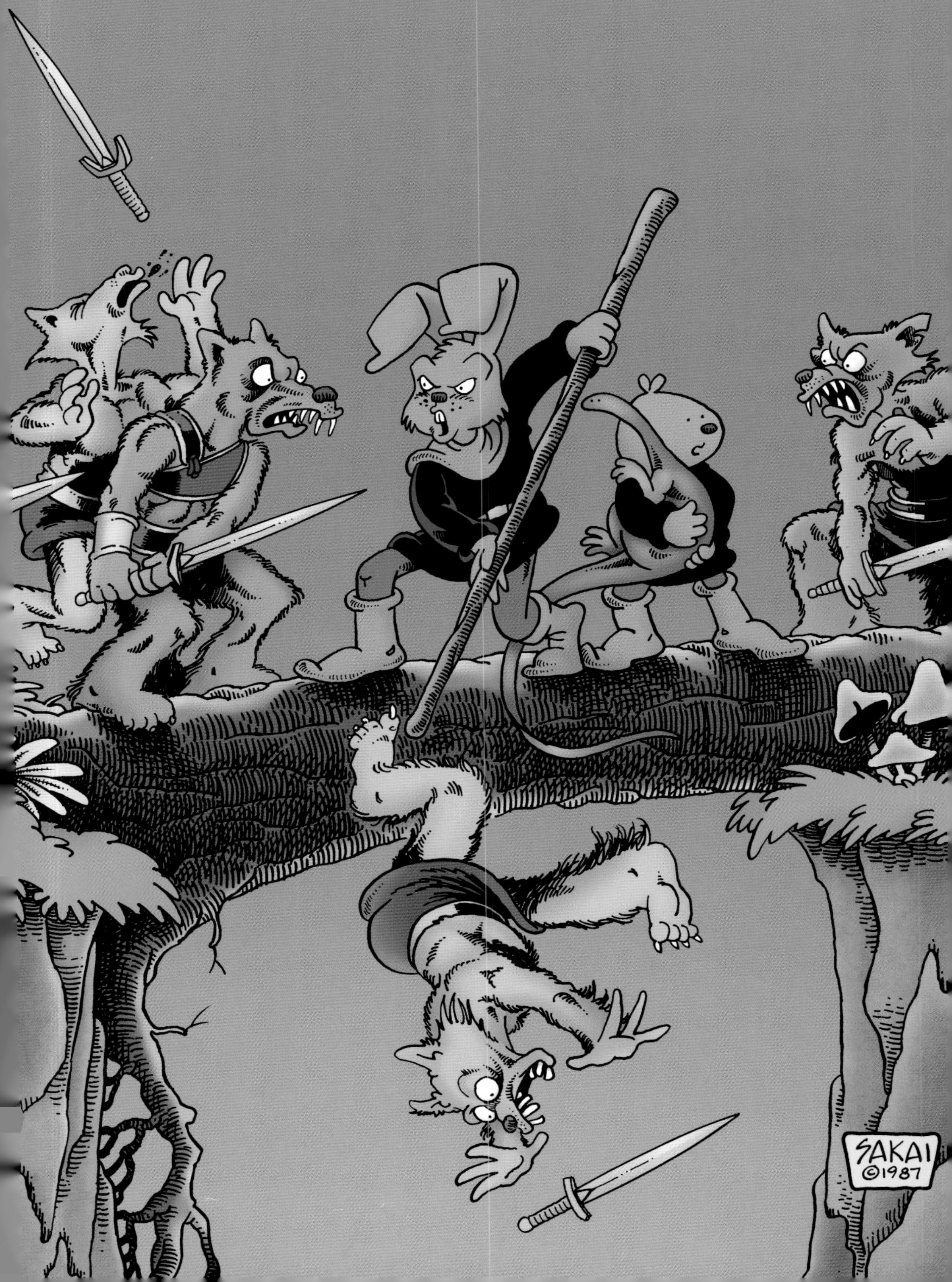
SAKAI
©1987

Cover art from *Critters* #27, published August 1988.

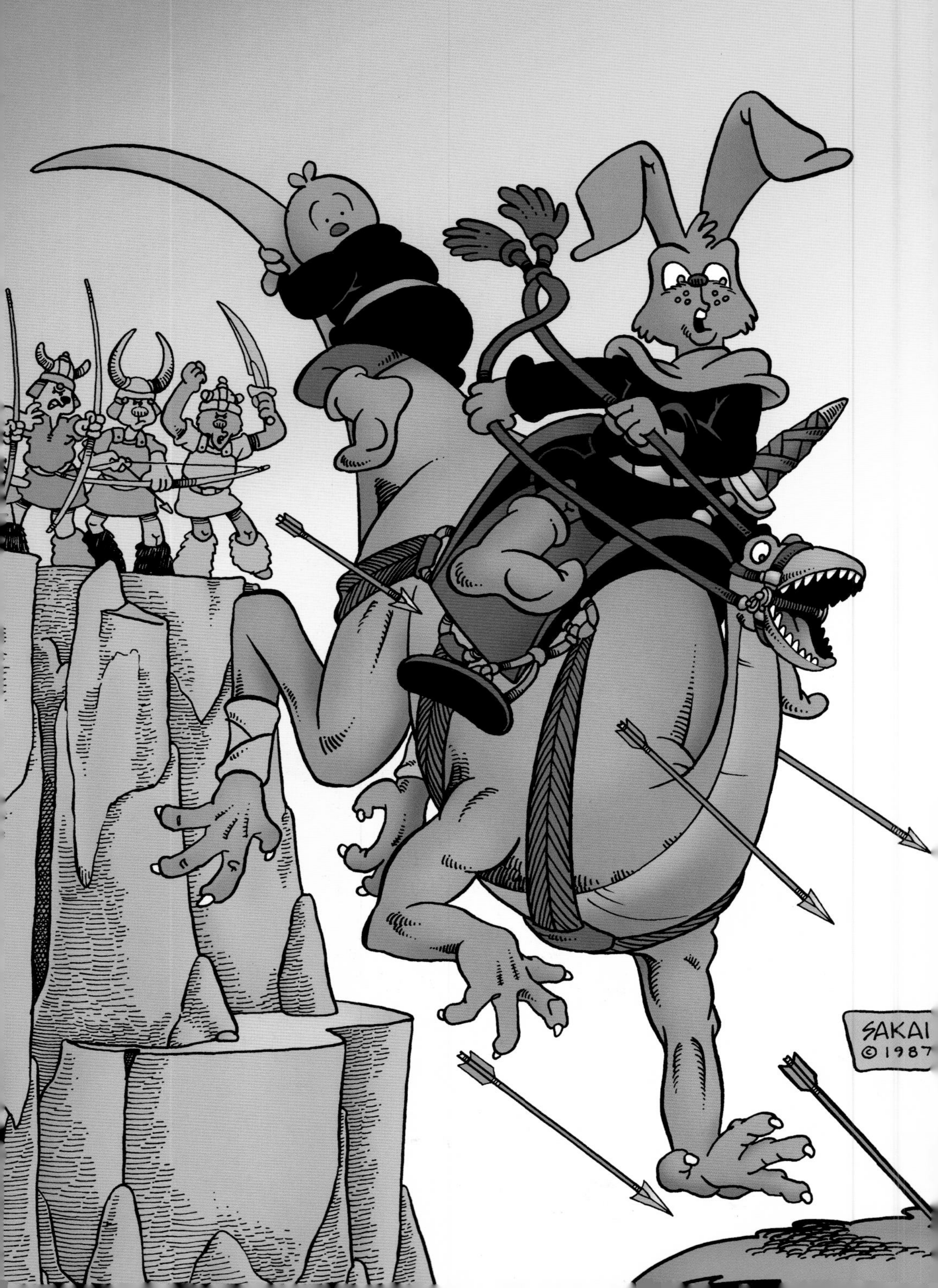
SAKAI
© 1987

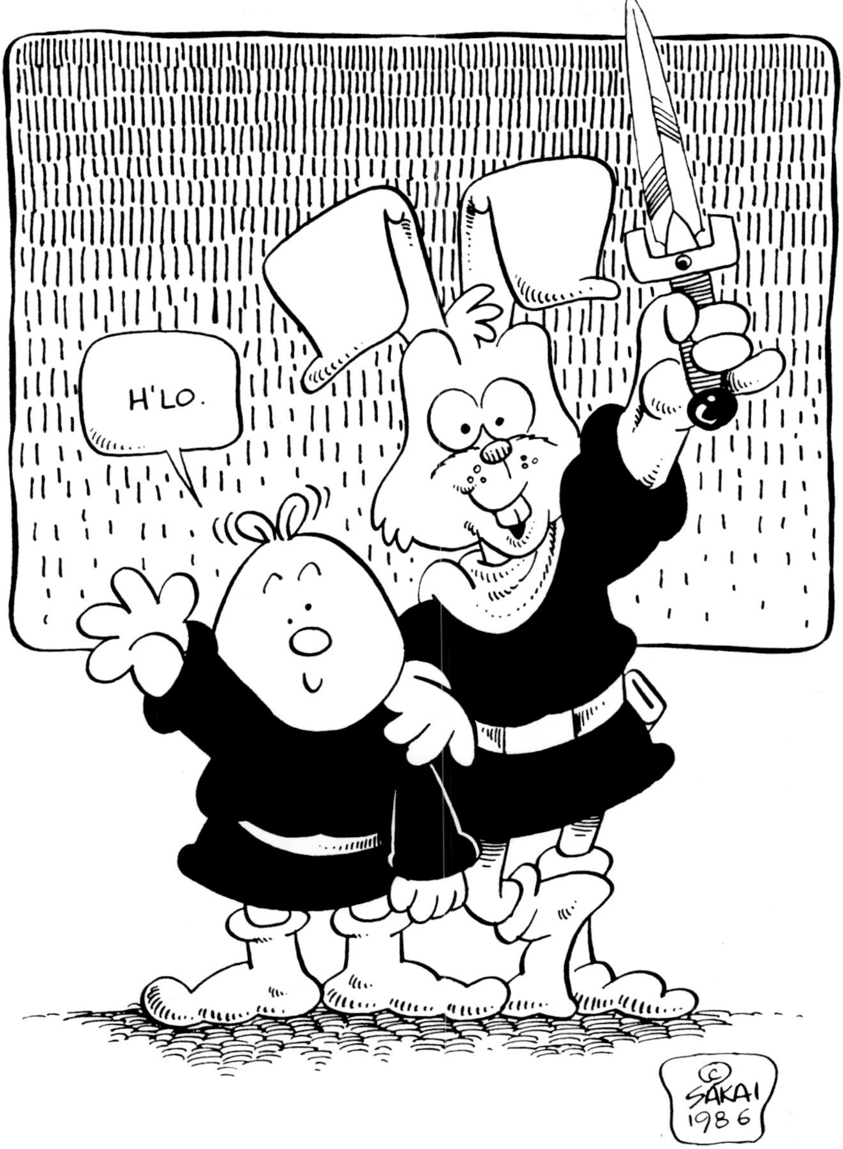
H'LO.
© SAKAI 1986

The Nilson and Hermy artwork awarded to the best answer in *Critters* #27's "Name That Critter" contest (see Stan's introduction).

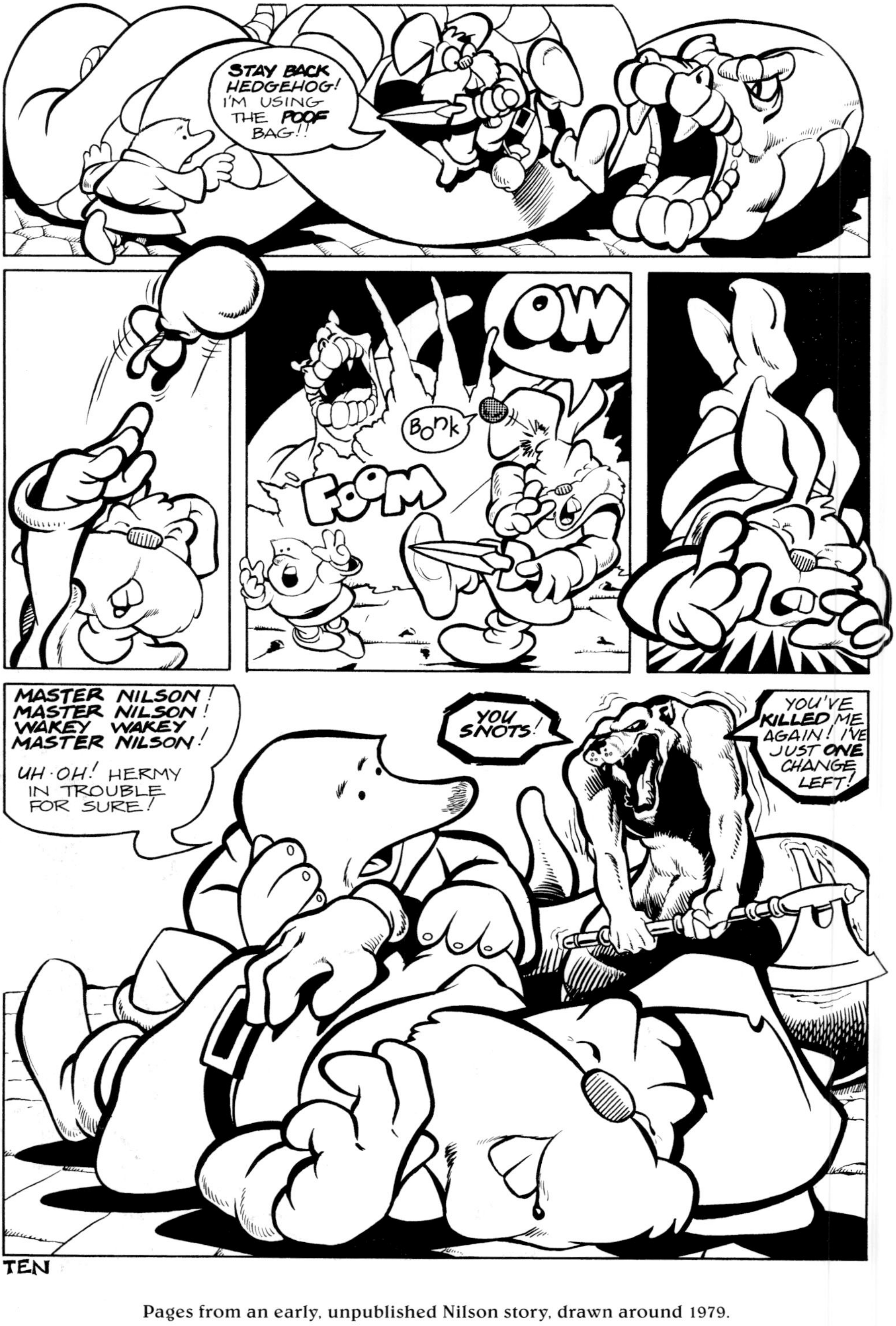
STAY BACK HEDGEHOG! I'M USING THE POOF BAG!!
OW
BONK
FOOM
MASTER NILSON! MASTER NILSON! WAKEY WAKEY MASTER NILSON!
UH-OH! HERMY IN TROUBLE FOR SURE!
YOU SNOTS!
YOU'VE KILLED ME AGAIN! I'VE JUST ONE CHANGE LEFT!
TEN

Pages from an early, unpublished Nilson story, drawn around 1979.

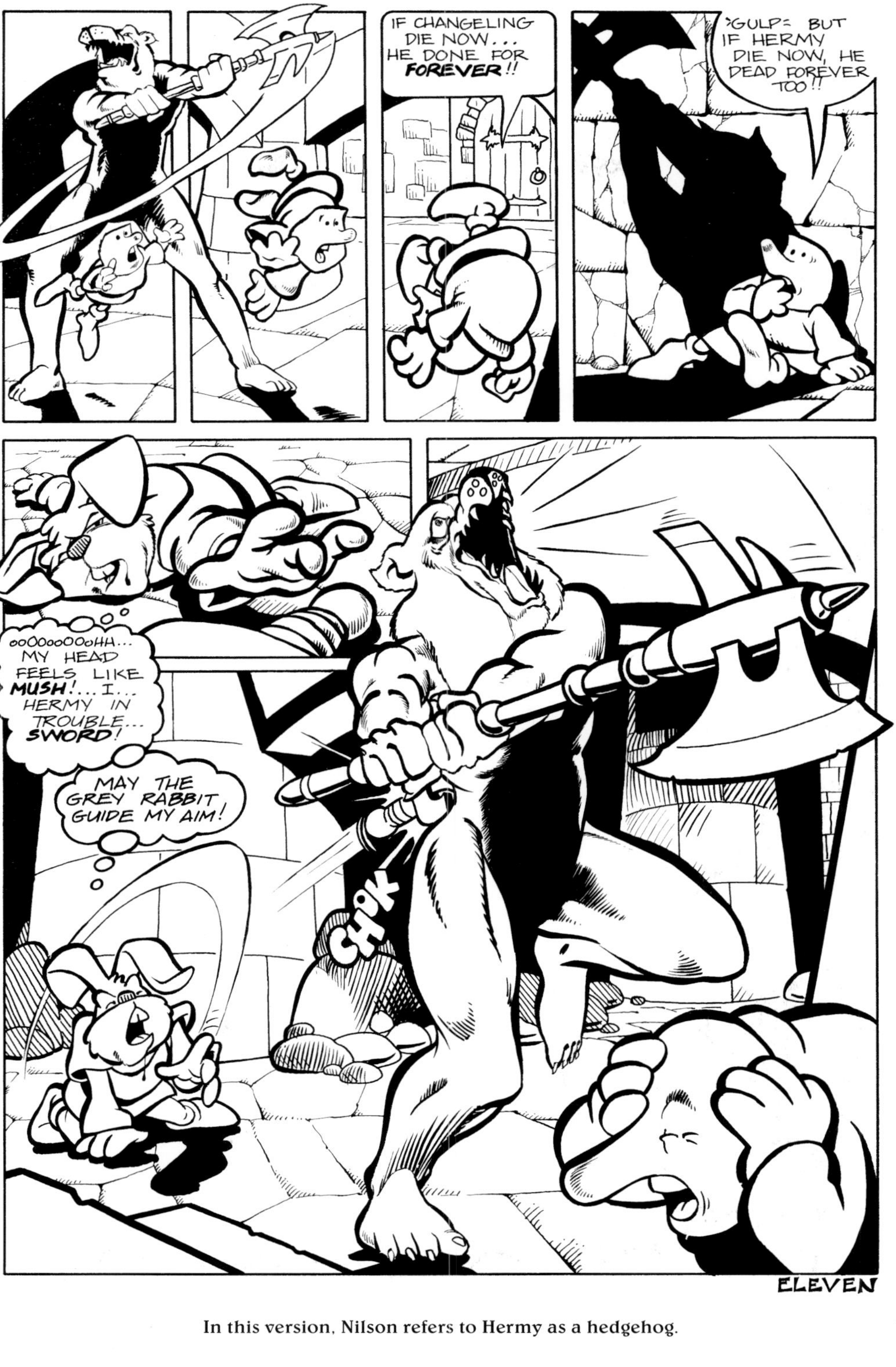
IF CHANGELING DIE NOW... HE DONE FOR FOREVER!!
>GULP< BUT IF HERMY DIE NOW, HE DEAD FOREVER TOO!!
ooOoooOOoHH... MY HEAD FEELS LIKE MUSH!... I... HERMY IN TROUBLE... SWORD!
MAY THE GREY RABBIT GUIDE MY AIM!
CHOK
ELEVEN

In this version, Nilson refers to Hermy as a hedgehog.

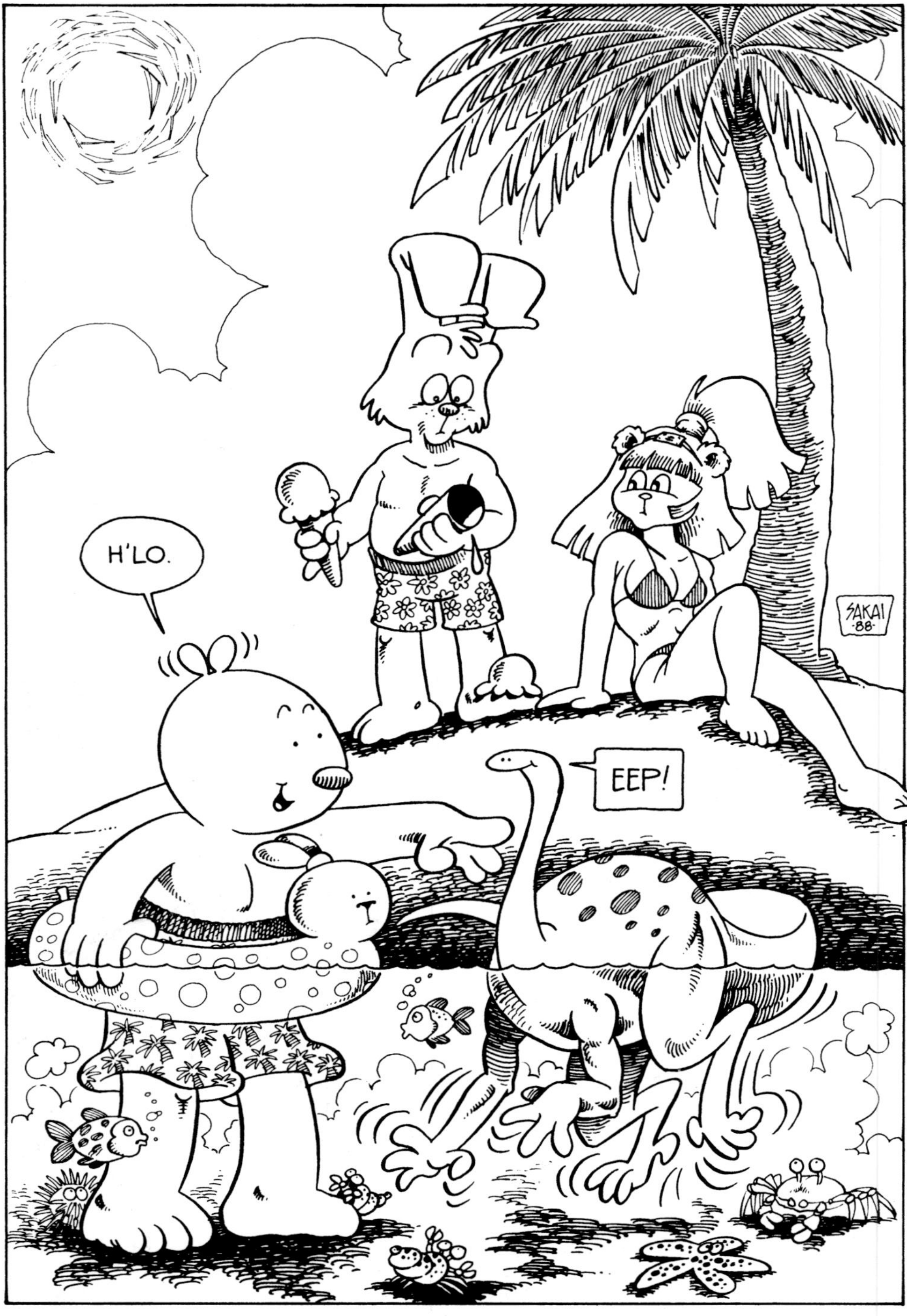
H'LO.
EEP!
SAKAI ·88·

Pinup from *Amazing Heroes* #138, the second annual swimsuit issue, published April 1988.

Nilson and Hermy don't appear in *Furrlough* #50, from February 1997, but Stan revisited his unwits for the cover.

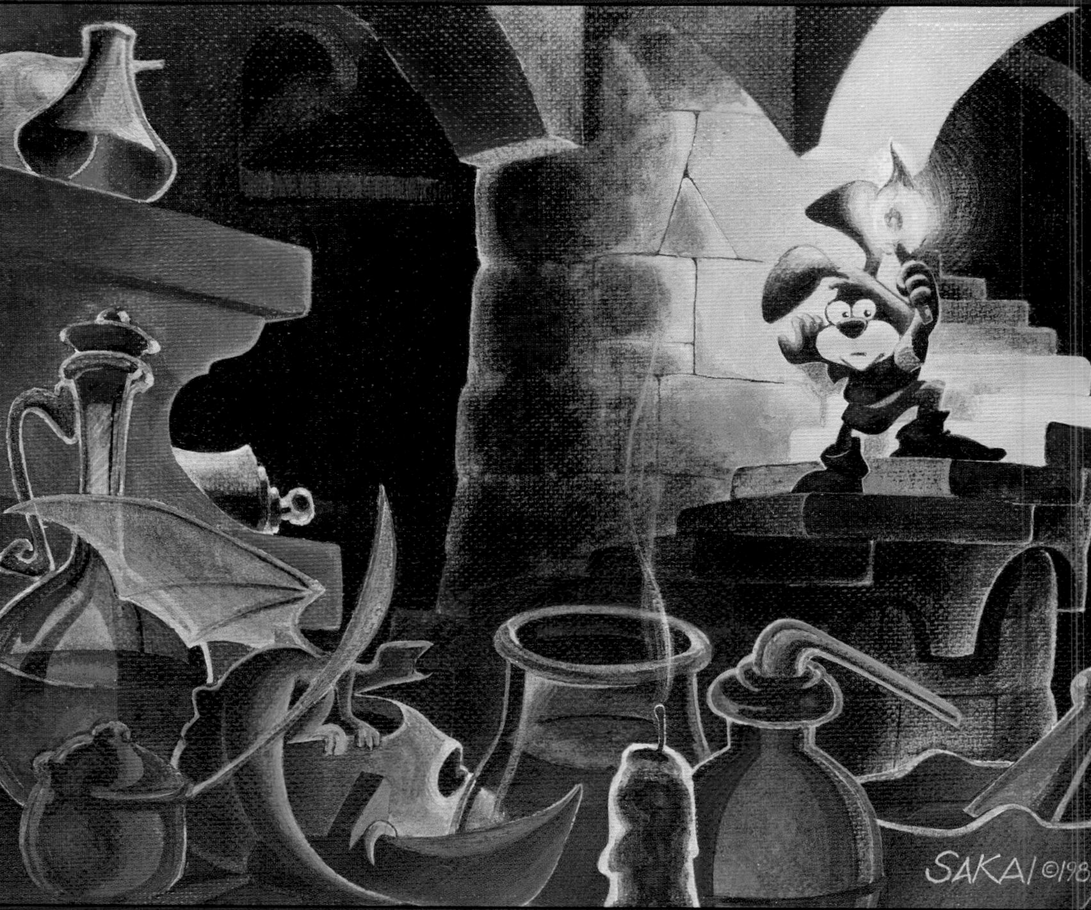
SAKAI ©198

An unpublished acrylic painting of Nilson, from 1982.
The original is 8" x 10".

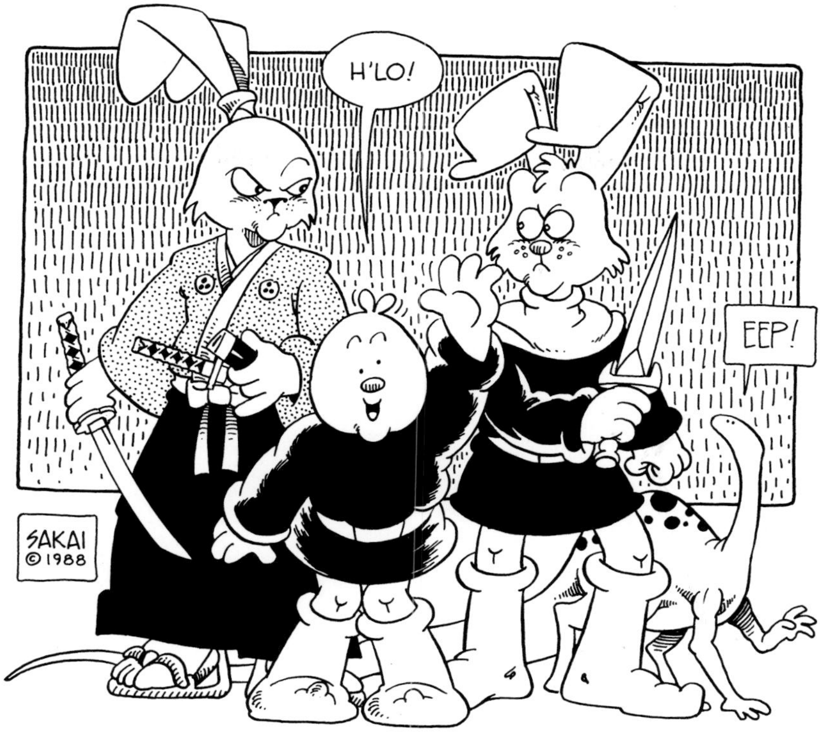
H'LO!
EEP!
SAKAI
©1988

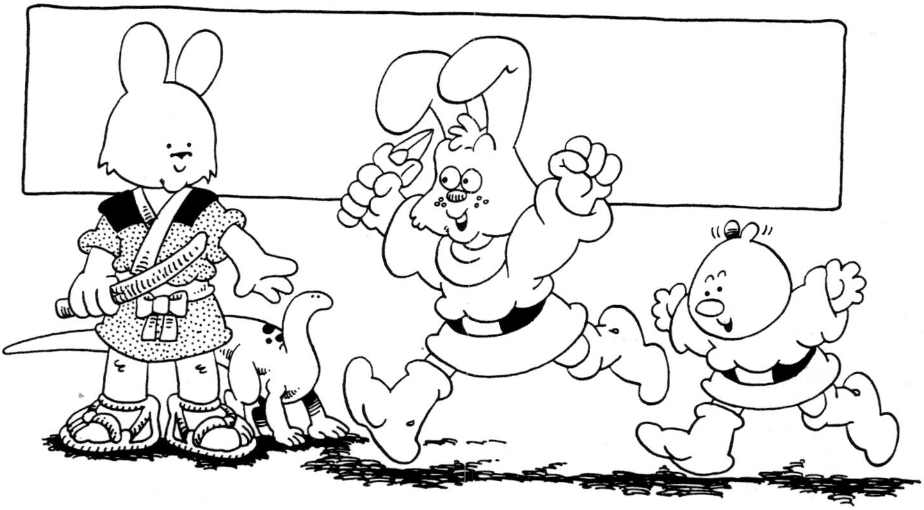

Convention sketches crossing over Nilson and Hermy
with Stan's more famous rabbit warrior, Miyamoto Usagi.

Stan Sakai in Gijón, Spain, in 2009. *Photo by Sharon Sakai.*

STAN SAKAI was born in Kyoto, Japan, grew up in Hawaii, and now lives in California with his wife, Sharon. They have two children, Hannah and Matthew. Stan received a Fine Arts degree from the University of Hawaii and furthered his studies at the Art Center College of Design in Pasadena, California.

Stan's creation, Usagi Yojimbo, first appeared in comics in 1984. Since then, Usagi has been on television as a guest of the Teenage Mutant Ninja Turtles and has been made into toys, seen on clothing, and featured in a series of graphic novel collections.

In 1991, Stan created *Space Usagi*, a series dealing with samurai in a futuristic setting, featuring the adventures of a descendant of the original Usagi.

Stan is also an award-winning letterer for his work on Sergio Aragonés's *Groo*, the *Spider-Man* Sunday newspaper strips, and *Usagi Yojimbo*.

Stan is the recipient of a Parents' Choice Award, an Inkpot Award, an American Library Association Award, a Harvey Award, four Spanish Haxtur Awards, and several Eisner Awards. In 2003 he won the prestigious National Cartoonists Society Award in the Comic Book Division, and in 2011 Stan received the Cultural Ambassador Award from the Japanese American National Museum.

USAGI YOJIMBO™

CREATED, WRITTEN, AND ILLUSTRATED BY STAN SAKAI

Available from Dark Horse Comics

Book 8: Shades of Death
$14.99 | ISBN 978-1-56971-259-7

Book 9: Daisho
$14.99 | ISBN 978-1-56971-292-4

Book 10: The Brink of Life and Death
$14.99 | ISBN 978-1-56971-297-9

Book 11: Seasons
$14.99 | ISBN 978-1-56971-375-4

Book 12: Grasscutter
$16.99 | ISBN 978-1-56971-413-3

Book 13: Grey Shadows
$14.99 | ISBN 978-1-56971-459-1

Book 14: Demon Mask
$15.99 | ISBN 978-1-56971-523-9

Book 15: Grasscutter II
$15.99 | ISBN 978-1-56971-660-1

Book 16: The Shrouded Moon
$15.99 | ISBN 978-1-56971-883-4

Book 17: Duel at Kitanoji
$16.99 | ISBN 978-1-56971-973-2

Book 18: Travels with Jotaro
$15.99 | ISBN 978-1-59307-220-9

Book 19: Fathers and Sons
$15.99 | ISBN 978-1-59307-319-0

Book 20: Glimpses of Death
$15.99 | ISBN 978-1-59307-549-1

Book 21: The Mother of Mountains
$15.99 | ISBN 978-1-59307-783-9

Book 22: Tomoe's Story
$15.99 | ISBN 978-1-59307-947-5

Book 23: Bridge of Tears
$17.99 | ISBN 978-1-59582-298-7

Book 24: Return of the Black Soul
$16.99 | ISBN 978-1-59582-472-1

Book 25: Fox Hunt
$16.99 | ISBN 978-1-59582-726-5

Book 26: Traitors of the Earth
$16.99 | ISBN 978-1-59582-910-8

Book 27: A Town Called Hell
$16.99 | ISBN 978-1-59582-970-2

Book 28: Red Scorpion
$16.99 | ISBN 978-1-61655-398-2

Space Usagi
$17.99 | ISBN 978-1-56971-290-0

Usagi Yojimbo: Yokai
$14.99 | ISBN 978-1-59582-362-5

The Art of Usagi Yojimbo
$29.95 | ISBN 978-1-59307-493-7

47 Ronin
Written by Mike Richardson
$19.99 | ISBN 978-1-59582-954-2

Available from Fantagraphics Books

fantagraphics.com

Book 1: The Ronin
Book 2: Samurai
Book 3: The Wanderer's Road
Book 4: The Dragon Bellow Conspiracy
Book 5: Lone Goat and Kid
Book 6: Circlesw
Book 7: Gen's Story

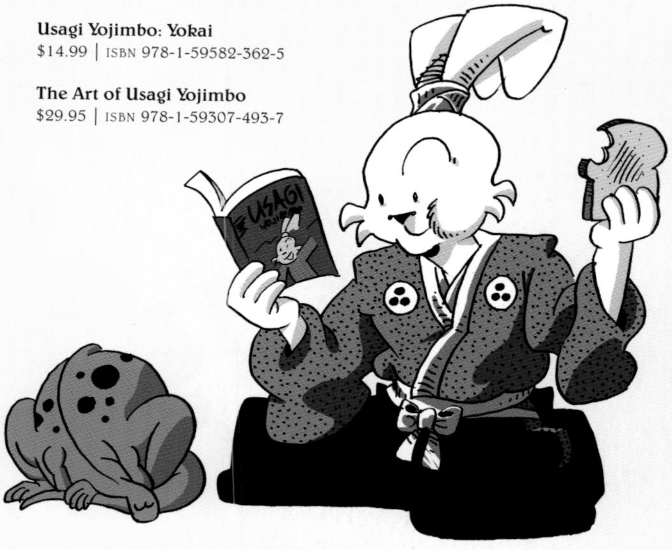
USAGI

AVAILABLE AT YOUR LOCAL COMICS SHOP OR BOOKSTORE

- To find a comics shop near your area, call 1-888-266-4226. For more information or to order direct:
- On the web: DarkHorse.com • E-mail: mailorder@darkhorse.com
- Phone: 1-800-862-0052 Mon.-Fri. 9 A.M. to 5 P.M. Pacific Time. *Prices and availability subject to change without notice.

DARK HORSE COMICS, INC.

President and Publisher
Mike Richardson

Executive Vice President
Neil Hankerson

Chief Financial Officer
Tom Weddle

Vice President of Publishing
Randy Stradley

Vice President of Book Trade Sales
Michael Martens

Vice President of Business Affairs
Anita Nelson

Editor in Chief
Scott Allie

Vice President of Marketing
Matt Parkinson

Vice President of Product Development
David Scroggy

Vice President of Information Technology
Dale LaFountain

Senior Director of Print, Design, and Production
Darlene Vogel

General Counsel
Ken Lizzi

Editorial Director
Davey Estrada

Senior Books Editor
Chris Warner

Executive Editor
Diana Schutz

Director of Print and Development
Cary Grazzini

Art Director
Lia Ribacchi

Director of Scheduling
Cara Niece

Director of International Licensing
Tim Wiesch

Director of Digital Publishing
Mark Bernardi

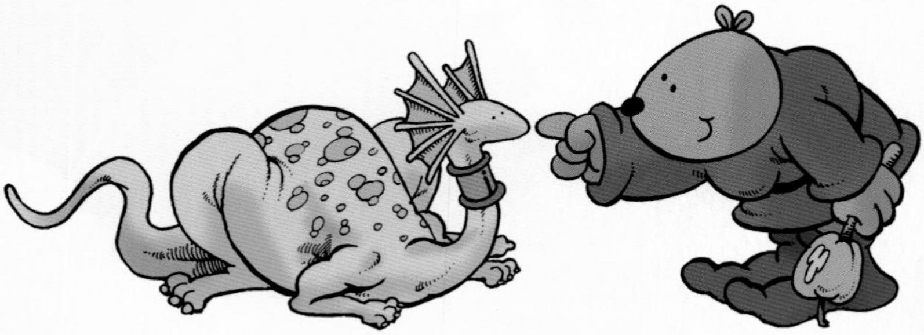